Thomas Cromwell
on
Church and Commonwealth

Thomas Cromwell
on
Church and Commonwealth

Selected Letters, 1523-1540

Edited with an Introduction by
ARTHUR J. SLAVIN

HARPER TORCHBOOKS
Harper & Row, Publishers
New York, Evanston, and London

THOMAS CROMWELL ON CHURCH AND
COMMONWEALTH

Introduction, Preface, headnotes, glossary, edition, and compilation copyright © 1969 by Arthur J. Slavin.

Printed in the United States of America.

First edition: HARPER TORCHBOOKS, 1969,
Harper & Row, Publishers, Incorporated,
49 East 33rd Street, New York, N.Y. 10016.

Library of Congress Catalog Card Number: 79-89498.

FOR ING
FOR ERINDRING OM LONDON

CONTENTS

PREFACE

Many histories have been written to explain the political, social, economic, and religious development of England in the sixteenth century. Within that vast literature there is an inevitable focus on the twin aspects of reform and revolution in both the secular and religious character of English life under Henry VIII. But the publication of documentary materials to support the study of early Tudor history is not nearly as far advanced as it ought to be—at least not in a form easily available to students of the period. Exception must be made, of course, for certain texts which have a literary as well as historical interest. Elyot's *Governor* and More's *Utopia*, for example. This collection of letters written by Thomas Cromwell is offered in that context and in the hope that those reading it will come away with a better understanding of the tremendous problems and exciting challenges of English Reformation history.

I cannot neglect to thank some people and institutions for sustaining the work of examining anew the manuscripts and completing this volume. First, I must acknowledge the inspiration and encouragement of Dr. G. R. Elton, Fellow of Clare College, Cambridge. To the Keepers of Manuscripts and Books in the British Museum and Public Record Office, London, I offer special thanks for the many services they offered, and I especially thank the staff of the photographic sections and the Keepers with whose permission material in crown copyright was used.

Special debts to Mr. J. Michael Phelps, my research assistant in the Center for Medieval and Renaissance Studies, University of California, Los Angeles, must be acknowledged. While I alone am responsible for any of the errors in this collection, Mr. Phelps checked the manuscripts, argued me out of erroneous readings, made the basic stock of notes drawn upon in the identification of people, places, and things, and in a hundred other ways made this work as much his as it is mine.

Finally, the inspection and filming of nearly four hundred letters of Thomas Cromwell in various English repositories was accomplished with the support of the Humanities Institute of the University of California and the American Council of Learned Societies.

NOTE ON
EDITORIAL POLICY

The spelling and punctuation of the Tudor originals of all documents have been modernized, but in most cases no reduction of complex Tudor sentences has been attempted. A minimum of half and full stops was commonly used in the sixteenth century, and some effort to help students construe certain sentences required the addition of commas, semicolons, colons, and periods. But I have kept these to a minimum. Technical terms have, for the most part, been treated in footnotes appended to individual letters. But where archaisms important to the language of a letter presented themselves, I have marked them with an asterisk. The very brief glossary at the back of this volume defines all such terms.

I have made an independent reading and a transcript of each of the Cromwell letters, all of which I have checked additionally from photographs in my possession. Even though all but one of the letters presented have appeared in print in R. B. Merriman's *Life and Letters of Thomas Cromwell*, I thought this necessary because other editors have not always been reliable, or they have employed conventions of editing not in accord with my policy. Often points of difference were trivial but, on some occasions, meaning as well as form has not been served well by Merriman or one of the editors of *The Letters and Papers, Foreign and Domestic, of the Reign of Henry VIII*.

To facilitate reference to other authorities, I have given a brief bibliographical description of every letter at its head. The top left-hand line refers to the manuscript call number. In each case there is a place of deposit (PRO for the Public Record Office, London; BM for the British Museum), followed by the particular collection (e.g., Harleian Mss.) for the British Museum material, and by E, C, or SP (Exchequer, Chancery, or State Paper material) for the Public Record Office. Below that material I have cited *The Letters and Papers, Foreign and*

Domestic, of the Reign of Henry VIII (referred to as *LP*, followed by volume number, part number, and document number, e.g., *LP*, XIII, ii, 413). This is followed by a semicolon and the item number in Merriman in arabic numerals. The date and place of composition are given wherever possible.

When some conjecture is made on my part as to a date of composition, or I supply material to cover defects or lacunae in the manuscripts, I have indicated this with brackets.

Official documents were often dated by the regnal year of the king then ruling. Sometimes this form was used to the exclusion of the year of grace, which might itself be variously dated. Regnal years spanned a calendar year from the day of accession. Thus, in the case of Henry VIII, a regnal year ran from 22 April of one year to 21 April of the following year. A letter dated 1 Henry VIII must therefore be placed between 22 April 1509 and 21 April 1510. But the year of grace was differently reckoned by different writers, each of whom might start from one of several important feasts of the Christian year. Modern historians use a historical year beginning on 1 January which can be traced back to the Roman civil year. But in the Middle Ages, the church wished to break with pagan customs and substitute for them reminders of Christ's grace. Bede, for example, began his year with the Nativity, Christmas Day. Matthew of Paris, the very famous chronicler of the thirteenth century, still used Christmas Day to begin his year. From the eleventh century on, English writers commonly used Lady Day, the Feast of the Annunciation on 25 March, which was in a sense a more logical starting point than the Feast of the Nativity, though they reckoned illogically from the Feast after Christmas as the opening of the year. For official purposes Englishmen continued to use 25 March as the beginning of the year until the calendar reform of 1752, which made mandatory in England the Gregorian calendar with its 1 January year opening, a usage accepted on the Continent in 1582. Thus a writer in the 1530's who wrote 10 June 1530 presents no problem. He is using the Julian calendar and reckoning from 25 March for his year. But if the same man wrote 27 February 1530, we should have to give the date 1531 to his letter if we remember that his year began the previous 25 March and would run through the following 24 March. Thus all dates between 25 March and 31 December 1530 in contemporary letters fall within the year 1530 as we reckon it, while all letters dated 1 January to 24 March 1530 would be in the year 1531. I have given all dates here in the New Style proclaimed in 1752.

Each letter has attached to it a headnote in which special circumstances or general background material is set forth. In three cases a single longer heading has been used to cover several letters, because the relationship among them seemed to make this the better course. Footnotes are provided for nearly all items important to the understanding of special subjects dealt with in the letters. In a few cases I have been unable to make any identification of people, places, or incidents and have so stated. Thus both a historical introduction and fairly complete notes should afford each reader an opportunity to comprehend fully the letters printed here. Endorsements, which may be signatures, remarks, or memorandums put on the backs of documents, are always noted. These are sometimes contemporary with the documents, e.g., some notation of the date of receipt or the name of the sender of the letter. Endorsements of a much later date were sometimes made by collectors or scholars, and are so described. A bibliography is given at the back of the volume in the hope that the student who wants to pursue a problem beyond the confines of this collection will know where to start.

Finally, a word about the arrangement of the letters. The simplest thing would have been to place the letters in the order in which they were written. But it seemed far better to group them under two broad headings: those about the affairs of secular government and politics, and those about spiritual matters. Cromwell exercised power in both realms and was as much the dominant figure in religious reform as he was in government, in the sense ordinarily understood of such things. In each of the two major groupings are some letters that could easily go into either classification. Thus Gardiner received letters from Cromwell which cast light on matters of religion. But they seem to belong more to the world of the politics of reform than to the history of reform itself. The letters to Lord Lisle, on the other hand, though they often touch affairs of secular government, seem to center on religious dissent and the entire problem of community of opinion and interest in religious reform. Again within the two major divisions I have attempted to gather related letters. Those showing lay interference in ecclesiastical patronage, for example, or those relating to the monasteries, are placed together in chronological order. The most difficult decision has been what to do with letters dealing with priests or other religious suspected of treason. Here, I have decided to put such letters with others of the same interest, which was primarily dynastic and political.

Arthur J. Slavin

Notting Hill, London
June 1967

INTRODUCTION

In a short essay it is difficult to evaluate the career of Thomas Cromwell or to reinterpret comprehensively his importance in the English Reformation. That difficulty is a striking admission of the large place he has come to occupy in all recent writing about reform in England in the 1530's. And it implies a contrast between the richness of modern historical studies and the poverty of a now discredited tradition in which Henry VIII's great minister appeared only as an evil genius whose sole purpose was the destruction of true religion and the creation of a tyranny.

While this is not the place to survey Cromwell's importance in the historical literature of the Reformation in England, we may well begin our examination of his role in reform by recalling the views of one of his near contemporaries as well as those of the late-Victorian editor of his letters and author of the standard account of his life. John Foxe the martyrologist considered Cromwell to be one of the heroes of the Reformation and a "valiant soldier and captain of Christ."[1] To Roger Merriman, however, Henry's minister was a thoroughly unscrupulous, Machiavellian timeserver whose infamous deeds against religion and virtue sprang from a contempt of both, as could be seen in the part Cromwell played in the entrapment and martyrdom of Thomas More.[2]

Foxe's account is clearly the bright end of the spectrum, while Merriman's is the dark one around which historians have gathered in drafting blue-black monochromes of Cromwell to match Holbein's somber and unflattering portrait. Until the last two decades it would have been difficult to enroll many as sympathetic to Foxe's view. But James A. Froude, who himself

[1] Quoted in A. G. Dickens, *Thomas Cromwell and the English Reformation* (London: English Universities Press, 1959), p. 173.
[2] Roger B. Merriman, *Life and Letters of Thomas Cromwell*, 2 vols. (Oxford: The Clarendon Press, 1902); especially, I, 118–122 and 130–1, as well as all of chap. 5.

charged Cromwell with a "long list of solemn tragedies," also wrote that the king's agent had taken upon himself tasks "beyond the ordinary strength of man"—securing the freedom of England and the destruction of idolatry.[3] These were in Froude's eyes objects transcending all other considerations in their excellence; and in moving toward their achievement Cromwell had to crush men threatening to check his mission. Here is his summary of Thomas Cromwell:

> [Thus] perished a statesman whose character will for ever remain a problem. For eight years his influence had been supreme with the king—supreme in Parliament—supreme in Convocation; the nation, in the ferment of revolution, was absolutely controlled by him; and he has left the print of his individual genius stamped indelibly, while the metal was at white heat, into the constitution of the country . . . and the polity of the Church of England remains as it was left by its creator.[4]

Against that view, in which Cromwell stood firmly as the defender of freedom and the builder of the English church and constitution, most have drawn their pens, dipped in venom, bent upon recording the evil done by the man Froude called the "universal authority."[5] Apart from Paul Van Dyke,[6] who nearly alone among early-twentieth-century historians emancipated himself from the spirit of hostility, writers in Merriman's train evolved fanatic and fantastic images hardly in keeping with the surviving evidence. Pollard labeled Cromwell the prime mover in Henry VIII's "progress to depotism."[7] Gustave Constant, echoing Cardinal Pole's dictum that Cromwell was born "with an aptitude for ruin and destruction," described him further as a man who "had no scruples" and one to whom "pity was unknown," as a man "covetous, active and determined" in the

---

[3] James A. Froude, *History of England from the Fall of Cardinal Wolsey to the Defeat of the Spanish Armada*, 12 vols. (London: Longmans, Green and Co., n.d.), III, 340.

[4] *Ibid.*, p. 339.

[5] "Whether it was an ambassador or a commissioner of sewers, a warden of a company or a tradesman who was injured by the guild, a bishop or a heretic, a justice of the peace, or a serf crying for emancipation, Cromwell was the universal authority to whom all officials looked for instruction, and all sufferers looked for redress." Froude, *op. cit.*, III, 339.

[6] Paul Van Dyke, *Renascence Portraits* (New York: Macmillan, 1905), contains a good essay on Cromwell; see also his work on Pole's account of Cromwell, in the *American Historical Review*, IX (1904), 696–724.

[7] Alfred F. Pollard, *Henry VIII* (London: Longmans, Green and Co., 1902), p. 259.

pursuit of evil, unaffected by sentiment or morality.[8] He was nothing less than the Reformation bureaucrat of destruction who had reduced evil to banality and so stripped even death of dignity. That image of the executor of public policy devoid of human values recommended itself to H. A. L. Fisher and through him to generations of students and scholars:

There are many features in his life and policy which deserve the hearty execration of posterity. He sent men to die without trial; he made use of torture; he was cunning, unscrupulous, truculent in the hour of success, slavish and abject in the moment of danger. . . . It has been disputed whether at heart he was not a Protestant. Heart he did not possess, but it is clear that his sympathies were with the new rather than with the old religion. . . .

To work his will, he had beneath him "a troop of henchmen, pliable, adroit, hard and exact in business," all men "schooled in Cromwellian methods" and eager to carry out "that great business arrangement of the sixteenth century which created a new landed aristocracy by means of the revenues of the medieval church." Theology and religion were of no consequence during his tenure of power. He was simply a man of business motivated by an abstract love of demonic efficiency in amassing personal wealth and in the process of state-building.[9]

In the past fifteen years such ideas have been sharply attacked from two directions. Dr. G. R. Elton focused attention on the reforms in Tudor government accompanying the revolution in ecclesiastical polity.[10] And, when his insistence on Cromwell's being the architect of a revolution in government based not on tyranny but on the consent of the community of the realm was challenged, he produced a series of articles documenting his essentially novel interpretation of Cromwell's personality, intentions, and achievements.[11] He did not, however, pay much atten-

---

[8] Gustave Constant, *The Reformation in England: The English Schism and Henry VIII, 1509–1547*, trans. R. E. Scantlebury (London: Sheed and Ward, 1934), p. 288. The remarks by Pole are to be found in the famous *Apologia ad Carolum V;* in Reginald Pole, *Epistolae Reginaldi Poli . . . et aliorum ad se*, ed. A. M. Quirini, 5 vols. (Brescia, 1744–1757), I, 127.

[9] Herbert A. L. Fisher, *The Political History of England, 1485–1547* (London: Longmans, Green and Co., 1928), p. 446–7; see also Philip Hughes, *The Reformation in England*, 3 vols. (London: Hollis and Carter, 1953), II, 224.

[10] Geoffrey R. Elton, *The Tudor Revolution in Government* (Cambridge, England: Cambridge University Press, 1953).

[11] See the list of his articles in the bibliography.

tion to Cromwell's role in reform or concern for ideas of reform apart from politics and the socioeconomic programs of the Commonwealth pamphleteers and propagandists. It remained for Professor A. G. Dickens to take up questions of Cromwell's interest in religion and religious reform, first in a brief biography and then in his masterful *The English Reformation*.[12]

Dickens drew attention to attainments beyond "sheer political and administrative energy." Following Elton in his emphasis on the radicalism of Cromwell's ministry, Dickens asserted what he took to be Cromwell's impact on the religious and intellectual history of England and Britian.[13] Whether with regard to North England or Wales, the Home Counties or the Midlands, Dickens stressed that Cromwell and his agents (not the "creatures" of the romanticists) were transforming "a lawless and faction-ridden people" into purposeful sections of English society:

When a worthy life of Cromwell comes to be written, it will devote many pages to the statesmanship which broke the feudal liberties and the sanctuaries, repressed the family factions, maintained peace and even co-operation with the Scots, promoted the overthrow of the Geraldines in Ireland, began the series of national poor-laws . . . who stopped the debasement and export of the coinage, solved by statute the old problem of uses, remolded and expanded the national system of financial courts . . . and perfected the development of a small and workmanlike Privy Council. In the field of the State, he was indeed a true "universal man of the Renaissance."[14]

But it was with regard to the church and religion that Dickens most surprised his readers:

In his Reformation-policy, just as in all other spheres, he was first and foremost a state-builder. The significance of the English Reformation is very far from being limited to religious and even to ecclesiastical history; it is a crisis and a resolution of a crisis in the history of the English state and people. . . . The main result of the Cromwellian phase was the transfer of the great ecclesiastical sector of English society and law to the sovereignty of the king in Parliament. . . .[15]

While reserving the strictly doctrinal aspects of this phase to theologians, Dickens insisted upon the religious context of the emergence of a society dominated by laymen. And that context was one in which Englishmen, laymen and clergy alike,

[12] *Thomas Cromwell and the English Reformation* (see note 1). The larger history was published in London: Batsford, 1964.
[13] *Thomas Cromwell*, p. 175.
[14] *Ibid.*, p. 176.
[15] *Ibid.*

rejected the primacy of doctrinal allegiances, preferred peace to a sword and embraced the vision of a paternal state, harsh against traitors yet mild with heretics. The early stages of this process may with all the greater confidence be ascribed to Cromwell and his group, since the king himself seems to have understood its implications none too clearly. . . . He [Cromwell] and his like show a vivid consciousness of the shortcomings of ecclesiastical administration and jurisdiction; behind the thin facade of courteous reverence, they entertained a strong resentment against . . . the easily won wealth, the hauteur and fundamental worldliness of their prelatical associates. . . .[16]

The crucial question remained: what linked mere resentment and the hunger for reform, the ardor for rationalization and the Cromwellian group's concern for sickness in society? How did a lay invasion of ecclesiastical privilege not executed by angels of light mix with the spirit of reforms specifically religious and pietistic in character?

On the face of it, Cromwell's hand was an unlikely one to wield the mixer. Yet that is precisely what Dickens has asserted as the truth of the matter. It was Foxe's "valiant soldier and captain of Christ" who grasped the principle that massive reforms could be initiated only by the monarchy. Using the best talent available—and this often meant clergymen—Cromwell's antiprelatical reform movement linked itself to religious reforms and clearly favored individual Protestant reformers. Cromwell was himself charged with heresy in 1540, and despite the fact that in historical literature his religious convictions play almost no part, Dickens saw in him the marks of serious Protestant religious convictions tempered by a distrust of dogma and some lack of spiritual ardor and fanaticism.

If we are to make acceptable the spectacular *bouleversement* explicit in the works of Elton and Dickens, if we are to see Cromwell as a tolerant, moderate, lay-minded reformer bent on parliamentary rule rather than despotic royal supremacy, and as the architect of a wise middle way rather than repression in religion, we must illustrate the relation between the maker of the great reform statutes of the 1530's and contemporary reform ideas.

The study of the relationships between general movements of reform and the Reformation in England was for many years handicapped by the poor form in which historians put their questions. Treating issues of priority, specificity, and nationality

[16] *Ibid.*, p. 178

as the great matters of sixteenth-century reform history, they created histories in which the very existence of an international community of like-minded men calling for similar reforms throughout all Europe had little or no place. From "une question mal posée," as Lucien Febvre once said, only bad answers follow.[17]

Recent historians have taken Febvre's lead and asked what was the character of reform thinking in various kingdoms, in order to determine its relationship to the complex and particular social, religious, educational, and political issues underlying the Reformation across Europe. What has emerged from that questioning is a notion of reform ideas linked to the broadest traditions of medieval Christendom and based on principles devoted to the simplification of doctrine and the practical reordering of society. Marcel Bataillon examined circumstances in Spain,[18] and Augustin Renaudet studied the advocates of reform and the shape of Reformation in Italy and France.[19] Lortz, Ritter, and Spitz[20] turned their attention to similar matters in the German-speaking world of Luther and Eck. Together, they broke ground in the study of how common norms of reform slowly penetrated particular societies and what the means of penetration were. Moreover, they agreed that reform movements shared a wide base of humanistic thought which might aptly be called Erasmian, especially inasmuch as it was skeptical of traditional authority and theology, at odds with a papacy grown fat and

[17] L. Febvre, "Une question mal posée: Les origines de la réforme française," *Revue historique,* CLXI (1929), 1–73.

[18] M. Bataillon, *Érasme et l'Espagne* (Paris: Bibliothèque de l'École des Hautes Études Hispaniques, 1937), vol. XXI. See also Beltran de Heredia, *Las corrientes de espiritualidad entre los Dominicos de Castilla* (Salamanca: 1941). The 1950 Spanish editiion of Bataillon's work was corrected because of the criticism of de Heredia.

[19] A. Renaudet, *Érasme et l'Italie* (Geneva: Droz, 1954); *Préréforme et humanisme à Paris pendant les premières guerres d'Italie* (Paris: Librairie d'Argences, 1953). See also Imbart da la Tour, *Les Origines de la Réforme* (Melun: Librairie d'Argences, 1944); and Delio Cantimori, *La riforma in Italia* (Milan: 1951); and J. Etienne, *Spiritualisme Érasmien et les Théologiens Louvainistes* (Louvain: 1955).

[20] J. Lortz, *Die Reformation in Deutschland,* 2 vols. (Freiburg: 1949); L. Spitz, *The Religious Renaissance of the German Humanists* (Cambridge, Mass.: Harvard University Press, 1963); for G. Ritter's numerous works see *Bibliographie de la Réforme, 1450–1648, Ier Fascicule, Allemagne—Pays Bas,* 2nd ed. (Leiden: E. J. Brill, 1961), p. 56, Nos. 1247–59. K. Oelrich, *Der Späte Erasmus und die Reformation* (Münster: 1961). For all questions of recent scholarship this bibliography and the companion volumes are invaluable.

venal, and loyal to independent-minded reforms and leaders.[21]

In England this "continental approach" gathered adherents slowly. But in the last decade it has come to characterize the best work done on the Reformation and its revolutionary impact in the 1530's. Historians have not abandoned the Divorce, schism, and supremacy entirely. But, increasingly, constitutional questions are subordinated to others: Were humanistic reformers active in government? By whom were they recruited? What tasks were they given? Were they in some sense part of an Erasmian community?[22]

The last question is in many ways the most interesting, because the answers given to it tend to imply answers to the others as well. For the English Erasmians advocated a simple piety in religion, to be realized through a basic reshaping of the techniques and objectives of education. This in turn necessitated that good counsel be readily available to royal councilors, so that the "Commonwealth" ideal (*respublica christiana*) of a conspiracy of Christians driven by *caritas*[23] and directed at the attainment of a just society could be rendered effective.

The ultimate goal of the English Erasmians was the realization of the *philosophia christi*,[24] wisdom consecrated to the service of God in a practical way—civic philosophy and not school philosophy, as More remarked in *Utopia*.[25] That civic philosophy was suspicious of subtlety and the late scholastic

---

[21] See the Introduction to a volume in this series: John C. Olin, "Erasmus and Reform," *Christian Humanism and the Reformation* (New York: Harper Torchbooks, 1965), esp. pp. 8–16. Olin, however, carefully distinguished Erasmian movements of reform from those definitely Protestant in character, while acknowledging the ground held in common.

[22] The best example of this work is James K. McConica, *English Humanists and Reformation Politics* (Oxford: The Clarendon Press, 1965).

[23] Charity must here be understood in a stricter sense than love or natural affection; it is specifically Christian love. St. Paul used it so in Rom. 8:39: "the charity of God, that is in Jesus Christ Our Lord."

[24] The relationship of this "philosophy of Christ" (seen as applied wisdom) to true theology, that is, a theology based on scripture, was spelled out by Eugene Rice, *The Renaissance Idea of Wisdom* (Cambridge, Mass.: Harvard University Press, 1958), 158–63.

[25] See St. Thomas More, *The Yale Edition of the Complete Works of St. Thomas More*, vol. IV, *Utopia*, ed. E. Surtz and J. H. Hexter (New Haven: Yale University Press, 1965), pp. 98–9, for the facing Latin-English texts, where the contrast is made between *philosophia scholastica*, which is fit for debates among friends (*apud amiculos in familiari colloquio*), and *alia philosophia civilior*, which knows its stage (*quae suam novit scenam*) to be the council of the king and to which statesmen attend (*eique sese accommodans*).

affection for definition; it was apt to prefer satire as the vehicle for announcing its intentions; and it was dedicated to a popular education in which people would be taught to eschew the corruption of the truly divine by the merely human in a sense mindful of St. Augustine. Fearful that for the masses of men Rome was killing Christ, Erasmus and his English followers, among whom we will remember Colet, Fisher, and More in the first generation, committed themselves to profound educational reforms as the condition of social and religious reform.[26]

In the event, the lay character of the movement emerged clearly. All people were called equally to sanctity by the flame at the center, charity, the fire of love. In the true Commonwealth there could be no special status for priests, since function did not imply merit. Properly considered the world itself was a monastery, a holy congregation. A well-ordered lay community in sixteenth-century Europe had no need of walls against a hostile world. Daily life in the world was itself a vocation, an asceticism in the world, guided by an ethical wisdom culled from scripture purified by the humanist revolution in scholarship. Neither legalism nor external piety had any place, only the simple imitation of Christ.

Thus, quite explicitly, the centuries-old monastic tradition was attacked. The many cults surrounding the sacraments were blasted. Treaties and methods of mystical knowledge were laughed at. No retreat from the struggles of very ordinary life was recommended, no substitute for pious living in the world. There could be no compromise with the truly revolutionary and total laicism trumpeted by these reformers, men who in a scant few years would find a new type of hero-saint in the most uncommon common lawyer, Thomas More, diplomat, undersheriff of London, councilor, and lord chancellor of England.[27]

The implications of their style of reform were many. Scriptures must be freely available to laymen in their own tongue. True theology—that based on the minimum that was revealed by God and ascertained by historical-philological criticism—must be restored. In education, languages and literature showed to

[26] Apart from F. Seebolm, *The Oxford Reformers*, (London: Longmans 1867), a classic work that must be used with great care, the best report of Erasmus' relations with his English followers before 1516 is in H. C. Porter's introductory essay to D. F. S. Thomson's edition of *The Cambirdge Letters of Erasmus* (Toronto: University of Toronto Press, 1963), pp. 3–103.

[27] For this characterization of English Erasmianism see McConica, *English Humanists and Reformation Politics,* chap. 2.

ordinary men the world in which Christ walked and worked;
these must be made basic in the reformed schools, through
translations whenever necessary. Hence Erasmianism was an
educational ideal leading toward true *amor dei*[28] through popular
instruction. But its social implication was a faith in a natural
human order, good in itself though perhaps corrupted by Roman
dogma and institutions. What was required was the restorative
action of Christian conspirators driven by love. And the remedies
for disharmony lay ready at hand to men moved by the vision
of a Commonwealth not hierarchical and prelatical in character
but horizontal and lay in spirit.

In England the enterprise had flourished before the great
crisis of the 1530's. The London reformers gathered strength
from Colet's early work, from his sermons and writings, but
even more from the lay and practical implications of his re-
founding of St. Paul's School, the curriculum of which rested
on translations of Erasmus and primers written by him. Their
spirit permeates Colet's *Statutes*.[29] From St. Paul's came scholars
and royal servants and future governors: Thomas Lupset,[30] John
Leland,[31] Sir Anthony Denny.[32] Grocyn's Oxford pupil Lily, the
famous grammarian, was St. Paul's second high master.[33] His

[28] Augustine's "love of God."

[29] Sears Jayne, *John Colet and Marsilio Ficino* (Oxford: The University
Press, 1963) best fits Colet into the activist tradition, opposed to earlier
scholars who saw in him a contemplative Neoplatonist. On the general
theme of Colet's friends and their relations to him, see the following:
Karl Bauer, "John Colet and Erasmus von Rotterdam," *Archiv für Re-
formationsgeschichte*, Ergänzungsband, V (1929), 155–87; W. A. Clebsch,
"John Colet and the Reformation," *Angelican Theological Review, XXXVII*
(1955), 167–77; D. J. Parsons, "John Colet's Stature as an Exegete,"
Anglican Theological Review, XL (1958), 36–42; W. E. Campbell, "John
Colet, Dean of St. Paul's" *Dublin Review*, CCXVIII (1946), 97–109;
and J. H. Lupton, *The Influence of John Colet upon the Reformation of
the English Church* (London, 1893).

[30] The helper of More, Linacre, and Erasmus in getting ready copy for
the press, Lupset (1498?–1530) was the first lecturer in rhetoric and
humanist literature under Wolsey's foundation at Corpus Christi College,
Oxford.

[31] The earliest of modern English antiquaries and royal librarian to Henry
VIII, Leland (1506–1552) was a priest and the author of *Itinerary* and
Collectanea, composed of six and nine volumes respectively.

[32] One of Henry VIII's favorite courtiers, Denny (1501–1549) was to
become a strong advocate of reform in the privy council.

[33] William Grocyn (1446?–1519) was England's first outstanding Greek
scholar. Despite his criticisms of Colet's lectures on *The Ecclesiastical
Hierarchies* of Dionysius, he was a leader in the circle of London reformers. William Lily (1468?–1522).

friends from Magdalene School and College,[34] among them More and Wolsey and the future bishops Lee[35] and Stokesley,[36] connected university reformers to those active in London and in government.

Thomas More's friends illustrated especially well the penetration of court and city by men bent on humanistic reform. Apart from Rastell,[37] Clement,[38] and Heywood,[39] More's early associates among the lawyers of the Inns of Court and Doctors' Commons gathered around a common table civilians and canonists, ecclesiastics and lay governors eager to discuss England's ills and the proper medicines.[40] Here was a center of discussion which cut across lines of ordinary influence and occupation, bringing together in the period from 1510 to 1530 many who in the thirties played opposite, critical roles: Tunstal,[41] Sampson,[42]

[34] The significance of Magdelene School and the Oxford college of the same name is developed by McConica, *op. cit.*, pp. 50, 84, 87.

[35] Edward Lee (1482?–1544) was archbishop of York from 1531 until his death. In 1519–1520 he broke with his early friends and came out against Erasmus, becoming increasingly conservative as he grew to be important in the royal government.

[36] John Stokesley (1475?–1539) was a fellow of Magdalene College, chaplain to Henry VIII, envoy to the Italian universities in the gathering of opinions in favor of the Divorce, critic of Reginald Pole and of radical Protestant doctrine as well. As Bishop of London he argued with Cranmer and Cromwell in the late 1530's.

[37] John Rastell (d. 1536) was a printer and lawyer who was of strong reform opinions by 1530. One son was the editor of More's *Works;* another ended as a Jesuit!

[38] John Clement or Clements (d. 1572) was a tutor in More's family and also held the Wolsey-endowed rhetoric lectureship at Oxford. An early advocate of humanistic reform, upon Henry VIII's death he went into voluntary exile at Louvain, returned under Mary, and again fled, this time to Mechlin, in 1559.

[39] John Heywood (1497–1580?) again illustrates the degree to which early favorers of reform cannot be easily comprehended with classical Protestant-Catholic distinctions. Though he was active in More's circle, he accepted the Supremacy in 1544 after a public recantation of his earlier denial. His plays are still important in dramatic history, though we have forgotten his very complicated spiritual odyssey.

[40] The Inns of Court were the schools of the common law, for which men prepared in the Inns of Chancery (ten in number as against four Inns of Court). Fortescue, in his *De laudibus,* chaps. 48 and 49, characterized them as minor and major Inns. Doctors' Commons on the other hand, was the college of doctors of the civil law. It was located in Paternoster Row, near St. Paul's and was later on to move to the former home of Lord Mountjoy, Erasmus' patron. Nearby were the homes of More, Fisher, and Richard Foxe.

[41] Cuthbert Tunstal (1474–1559), bishop of London and Durham, a great lawyer, skilled in Greek, Hebrew, and mathematics, was especially

Bonner, [43] Petre,[44] Abbot Faringdon,[45] John Tregonwell,[46] and others too numerous to list.

That is not to say that the lines connecting the council chamber and the study depended only on the accidents of conversation. Queen Catherine's[47] influence helped to link More, Vives,[48] and Erasmus, though it was Cardinal Wolsey himself who actually enticed the Spaniard from Alcalá to Oxford. She also helped recruit Linacre[49] and Leland, so continuing the work of Margaret Beaufort, the king's grandmother, and her chaplain John Fisher, whose circle included Warham,[50] Foxe,[51] Elyot, and More.

---

esteemed by More and Erasmus. Long after they had died, he showed the justice of their praise; for despite his own rather conservative theology, he refused to persecute Protestant dissenters under Queen Mary.

[42] Richard Sampson (d. 1554), bishop of Coventry and Lichfield, had risen in Wolsey's service through ambassadorial skills. He wrote theological treatises, rather conservative in character, late in life.

[43] Edmund Bonner (1500?–1569) ended as bishop of London. After a long career in the service of the Henrician reforms, he became increasingly conservative, opposing the Edwardian reforms, as did so many of the administrative bishops.

[44] Sir William Petre (1505–1572), secretary of state in Henry VIII's last years, had earlier legal ambitions in chancery.

[45] Hugh Faringdon, *alias* Cook (d. 1539), was a remarkable monastic reformer and supporter of Henry VIII's divorce. At Reading Abbey he collected a great library, which he lent willingly to royal agents and humanists alike. But that did not save him in 1539, when he was executed for treason, perhaps because of his strong connections with the Pole family.

[46] Sir John Tregonwell (d. 1565) was a well-known civilian lawyer who was one of Cromwell's agents in the Dissolution, an unusual distinction among Queen Mary's favorites.

[47] For all matters relating Catherine's reform attitudes to humanism, see G. Mattingly, *Catherine of Aragon* (London: Jonathan Cape, 1941).

[48] Juan Luis Vives (1492–1540) had studied in Paris and taught in the Netherlands, achieving early fame for his commentary on Augustine's *City of God*. A voluminous writer, his main fame today rests on his educational writings.

[49] Thomas Linacre (1460?–1524) was a classical scholar and royal physician before he turned to the priesthood very late in life. He was the future Queen Mary's tutor and the author of books on grammar in the Erasmian tradition.

[50] William Warham (1450–1532) is chiefly remembered for his eleventh-hour opposition to the Reformation Parliament's revolutionary actions. But he had earlier befriended Erasmus, if not Colet, against whose ideas he fulminated as archbishop of Canterbury.

[51] Richard Foxe (1448?–1528) was bishop of Winchester and had been one of the chief councilors under Henry Tudor and his son. He was the translator of St. Benedict's *Rule for Women* and also a patron of educa-

With Fisher stood Wolsey in all efforts to carry the ideal of reform deep into the bodies of Cambridge and Oxford. Their collegiate statutes and foundations reveal this clearly, as do those of their companion Richard Foxe. By the early 1520's preaching in English, scriptural study, public lectures in the classics, and language instruction *pro philosophia christi* were all well established and gaining ground throughout the university world, not alone in the allegedly Protestant "Little Germanies" in Cambridge taverns.[52] New studies were respectable on the eve of Wolsey's great foundation, while in 1518 More's famous letter to the Oxford "Trojans" had expressed grave pessimism about the future of humanistic studies and reforms.[53] In the decade between 1518 and 1528 there was an international movement of scholarly reformers to England from Paris, Louvain, Bologna, Turin, Padua, Orléans, Cologne, and even Wittenberg. And while we will always be ignorant about all that they thought and taught, we do know that in 1521 more of Erasmus' work was being sold at Oxford than was Aristotle's.[54]

This peaceful permeation of England by humanist notions of reform supposedly was shattered by the "King's great matter." The Divorce and consequent schism spelled the end of humanism's halcyon days. That we have been carefully taught for generations. But we may fairly question whether the program and enactments of the Reformation Parliament from 1529 to 1536 and the ministry of Thomas Cromwell (1532–1540), if carefully examined, sustain such a thesis. In fact we may even wonder whether reform activity in and out of government in the years of Cromwell's power does not coincide in a way that will best provide understanding of the ideas and events of the 1530's, while avoiding premature distinctions between Catholic and Protestant.

That when Cromwell achieved great power in the king's

---

tional reform through his foundation of Corpus Christi College, Oxford, as well as of grammar schools at Taunton and Grantham. Finally, he was also the benefactor of several other Oxford and Cambridge colleges.

[52] See the analysis in McConica, *op. cit.*, chap. 4, "Humanism in the Universities," where a different emphasis is found than that in Mark Curtis, *Oxford and Cambridge in Transition* (Oxford: The Clarendon Press, 1959).

[53] See letter 19, written by More to the university officers and masters on 29 March 1518, in Elizabeth Rogers, *St. Thomas More, Selected Letters* (New Haven: Yale University Press, 1961), as well as the informative introduction to the letter.

[54] See the discussion of booksellers and inventories in McConica, *op. cit.*, pp. 89–92.

council in 1532 there existed serious divisions among reform-minded men is not worth debating. In May of that year More resigned the chancellorship; Reginald Pole returned to Italy, where he finally turned against his royal cousin and his reformation; Stephen Gardiner, Wolsey's brilliant protégé, had slipped from favor. Moreover, Cromwell had power; and according to traditional accounts, he was no friend of humanism or reform, Erasmian notions, or any other idea close to the minds of men laboring for the edification of a Christian Commonwealth. But that these divisions and Cromwell's power were incompatible with the continued vitality of the reform movement seems to me the contrary of the truth.

Elton proved this long ago with regard to what he called the "revolution in government." Cromwell, who came to the court in Wolsey's service, had been conversant with every aspect of the cardinal's power. It is doubtless true that he was the man best placed to wind up the complicated political bankruptcy of Wolsey.[55] But was Wolsey's legacy bankruptcy only? Certainly not, if we remember that he was a leader in the support of humanist reforms in the universities; that he had been regarded by More as England's best hope in the building of a true Commonwealth;[56] that he had begun the large-scale dissolution of monasteries in order to supply the fabric of the new colleges which were to be his monument;[57] or that with regard to those colleges he said they were Cromwell's work.[58]

Opera manuum tuarum! In Wolsey's service Cromwell had done hard things and reaped a crop of abundant hatred. He had mastered the skills of royal administration. He had developed unmatched understanding of Parliament's weakness and strengths. He had offended dukes and taken possession of the lands and plate of dispossessed abbots and priors. And he had also deepened friendships among men who would in the 1530's

[55] A. J. Slavin, *Politics and Profit: A Study of Sir Ralph Sadler* (Cambridge, England: Cambridge University Press, 1966), pp. 14–30.

[56] J. H. Hexter, *More's Utopia: The Biography of an Idea* (New York: Harper and Row, 1965), pp. 146–55, where Hexter sketches Wolsey's programs as lord chancellor against the backdrop of More's designs to abate the fury of the conspiracy of rich against poor that had prevailed in England.

[57] A. F. Pollard, *Wolsey* (Longmans, Green and Co., 1929), 165–216, for a discussion of Wolsey's use of his legatine power, esp. 202–4 and 324–6, about the colleges.

[58] In a fit of anxiety about the fate of his colleges at the time of his fall, Wolsey asked Ralph Sadler, Cromwell's clerk, to look after their fate and remind Cromwell that they were "in a manner *opera manuum tuarum*," the work of Cromwell's hands. (Slavin, *Politics and Profit*, p. 17.)

help him to formulate and carry through a reform program that profoundly affected English life for generations.

This has been most clearly recognized with regard to the social and political ideas put forward by Elyot,[59] Starkey,[60] St. German,[61] Taverner,[62] and Marshall.[63] With all of them he had close ties; to them he extended patronage; with some he developed very deep friendships. Their amity arose out of the qualities in Cromwell perceived by humanists and reformers but often missed by historians. Elyot's admiration was not founded on the minister's hunger for power or any alleged rapacity. Elyot himself stressed always their interests in similar studies, a remark especially important in the light of his insistence that the best possible basis for friendship lay in shared views about important things, particularly religion.[64] Cromwell attracted the flower of England's second-generation humanists to government service, because he was himself a "man for all seasons." Charles V's ambassador Chapuys knew this when he described him as one who loved hawking, the lending and borrowing of good books, moments stolen from the struggles of the council board that could be spent along the banks of the Thames in talk about politics, scholarship, Antwerp's goldsmiths, ancient sculpture, painting, and contemporary Italy.[65]

[59] Sir Thomas Elyot (1490?–1546), the brilliant humanist and courtier, was a crown agent active in administration and diplomacy. His works showed Italian and Erasmian influence.

[60] Thomas Starkey (1499?–1538) spent his early career in the service of the future Cardinal Pole, before becoming Henry VIII's chaplain.

[61] Christopher St. German (1460?–1540), a legal writer and controversialist in religious matters, also the author of *Doctor and Student,* a law textbook in Latin translated into English and widely republished through the eighteenth century.

[62] Richard Taverner (1505?–1575) was chiefly a religious writer and reformer whose first patron was Wolsey. He wrote many works for Cromwell in support of Reformation policies.

[63] William Marshall (fl. 1535) was another reformer, translator, and printer of polemical works in Cromwell's service. He is especially remembered as the translator of *Defensor pacis.*

[64] For the points made here, see Pearl Hogrefe, *The Life and Times of Sir Thomas Elyot* (Ames, Iowa: Iowa State University Press, 1967), pp. 298–300. The Elyot "renaissance" includes very good studies of his government service and writings: see Stanford E. Lehmberg, *Sir Thomas Elyot, Tudor Humanist* (Austin, Texas: University of Texas Press, 1960) and John Major, *Sir Thomas Elyot and Renaissance Humanism* (Lincoln, Nebraska: University of Nebraska Press, 1964).

[65] Eustace Chapuys-Nicholas Perrenot, Sieur de Granvelle, 21 November 1535, in *Letters and Papers, Foreign and Domestic, of the Reign of Henry VIII,* ed. J. S. Brewer *et al,* 21 vols. in 33 parts. (London: Stationery Office, 1852–1929), IX, 862.

He was a man whose learning and wit were responsive to like qualities in other men. These helped create the common ground upon which he stood with the humanists in fashioning a new ideal of a commonwealth in which royal power would be used to shape programs of reform too long discussed and not embodied in any effective actions. Several historians have recently described in detail the political- and social-reform ideas freely moving in Cromwell's circle. They have argued for the continuity of such ideas with earlier efforts concerning enclosure, good counsel, poor relief, abuses of aristocratic and ecclesiastical power and influence, the corruption of justice and consequent discord which debased the quality of life in England. They have also argued that Cromwell's active interest in these causes led him to promote reformers at court and engage them in ceaseless dialogue about how best to make reform work.[66]

Perhaps the best example of this is in Cromwell's influence upon Thomas Starkey, the ablest of the many humanist reformers of the 1530's. Not only did Cromwell bring Starkey to court, but the famous *Dialogue Between Master Lupset and Cardinal Pole* was itself the result of Cromwell's prodding. Starkey had applied his learning to studies fashionable in Padua, after an Oxford education. Joining philosophy to Latin and Greek, he had delighted in the "contemplation of natural knowledge" until moved by Christian charity; with philosophy set aside, he turned to patristic literature and holy scripture, "judging all other secret knowledge not applied to some use and profit . . . to be but a vanity." Because his purpose was then to live "in the political life," the once contemplative priest turned to the political order and customs of his native land.[67] In fact he sought employment by dedicating the short essay "What is Policy after the Sentence of Aristotle" to Cromwell, who had made of him a request that he perfect what pagans said by the application of Christian policy. When Cromwell read the short piece he complained that the theme was too tersely treated, especially where it touched how order was derived from "a multitude of men as it were conspiring together to live in all virtue and

---

[66] Franklin Le Van Baumer, *The Early Tudor Theory of Kingship* (New Haven: Yale University Press, 1940); Fritz Caspari, *Humanism and the Social Order in Tudor England* (Chicago: University of Chicago Press, 1954); Arthur B. Ferguson, *The Articulate Citizen and the English Renaissance* (Durham, N.C.: Duke University Press, 1965); and W. Gordon Zeeveld, *Foundations of Tudor Policy* (Cambridge, Mass.: Harvard University Press, 1948).

[67] S. J. Herrtage, *England in the Reign of Henry VIII: Starkey's Life and Letters* (London: Early English Text Society, 1878), p. *x*.

honesty." So Starkey wrote his *Dialogue;* "to create a satisfactory apologetic, Thomas Cromwell turned to such humanists as Starkey."[68]

"Order" was nothing less than the Cromwellian polity, which was discussed by Pole and Lupset and which was required to be set forth by Parliament, the true common authority of the realm and alone able to remedy defects and reduce disorder and so edify a "very and true commonweal." No aspect of contemporary society was immune to scrutiny, whether it was the reduction of ecclesiastical wealth, the application of it to lay purposes, especially educational reform, or the radical transformation of the law touching the poor and hopeless vagabonds and beggars of Tudor England.

In every such effort the hand of Cromwell linked legislation to ideas. We have recently learned how under his aegis William Marshall redirected poor relief between 1531 and 1536.[69] Joan Simon has stressed that humanist educational ideas were taken up and adapted in various ways in the 1530's, first by the poet Wyatt, who was one of "Cromwell's entourage," and then by Elyot, whose program was the model employed in the tuition of Cromwell's own son Gregory.[70] She has also described the influence of Starkey and Richard Morison,[71] the latter a thoroughgoing Erasmian, in suggesting reform programs actually submitted to Henry VIII late in 1535. More to the point, Miss Simon has demonstrated that Cromwell was critically active in formulating plans to use church wealth in order to improve the schools and universities and in other effects to revive monastic education before the dissolution. Latimer looked upon it as one of Cromwell's good works, that he was cleansing the colleges. Specifically, he initiated a plan for tax concessions for the universities, specifying that they be exempt from the payment of tenths on the condition that they contribute to the support of public lecturers.[72] This was a scheme joining two key Erasmian

[68] On the composition of the *Dialogue* see W. Gordon Zeeveld, "Thomas Starkey and the Cromwellian Polity," *The Journal of Modern History,* XV (1943), 177–91, esp. p. 178 for Zeeveld's view of Cromwell's role.
[69] G. R. Elton, "An Early Tudor Poor Law," *Economic History Review,* 2nd ser. VI (1953), 55–67.
[70] Joan Simon, *Education and Society in Tudor England* (Cambridge, England: Cambridge University Press, 1966), p. 155.
[71] *Ibid.,* p. 158. On Richard Morison (d. 1556) see W. Gordon Zeeveld, "Richard Morison, Public Apologist for Henry VIII," *Publications of the Modern Language Association of America,* LV (1940), 409–10; 416–18.
[72] Simon, *op. cit.,* pp. 160, 201–2.

ideas: public instruction *pro philosophia christi* and the general reform of higher education. And the universities recognized the fact, voting thanks for policies which promised to make excellent use of wealth that had earlier been "unprofitable, nay pernicious, to the Christian religion."[73]

What was taking place was the steady application of humanist ideas of reform to the actual business of the Reformation as it touched politics, the church, social and economic affairs, and education. Hostile to the stultifying influence of the old hierarchical notions which were enjoying their Indian summer, Cromwell was making policy along humanist lines and using the humanists themselves to explain it to the community. More important even than that, however, was the action he took to translate policy into effective reform, coupling good counsel with the energy of a lay-minded revolutionary bent on making work new solutions to old problems. Having settled on certain purposes, he was also organizing for home consumption a campaign of persuasion unprecedented in English history:

The patronage of Cromwell coincided with, if it did not actually create, the first significant growth of public discussion. . . . Cromwell's fall from the royal grace was followed by a relatively barren period. The extent to which the blight can be explained by the fall of the Vicar-General himself depends, of course, upon the amount of credit he deserves for stimulating discussions in the years of his ascendancy. The fact remains that, after Cromwell's fall, Henry's conservative tendencies in religion were accompanied by a repressive attitude toward the discussion of such matters. The resulting atmosphere at court must have been discouraging also to the discussion of other issues as well. And, in the country as a whole, the potentially articulate citizen could have found little encouragement in the ominous shadow of the Henrician law of treason and the act "abolishing diversity in opinions." Certainly the humanists as a group were not much in evidence as official spokesmen after Cromwell's fall.[74]

Cromwell directed and channeled the "Erasmian enthusiasm for social reform"[75] which was a characteristic of the 1530's. His patronage gave meaning to the Renaissance ideal of the citizen-

---

[73] John Strype, *Ecclesiastic Memorials, Relating Chiefly to Religion and the Reformation of it . . . Containing Original Records*, new ed. 6 vols. (Oxford: The University Press, 1822), I, *i*, 484–5.
[74] Ferguson, *op. cit.*, pp. 138–9.
[75] *Ibid.*, p. 140.

councilor; and it was this fact which Clement Armstrong[76] honored when in 1536 he sent this note to Cromwell along with some writings on social problems:

> Please it your mastership to consider where I have been your servant *in my mind* this three years, taking time, labor, and pain to help set forth the knowledge of the right order of commonweal of all people in the realm, to the intent that ye should help the King to set it up to be administered in exemplum to all other realms.[77]

Social and educational reforms were to bear fruit in many ways, but even these achievements seemed less immediate matters of concern to reformers than did religious affairs. As we have already shown, English humanists aimed at an undogmatic transformation of popular religion, based on their scholarship and an urgent sense that life in the world was a true calling. But Erasmus, whose work was so basic to the movement, wrote only in Latin. If his ideas were to penetrate English society, two things were needed: a program of translation into the vernacular, and royal councilors willing to make humanist reform motifs the policy of government.[78]

The role of Thomas Cromwell in meeting both needs was striking. From 1522, when William Tyndale Englished the *Enchiridion*, until the middle of the century, the stream of translations flowed steadily. While Tyndale's work was not published until 1533, under Cromwell's patronage, in More's circle both translation and publication of Erasmus was established in 1524. More, Fisher, and the Pole family took an active part in spreading the *philosophia christi* to "plowmen and weavers."[79] But it was only after Cromwell came to power in 1532 that the stream became a flooding torrent.

The first humanist reformer to put Erasmus in the new context of the English Reformation was Richard Taverner, one of the numerous Cambridge men who had migrated to Wolsey's

---

[76] For Clement Armstrong (fl. 1535) see S. T. Bindoff, "Clement Armstrong and His Treatises of the Commonweal," *Economic History Review*, XIV (1944), 64–83.

[77] Quoted in Ferguson, *op. cit.*, p. 154, from R. Pauli, *Drei Volkswirtschaftliche Denkschriften aus der Zeit Heinrichs VIII von England* (Göttingen: n.p., 1878), pp. 49–51. I have changed the spelling and punctuation.

[78] See the recent summary of E. J. Devereux, "English Translators of Erasmus, 1522–1557," in *Editing Sixteenth Century Texts* (Toronto: University of Toronto Press, 1966), pp. 42–58.

[79] Erasmus' words in *Opera Omnia*, ed. J. Clericus, 10 vols., (Leiden: 1703–1706), V, 140.

Oxford foundation under Cromwell's stewardship. What is especially interesting about Taverner's translation of Erasmus' book on matrimony is its dedication to Cromwell. Taverner used the timely book to offer his services to the newly established chief councilor, telling him how he

began besily to revolve in mind, how he agayne on hys parte myght somewhat declare his fervent zele of herte towardes hym. Whiche he thus revolvinge, lo soddenly (as god wolde) a certayn Epystle of Doctor Erasmus . . . offered it selfe unto hys syght. Whiche so sone as he began to read, he thought it a thyng full necessarie and expedyent, to translate . . . and so under your noble protection to communicate it to the people, namely when he considered the blynd superstition of men and women, which cease not day by day to professe and vowe perpetuall chastyte before they sufficyently knowe them selfes and the infirmitie of theyr nature.[80]

A recent critic has said: "Word seems to have gotten around that Cromwell's patronage would be given for English versions of Erasmus' works, particularly those straightforward enough for plain people, those that contained the simple Erasmian *philosophia christi.* . . ."[81] The call was quickly answered. When Martin Tyndale sent to Cromwell a version of the famous *Epistle to Jodocus Jonas,* which contained brief lives of John Colet and Jean Vitrier, he assumed that Cromwell was actually organizing a secretariat to deal with such works. His letter implied that Taverner would check the book, along with William Marshall perhaps, but that Cromwell himself would make the decision to accept or reject the work.[82] At about the same time Cromwell began to pay the expenses of the publisher John Bydell, one of Wynkyn de Worde's men, who was to be very prominent in the publication of reform tracts and especially Erasmus' books. In April 1534 Cromwell helped to finance the Erasmian catechism.[83] Again, when Thomas Cox sent his version of the *Paraphrasis* to the bookseller John Toy, he noted that it must

---

[80] *The Epystle in laude and prayse of matrymony* (London: R. Redman, 1531?) was Taverner's version of *Encomium Matrimonii.* On the circumstances of consultation between Taverner and Cromwell, see McConica, *op. cit.,* pp. 116–9.

[81] Devereux, "English Translators of Erasmus," p. 49.

[82] *Ibid.,* p. 50.

[83] See *Letters and Papers,* VI, 299, items II and VII, as well as 923, item iv. On Bydell, see E. Gordon Duff, *The Printers, Stationers and Bookbinders of Westminister and London from 1476 to 1535* (Cambridge, England: Cambridge University Press, 1906), pp. 138–40; 203–4.

first be sent to Cromwell to see whether it should be printed.[84] Gregory Cromwell's tutor Henry Dowes translated *Pietas puerilis*,[85] a colloquy dealing with the concept "adiaphora," or things indifferent to salvation, which was soon followed by the anonymous rendering of *De esu carnium,* on the same theme.[86]

Between 1534 and 1537 the campaign reached its crest when *Colloquies* and the *Julius Exclusus* were printed. Even more to the point was the *Peregrinatio religionis ergo*, in which Erasmus and Colet engaged in lively criticism of pilgrimages, superstitious devotions, and other "dampnable allusyones of the devylle . . . contrary to the immaculate scrypture of God." The monasteries were then being dissolved.

While humanist ideas of reform were thus advancing, the Cromwellians also acted on the truth that one could not throw a body from a tower and bid it stop halfway down. England was caught up in the great European movement of the Reformation. And for Cromwell Erasmianism was not an end in itself. Rather it was a steppingstone toward moderate Protestantism. Between 1525 and 1547 over eight-hundred separate editions of religious works were printed in England in English, and a large part of these were books of markedly Protestant tone by Barnes, Coverdale, Becon, Taverner, Roy, and Joy, as well as translations of Melanchthon and Luther. The Ten Articles of 1536 drew heavily on the *Augsburg Confession* of 1530 and the subsequent *Apologia* of Melanchthon. Both German books were translated and printed at Cromwell's urging by Richard Taverner and bore dedications to the king's minister. A year earlier Melanchthon's *Loci Communes* appeared in an English version dedicated to Henry VIII. The 1537 *Bishops' Book* owed much to Luther's *Catechism,* and even the supposedly reactionary *King's Book* of 1543 owed a great deal to the official formularies of the 1530's, tinged as they were by Lutheran ideas. Hence it will no longer do to say that the Reformation over which Cromwell presided from 1532 to 1540 was 'Catholicism without the Pope." While he lived and held the reigns of

---

[84] *Letters and Papers*, VII, 659.

[85] *Ibid.,* 1135.

[86] Erasmus dealt plainly with the distinction between those things necessary for salvation and ordained by God and those things which were human additions and so indifferent. The degree to which Erasmus' moderate questioning of traditional points of view masked his radicalism is discussed in H. A. Enno Van Gelder, *The Two Reformations in the Sixteenth Century,* (The Hague: M. Nijhoff, 1964); esp. in chap. 4, "Erasmus."

power, England took long strides toward Continental reform. We must grapple with these facts if we hope to understand the English Protestanism of Edward VI's reign or that of his sister Elizabeth's long rule.

By late 1539 Erasmus had served his turn. When Cromwell fell, the translation of books attacking the external framework of the old religion ceased, and Erasmus was represented by editions of *Exomolegesis* and *An Epistle to Balthasar Mercklin,* works in defense of auricular confession and the real presence in the eucharist. The reaction came with the Six Articles, an act implying strict control of ideas, whose purpose was mirrored in its title: *An Act to Abolish Diversity of Opinion.* It was a watershed in Reformation history in England. And so was the execution of Cromwell in the following year.[87]

Cromwell had been more than the patron of printers and translators. He had put into practice Erasmian notions, as even the casual reader of his letters will quickly recognize. In his official correspondence we find basic humanist ideals of reform at work: a religion purged of superfluous ceremonies and fantastic ritual; doctrine not burdened with finely spun out distinctions and assumptions of priestly domination; scholarship put to work in the basic task of purification of scripture and in the setting forth of books conducive to popular piety; a concept of vocation reserved neither to the monk nor parish priest but instead the common property of every man and woman in the world. Had he been the author of treatises on reform, Cromwell could not have been more explicit about his desire to see humanist programs permeate English society. And what he did write was more effective than any book. He gave to the newly founded Church of England his *Injunctions,* which are the most important texts of official Erasmianism in search of that Christian conspiracy we have so often noted. The *Injunctions* throw a clear light on the justice of the charges laid against Cromwell in 1540: that he had spread false books of religion into all English shires; that he had affirmed heresies; and that he had them translated into "our maternall and English tongue."

Let us reconsider the case we have made. While we have given due emphasis to the development of reform sentiment in the period before Cromwell's domination of politics and patronage, we have also paid attention to its alterations and difficulties in the swirling currents that drowned Wolsey and broke the

[87] Devereux, *op. cit.,* pp. 51–3.

bonds of church unity. We have maintained that the ebb and flow lacked direction until it was channeled by Cromwell. James K. McConica has put it succinctly:

> The turning point is the year 1532, when the appearance of distinguished opposition to the King's policies, followed within a year by the decisive break with Rome, made the creation of a royal apologetic a matter of urgent necessity. It seems that it was in these months that Thomas Cromwell decided to supplement the theories put forth about the King's relationship to the English Church with a substantial body of Erasmian matter in translation, which associated the King's design with the cause of humanism and reform.[88]

And:

> In retrospect, it is clear that Cromwell's propaganda extended far beyond the political treatises which first attracted scholarly attention. As his contemporaries knew, he was the center of a great publication programme in which popular doctrinal works were the main theme. The influence of these ideas can also be traced in the official and semiofficial formularies of the early Henrician Church, and the keynote is always Erasmian reform [89]

Cromwell's program was intensely English only in its political dimensions. Its Erasmian skepticism and hostility to the papacy were not native or peculiar to England. But Erasmianism blended with the crisis of the 1530's to produce a movement that defined the character of the English commonwealth for centuries. When Cromwell climbed the scaffold on 28 July 1540, murmuring Erasmus' *In gravi morbo*,[90] he had already helped to put down roots of reform that would defy attempts to graft on radical stock or to root them out under Edward VI and then Mary. Subsequent generations of Englishmen developed and completed the work begun in the circle of Cromwell, while all the time execrating his memory.

The reasons for that execration were themselves real enough in men's minds and must be apparent also to those who read Cromwell's letters. During his tenure of power profound changes were brought about, and attempts were made to permeate society with new motifs of government in both church and commonwealth. Active commitment by subjects to these new trends

---

[88] *Ibid.*, p. 148.

[89] *Ibid.*, p. 194.

[90] Many writers have discussed this beautiful prayer, but the only one to identify it is Devereux, *op. cit.*, p. 53, with references to C. S. Coldwell, *The Prayers of Erasmus* (London, 1872) p. vii. Hall's *Chronicle* and Foxe's *Book of Martyrs* report Cromwell reciting the prayer.

was often lacking, despite the campaign for home consumption. Resort to force was thus sometimes necessary, unless the government chose to suffer the existence of men whose conduct did not conform to what was expected of them. Cromwell was the maker and enforcer of reform, once the sense of the community of the realm was arrived at in Parliament. The degree to which there was struggle and protest within the kingdom had helped to make Parliament the focal point of a revolution by consent. But it also meant that new powers spelled out there were put into effect in the shires under Cromwell's direction. He was the king's chief minister in secular affairs, but he was also vicar-general of the Church of England. And so all the unlovely aspects of heresy and treason appear side by side with Erasmian exhortations in his papers.

He had daily to "struggle with problems beyond the strength of men," as Froude justly said, especially those touching the use of a royal supremacy not clearly limited by law but yet impinging daily upon men's lives in novel ways. Where grievances were many and unrelieved, rebellion came, as in the Pilgrimage of Grace. Where the adjustment of the relations between crown and commonwealth touched the church, some men proved as hearty in resistance as Cromwell proved strong in his loyalty to reform. He was thus an actor in scenes dramatized out of proportion. For we will never grasp the nature of his achievement if we cannot for a moment forget that Fisher and More were cruelly killed. The great struggles of the 1530's were not between right and wrong, but rather, as Hegel said of the struggles between Creon and Antigone, between two rights. So Cromwell led a reformation in a country torn by chronic poverty, dangerous religious passions, rebellion at home, and threats from abroad, in a situation of political crisis without parallel since the Norman conquest of England.

In that struggle Cromwell was for the policy of the open Bible and the dimunition of ecclesiastical wealth, power, and prestige. He stood for a policy which at times seemed frankly Protestant, but which can be better understood in the context of humanist reform. He stood for a policy in which sensitivity to educational reform and amelioration of social injustice were considered to be instruments useful in the perfection of a Commonwealth. Increasingly, he seemed also to stand for a policy that moved more rapidly than Henry VIII would follow.

Above all else Cromwell stood for a policy that we can identify with the origins of Anglicanism. He was deeply involved with reform-minded men who were moving toward views that were daring and dangerous. He had seized upon the English Bible as the best weapon in his struggles, an interest which must be explored anew in the light of some startling circumstances not yet fully understood.[91] He worked toward an ideal of an independent English church midway between Rome and Wittenberg, eschewing alike the heresies of the radicals and the old superstitions of the conservatives. The revolution over which he presided was, as Dickens has rightly noted, therefore as much religious as it was legal, a revolution in which a simple doctrine of faith based on scripture was set forth by Parliament and carried to the people by the press and pulpit. Always mindful that good order in both church and commonwealth were twin aspects of a single society, Cromwell pursued the Christian conspiracy relentlessly and insisted that it be guided by charity. That he made martyrs is thus ironic.

Already the government and the intellectuals were groping their way toward a Reformation of compromise and detachment . . . most of all because the divisions among Englishmen made it safer to attempt a settlement based on balance and comprehension rather than upon a narrow orthodoxy. However one measures these forces, it remains imperceptive to date the genesis of Anglicanism from the accession of Elizabeth, or even from the publication of Cranmer's first prayer book.[92]

Opera manuum tuarum indeed!

[91] Mr. Abraham Hoffman, one of the students in my doctoral seminar, has been working on the probability that Cromwell may have offered to intervene in admiralty matters between German merchants and the brother of the constable of France in order to secure the release of the English Bible seized from printers by Parisian authorities. Upon his fall in 1540 he was accused of having illegally manipulated the proceedings for his personal gain.
[92] *The English Reformation,* p. 179.

I

Letters on the Commonweal:

Secular Governance

1. To John Creke

PRO SP1/28/153
LP, III, 3249; 1

17 August [1523]
London

BETWEEN 1520 and 1524 Cromwell was busy as a solicitor, arbitrator, and attorney in London and in the circle of the Marquis of Dorset. Both his city connections and those with the Grey family threw him into contact with men important in the politics of the period and in government. In 1523 he was a member of the House of Commons. In the debates of that year he took a very active part, standing against Wolsey's financial demands and the war policy in France that necessitated taxes beyond the capacity of subjects' pockets. He also proposed a union with Scotland as a more effective curtailment of French threats to England than any renewal of continental wars. This letter is more sardonic and ironic than it is hostile to Parliament, and cannot be seen in terms of any alleged contempt for representative institutions. Perhaps Wolsey noticed Cromwell's clever and stubborn independence on that occasion, for in 1524–1525 the Cardinal counted Cromwell among his counselors. The political career of Thomas Cromwell had begun.

Master Creke[1] as heartily as I can I commend me and in the same wise thank you for your gentle and loving letters to me sundry times sent. And where as I accordingly have not in like wise remembered and rescribed it has been for that I have not had anything to write of to your advancement, whom, I assure you, if it were in my little power I could be well contented to prefer as far as any man living. But at this present, I being at some leisure, contending to remember and also to remunerate the old acquaintance and to renew or not forget sundry communications, supposing you desire to know the news current in these parts, for it is said that news refreshes the spirit of life,

---

[1] John Creke was a merchant tailor and factor to a London trader named William Munkcaster or Moncaster. He became a servant of Cranmer in 1533 and subsequently was esquire beadle in Oxford University.

wherefore you shall understand that by long time I among others
have endured a parliament which continued by the space of
seventeen whole weeks.[2] Where we communed of war, peace,
strife, contention, debates, murmur, grudge, riches, poverty, pen-
ury, truth, falsehood, justice, equity, deceit, oppression, magna-
nimity, activity, force, attemprance,* treason, murder, felony,
conciliation, and also how a commonwealth might be edified
and also continued within this our realm. Howbeit, in conclusion we have done as our predecessors have been wont to do.
That is to say, as well as we might and left where we began.

You shall also understand that the Duke of Suffolk,[3] furnished
with a great army, goes over in all goodly haste, whither I
know not. When I know, I shall advertise you. We have in
our parliament granted unto the king's highness a right large
subsidy, the like whereof was never granted in this realm.[4]

All your friends to my knowledge be in good health and
specially they that you wott of. You know what I mean. I think
it is best to write in parables, because I am in doubt.[5] Master
Vaughan[6] fares well and so does Master Munkcaster.[7] Master

[2] Internal evidence (the war subsidy, Suffolk's command of the army,
and the length of the Parliament, make it certain that the Parliament is
that of 1523. This parliament first met on 15 April, after a period of
eight years in which none had been summoned. Cromwell's statement
of 17 August about the seventeen weeks during which he endured parliament is a precise one.

[3] Charles Brandon (d. 1545) had married Henry VIII's sister Mary.
There is no adequate life of Suffolk, whose skills as either soldier or
statesman never rose above mediocrity. The army he led invaded France,
threatening Paris in league with the rebelling Duc de Bourbon. But
Bourbon's treason was discovered and he fled to the emperor. Nothing
of substance was accomplished.

[4] In 1522 Wolsey raised a forced loan among Henry's wealthier subjects
in an amount equal to double the subsidy of 1514. The subsidy was a
form of direct parliamentary taxation to supplement royal income from
ordinary sources (customs, land revenue, and the profits of justice, among
others). But the income of the loan was spent, and the needs of war
finance prompted Wolsey to seek about £800,000, at a rate of four
shillings in the pound, on both lands and goods. The Commons offered
half that amount, to be spread over two years, a twentieth in 1523 and
another in 1524. A compromise between the two figures resulted from
the mediation of the Speaker, Thomas More.

[5] Whether the reference is to some business Cromwell had in hand and
concerning his friends must remain obscure.

[6] Stephen Vaughan (d. 1549) was a merchant and diplomat who was
in Cromwell's service as early as 1523 or 1524. He had been among
Cromwell's friends from about 1520. He played an important role in
Cromwell's administration at home and abroad, especially with regard

Woodall[8] is merry without a wife and commends him to you.
And so also is Nicholas Longmede,[9] which has paid William
Wilford.[10] And thus as well fare you as I would do myself. At
London the seventeenth day of August. By your friend to all
his possible power.

Autograph letter. Addressed: "To his special and entirely beloved friend John Creke be this given."

2. To William Claybrook

PRO SP1/55/23   [July 1529]
LP, IV, 5812; 11   [London]

IN THE SUMMER of 1529 resentment of Wolsey and the loss of
the king's confidence portended his fall. There were many
ominous signs, the fervor with which Wolsey's policies were
criticized by laymen and clergy as well as popular derogatory
poems and the intrigues of courtiers. Crown lawyers were in-
vestigating various aspects of Wolsey's exercise of power, and
it is doubtless in this connection that Cromwell wrote to one
of the Cardinal's most active agents, William Claybrook. If the
date given by Brewer and Gairdner in *LP* is correct (the end
of July), plans to bring Wolsey down must have been in hand
immediately after Campeggio broke off the hearings on the Divorce. To this letter Claybrook replied, denying that he had ever
had custody of Toney's registers or other relevant documents.
But he did arrange a meeting with Cromwell at Blackfriars the
following day, for which reason this letter is placed in London.
Also, in the reply to Cromwell, Claybrook mentions specific legal
problems raised by the king's attorney, which may well support
Pollard's contention that the letter printed here belongs to October 1529, since the king summoned the council to Windsor on

---

to the Antwerp money market and the negotiations for the delivery of
William Tyndale into English hands. See W. C. Richardson, *Stephen
Vaughan* (Baton Rouge: Louisiana State University Press, 1952).
[7] For Munkcaster, see *LP*, IV, 3086, and III, 3028; also note 1 of this
letter.
[8] Another of Cromwell's merchant friends, see *LP*, III, 2624.
[9] Longmede owed a debt to Cromwell (*LP*, IV, 5330) and was in a
list of correspondents (*LP*, IV, 955).
[10] Impossible to identify.

1 October to discuss Wolsey's fate. Cromwell, contrary to charges that he was looking to his own interests only, was faithfully doing Wolsey's business right in the eye of the storm.

Master Claybrook.[1] This is to advertise you, as ever you wanted to do my lord service or pleasure, that you sort out the register of Master Toney[2] and also all other registers, with also the bulls of my lord's legacy,[3] to the intent that said may be showed this night to the king's attorney, for such causes as I declared unto you at my last speaking with you.[4] Of answer by this bearer I pray you that I may have knowledge. And fare you well. Your friend.

Autograph letter. The answer Cromwell requested was in fact written on the back of the letter. The letter sent by Cromwell lacks address and endorsements.

[1] William Claybrook, also known as Clayborough and Claiburgh, LL. D., canon of York, prothonotary in the legate's divorce court and as such familiar with all of Wolsey's then pressing business, had worked with the cardinal for nearly a decade. He was later a member of the king's counsel in the trial of the case before Cranmer at Dunstable in 1533.

[2] A "Master Toney" appears in Wolsey's service as early as 1514, perhaps the Robert Toney who was in Princess Mary's suite and attestor of her marriage to Louis XII of France. If so, he steadily rose in Wolsey's service, while holding canon's office in Lincoln and York cathedrals. That Dr. Robert Toney had been of Wolsey's council, but had died in 1526, in which case Claybrook's denial that he had ever had custody of Toney's registers makes good sense.

[3] The registers in question were doubtless books in which regular entries were made of the details of Wolsey's affairs touching the exercise of legatine powers and in which copies of letters were kept. Specifically, bulls granted to Wolsey in which the pope had ceded certain powers to him pertaining to "preventions," or actions in which Wolsey claimed superior powers to forestall official acts of inferiors, including the archbishop of Canterbury, were meant.

[4] The exact subject of the conversation alluded to grew out of Claybrook's letter to Cromwell (*LP*, IV, 5810), in which Cromwell was asked to bring to Kingston all books and writings relevant to the colleges at Ipswich and Oxford, which Pollard argues was 23 October 1529, *after* Wolsey had been deprived of the great seal, a fact of some importance in assigning this letter to October 1529 in place of July.

3. To Cardinal Wolsey

PRO SP1/57/92–3   5 May [1530]
LP, IV, 6368; 14   St. James's Palace

THIS LETTER of necessity is more important for what it does not
say than for what it does. Here we have the anguish of a man
accustomed to command cardinals and move kings. During the
Easter season of 1530 Wolsey slowly made his way north, to
the archbishopric of York which he had never visited in his
years of power, into an exile more terrible with every mile he
rode. By 20 April he had reached his house at Southwell, but
the manor house was under repair and Wolsey had to stay with
a friend to whom he had given favor in better days. His every
move was watched at court, especially by those who feared he
would try some tricks to win again the king's favor. Cromwell,
who was with the king, knew the machinations of Wolsey's
enemies, and he urged his master not to give them any grounds
for new moves against him. In that regard, he counseled humility
and consent to any demands Henry VIII might make. What the
particular matters at issue were, it is difficult to say. But some
difficulty over the king's not honoring Wolsey's debts may be
involved. When Wolsey's great income was confiscated by Henry
VIII, he had promised to meet the debts due Wolsey's creditors.
But in some instances he reneged, and Wolsey perhaps showed
his impatience by obstructing some purpose of the king.

After my right hearty commendations to your grace. According to your desire specified in your letters of answer to the request made unto you by the king's majesty, for the treasureship
of York, I have so solicited the matter both to his highness and
to Doctor Leighten[1] that both be content your gift shall stand,
so as your grace do accomplish the tenor of his highness' letters
now eftsoons* directed unto you. Which mine advice and counsel is that you shall in any wise ensue* and that your chancellor[2]

---

[1] Dr. Richard Leighton (1500?–1544), dean of York, and one of the
chief agents in Cromwell's administration of the suppression of the
monasteries.

[2] For evidence that Wolsey's household administration and curial service
possessed a chancellor, see *LP*, IV, 2052, 4529. The most important
Henrician official to serve Wolsey in that capacity was Sir William
Bulmer (*LP*, III, 3447).

shall do the semblable in an other request made by his majesty
unto him, without stay, tract, or further sticking. And in anything else, wherein I may do unto your grace* stead or pleasure,
I shall be as glad to do the office of a friend as you shall be
to require the same of me. Thus most heartily fare you well.
From St. James beside Westminster,[3] the fifth day of May.

Copy, unsigned, in the hand of Thomas Wriothesley, Cromwell's
clerk. There are neither address nor endorsement clauses.

4. To Sir Anthony Fitzherbert[1] and Walter Luke[2]

PRO SP1/78/20   19 July [1533]
LP, VI, 872; 49   London

THE SOCIAL institution of wardship developed within the rules
of descent and the government of real property. The basic intent
was to protect the property of minor heirs. But over the centuries
a great competition for wards grew up, even where the value of
the property to which a minor was heir was itself quite trivial.
For beyond regulations against the wasting of an inheritance by
guardians or the enforcing of an unsuitable marriage, it was a
fact that county politics and alliance systems often turned on
the control conveyed by the crown with a wardship. The traffic
in wardships embraced men of all classes and all professions,
from the servants of Cromwell's household, or the minister himself, to the most eminent men of the realm. During the 1530's,
before the creation of a Court of Wards out of the earlier Office
of Wards, Cromwell, as the king's leading minister, was no less
closely connected with that office than he was with the monasteries or other crown rights that promised to meet rising expenditures of government. Cromwell apparently exploited the
existing machinery, while also formulating plans to reform it, a
thing more necessary as the crown's assumption of ecclesiastical

[3] St. James's Palace, Westminster, where the king kept court in the
spring of 1530, from which circumstance this letter can be dated.
[1] Sir Anthony Fitzherbert (1470–1538), judge and barrister; justice of
common pleas from 1522–1538; author of the earliest systematic abridg-
ment of the common law.
[2] Walter Luke, sergeant-at-law and judge of king's bench.

jurisdiction increased tremendously its interests in wardship. The issues involved were often matters for the common law courts as well as the church courts, since property rights involved in wardship were part of the common law of real property applied to private wardships. Side by side with royal claims and those of lords over tenants on their estates, officials closely connected with the Office of Wards (or the later Court) enjoyed the opportunities of their office and, as Cromwell reveals here, they often used all of their influence to prevent the defeat of their interests.

After my right hearty commendations. Forasmuch as there is a *nisi prius* passed out to be tried before you at the next assizes[3] to be holden at Lincoln, concerning the trial of the title of Anthony Styldolfe,[4] who is my ward, which *nisi prius* is secretly sued out and passed without my knowledge, so as per case the same may be much prejudicial unto me in that thing whereunto I have good, just and lawful title, as you shall apperceive by

[3] The matter of *nisi prius* must be treated with that of assize. By the late thirteenth century, trial by jury was the usual mode of trying most civil and some criminal matters. When an action in one of the courts fixed at Westminster was ready for trial, that is, when the parties had *raised some issue of fact* in their pleading, it had been the practice to summon to the court a jury from the county to which the case belonged. In a Lincolnshire case of the kind Cromwell relates in this letter, the sheriff of Lincolnshire would be directed to send jurors to Westminster. But this was burdensome and expensive. In 1285, to correct this absurd condition, it was ordained that the trial of such actions should be before justices of assize, that is, by men among whom one professional judge sat to dispose of ordinary civil matters of the county. The court before which the action was pending would then bid the sheriff to send the jurors to Westminster on a certain day, unless first *(nisi prius justiciarii veniant)* justices came into Lincolnshire to take the assizes. As a matter of course, then, justices of assize would come around before the day named in the *nisi prius* writ; that is, the case would in fact usually be heard by a judge under royal commission, at *nisi prius* and not at Westminster. Here the question of fact is Cromwell's claim to exercise a wardship, which he fears will be defeated by a *nisi prius* to be heard by Fitzherbert and Luke and which has been so secretly begun and continued as to raise a suspicion of four play.

[4] Apparently Anthony Styldolfe was the ward of his uncle, Thomas Styldolfe, until 16 July 1533, at which time Cromwell's servant William Body paid £4/2/11 to Thomas Styldolfe for the wardship of Anthony (*LP*, VI, 841). That Thomas Styldolfe may have been involved in some attempt to defeat Cromwell's lawful interest seems unlikely. But many years later Cromwell intervened in a case between Sir Ralph Sadler and Stydolfe, to help Sadler defeat Styldolfe's claim to exercise the stewardship of a manor belonging to the crown.

such deeds and writings as my friend this bearer shall show unto you; I, therefore, considering your worships and good indifferencies, trusting that you will do me none injustice in this behalf, do most heartily require and pray you to stay the trial of the said *nisi prius*, until you shall have further knowledge of the matter, the rather for that I am credibly informed that the inquest is already so partially empanelled that undoubtedly it is thought they will pass directly against the truth. Eftsoons, therefore, most heartily requiring you to provide and foresee mine indemnity in this part, and for the good acquittal of your gentleness to be showed unto me herein, if there be anything wherein my poor powers can extend to do you pleasure, I shall not fail to accomplish the same to the uttermost of my little power. And so heartily fare ye well. At London, the 19th day of July. It may please you to give firm credence unto this bearer in such things as he shall declare unto you on my behalf. Your assured friend.

Clerk's hand, signature autograph. Addressed: "To the right worshipful Sir Anthony Fitzherbert knight, one of the king's justices of the common bench, and to Mr. Walter Luke, esquire, and to either of them."

5. To Henry VIII

PRO SP1/82/98   January [1534]
LP, VII, 73; 67   London

CROMWELL'S REFERENCE to a statute limiting the number of sheep permitted to a single sheep farmer is to 25 Henry VIII, c. 13, whereby a farmer might keep a maximum of 2,400 sheep. While there were several exceptions allowed to lay and clerical entrepreneurs, the most interesting thing about Cromwell's advocacy of this bill is the relation between his opinions and those of humanist reformers, among whom we might list More, Starkey, and John Hales. Perhaps the most famous passage in *Utopia* is that diatribe against enclosing landlords, in which More recognized the tide running in favor of the large- and medium-size producers whose enthusiasm for wool and the cloth trade seemed to More to threaten depopulation on a massive scale. The strain More espied was that of powerful and undisciplined market competition in the early Tudor period, which reached a peak in the thirties and forties, with the insistent demand for ever more wool the driving force. But it was not only from More that Cromwell learned of the problems of sheep-running, enclosure, and depopulation. Wolsey had given ear to the complaints of the peasants and yeomen against enclosing landlords. In the matter of sheep-running he threw the weight of his administration with the poor. In 1517 his commissioners of depopulation made an inquest into all lands enclosed since 1485. Names of depopulating landlords came to the cardinal's hands in his famous "domesday of enclosures." Among them we find yeomen, gentry, aristocrats, high officers in both lay and clerical administration. What we do not know is how effectively his decree to throw over recent enclosures was executed. We do know that of 101 cases brought in chancery under writs issued because of the decree, 25 received a stay only on condition that they would comply in a specified time, while another two dozen offenders proved their compliance. For years after Wolsey's own fall, cases arising out of the 1517 commission came into court under the watchful eye of Cromwell—who in characteristic fashion preferred statute to equity jurisdiction in chancery as a remedy for the ills of the commonwealth.

Please it your most royal majesty to be advertised that according to your most high pleasure and commandments I have made search for such patents and grants as your Highness and also the most famous king your father, whose soul our Lord pardon, have granted unto Sir Richard Weston knight, your under-treasurer of your exchequer.[1] And the same I have sent to your Highness here enclosed.

It may also please your most royal majesty to know how that yesterday there passed your Commons a bill that no person within this your realm shall hereafter keep and nourish above the number of two thousand sheep and also that the eighth part of every man's land being a farmer shall for ever hereafter be put in tillage yearly. Which bill, if by the great wisdom, virtue, goodness and zeal that your Highness bears towards this your realm, might have good success and take good effect amongst your lords above, I do conjecture and suppose in my poor, simple and unworthy judgment, that your Highness shall

[1].Sir Richard Weston (1466–1542), courtier, governor of Guernsey, knighted 1514, treasurer of Calais 1525, and undertreasurer of England, 1528–1542, was a constant attendant on the king and a close friend of Henry VIII's for nearly thirty years.

do the most noble, profitable and most beneficial thing that ever
was done to the common wealth of this your realm. It shall
thereby increase such wealth in the same amongst the great
number and multitude of your subjects as never was seen in
this realm since Brutus' time. Most heartily I beseech your
highness, and prostrate at the feet of your majesty, I beseech
your highness to pardon my boldness in thus writing to your
grace; which only proceeds for the truth, duty, allegiance and
love I do bear to your majesty and the common wealth of this
your realm, as Our Lord knows, unto whom I shall, as ever I
am most bounden, incessantly to pray for the continuous and
prosperous conservation of your most excellent, most royal and
Imperial estate long to endure.

Holograph draft, much corrected. Note that the phrases struck
through in Cromwell's draft contain some interesting populist
sentiments. For example, when the commonwealth is spoken
of, where the text now reads "ever was done to the commonwealth of this your realm. It shall thereby increase . . . ," the
original corrections, afterward excised, read "ever was done to
the common wealth of this your realm and your most humble
and obedient subjects in whom consisteth the strength, puisance
and magnificence of your most royal majesty. . . ."

6. To the University of Oxford

PRO SP1/83/252–3   [1534]
LP, VII, 618; 92

THE INTERESTING aspect of this letter is that it throws some light
on Cromwell's exact role in government. He was appointed secretary of state early in 1534, and it was normal for the secretary
to receive and answer royal correspondence in the king's name.
But here we have something more. When informed of the mis-
deeds of the university against townspeople, an episode in the
long history of town-gown strains and riots, Cromwell states
clearly that the king knows the university acted badly. Moreover, the king's council intended to make an end of the abuses
of townsmen by scholars and officials of the university, perhaps
in the form of an award determining disputed privileges. There
is in this case a letter from the commissary of the university to

Sir William Fitzwilliam, himself a member of the king's council, which shows that when the commissary and the mayor of Oxford came before the "council" they saw only Cromwell and the lord chancellor, Audley. Cromwell not only was dominant in the council; he was in many respects the effective council, acting in harmony with dependents like Audley. The evidence for an understanding of this among Cromwell's contemporaries, who knew to whom to address council matters touching reform of abuses, is well presented in Elton's *Tudor Revolution in Government*, pp. 349–58.

I commend me unto you, advertising the same that where the king's highness is credibly informed of your abusions, usurpations and ungentle demeanor used towards the king's highness, his subjects and inhabitants of that his town of Oxford and suburbs of the same, I cannot but marvel that you, being men of learning and in whom should remain both wisdom and discretion, will in such wise demean yourselfs; not only in making of laws and ordinances amongst yourselves to their hinderance, hurt and prejudice, but also contrary to the king's laws, which appears in you to have proceeded of nothing but mere malice. Wherefore, intending to conduce and allect* you to some good conformity and quietness, the king's highness therefore has commanded me to advertise you not only to restore all such persons as you have discommoned,[1] permitting them to do and occupy as they did before, without maintaining or suffering any scholar or their servants to occupy within the town or suburbs of the same as a burgess* there does, except he or they agree therefore with the said burgesses; but also that in no wise you do, vex, trouble or inquiet any of the said inhabitants—by suspension, excommunication, ensummoning,* banishment or otherwise. Using such discretion that all variances may cease and be stayed amongst you, so as all malice and evil will being condemned and expulsed from you, good amity, peace and quietness may take place accordingly.

And doubt you not, or it will be long the king's council by his gracious commandment will and have determined to set such an end and redress amongst you, as God willing shall be

[1] The specific town-gown problem alluded to is inherent in the meaning of the term "discommon." In the universities of Oxford and Cambridge, tradesmen had certain charter rights to trade with the undergraduates. As burgesses, they also had some rights of commoning stock on certain lands in which the universities had an interest. But denial of common rights in this context refers to trading privileges and not grazing.

an establishing of a perpetual peace, good unity and accord amongst you for ever. Fail you not this to do, as you will answer the king's highness and avoid the danger of his indignation and high displeasure. And so fare you well.

Clerk's hand, no signature. Addressed: "To the Chancellor[2] and Commissary[3] with other the Heads and Members of the University of Oxford be this given." Endorsed: "A copy of a letter to Oxford."

7. To Sir Richard Rich[1]

PRO SP1/92/30–1   20 April [1536]
LP, VIII, 563; 102   London

In 1361, Edward III's Parliament passed into law an act giving judicial powers to local gentry and lords who had before that time acted as conservators of the peace in each shire. He could scarcely have foreseen the place his conservators would occupy in Tudor local government, when the humble amateur policemen of Edward III, c. 16, became the backbone of magistracy as justices of the peace. Throughout the Tudor century "not loads, but stacks of statutes" were piled on the justices' backs, as Lambarde wrote in the 1602 edition of *Eirenarcha.* The essence of their judicial work was in the county quarter sessions, which from 1368 were conducted four times a year. But the "petty" session routine carried out by amateurs rested entirely on the professionals known as the "clerks of the peace," the pivotal figures in magistracy. Without them, there would probably have been no quarter sessions and no amateur county governors. The clerk of the peace was the chief channel and the chief instru-

---

[2] The chancellor of Oxford was John Longland (1473–1547), Bishop of Lincoln.

[3] Dr. William Tresham (d. 1569), commissary and vice-chancellor of the University.

[1] Sir Richard Rich (1496?–1567), first Baron Rich and later lord chancellor of England. He had risen rapidly between 1533 and 1536 under Cromwell's aegis, having represented the crown in a number of the important cases arising out of the supremacy and succession statutes. Cromwell favored him as an ambitious and loyal agent. By 1536 Rich was knight of the shire for Essex and also chancellor of the newly erected Court of Augmentations.

ment for coordinating the justices' work. He preserved the
quarter sessions' records and drafted indictments, processes, and
other legal instruments. He was therefore both deputy to the
custos rotulorum (keeper of the rolls) of Shakespeare's witty
scenes and clerk of the court of law. He was responsible for the
easy functioning of the court in its exercise of a complex and
expanding jurisdiction. If he was deficient, the justices were
themselves liable to the king for errors; thus it was incumbent
on them to choose wisely. As the recipient of virtually every
communication directed to the county courts from central agen-
cies, he was the key to any effective liaison between Cromwell's
administration, the council, and local governors. Moreover, the
money and prestige garnered from the office made it one hotly
contested for and a reflection of factional tensions in county
politics. Hence the patronage aspect of this letter, in which
the knight of the shire is asked by the king's secretary to help
the clerk against the power of one of the local, office-holding
gentry. Much of the success of Cromwell's reform-minded re-
gime depended on loyal agents in the county.

After my most hearty manner I commend me unto you. And
even so I pray you at this my request and contemplation to be
good master and friend unto Edward Campion,[2] clerk of the
peace within the shire of Essex and in all such his business
touching the same his office. And to be a means for him in the
same unto Mr. St. Claire,[3] him to desire to put the said Campion
to no further vexations and suits for the said office, as he has
hitherto done. In doing whereof you shall administer unto me
right singular pleasure, which, God willing, I shall not forget
semblable to requite as shall lie in my little power. And thus
heartily fare you well. At London, this 20th day of April.[4]

[2] The only Edward Campion who can be traced to Essex in the mid-
thirties is mentioned in a complaint of the Abbot of Tiltey, who states
that the man had intruded on a benefice given to the abbot; see *LP*,
VII, 1658. It is not likely that a priest would hold the clerk's office.
[3] It seems likely here that Sir John St. Claire or Sinclaire is meant; he
was an Essex landowner and frequent suitor to Augmentations.
[4] I cannot follow either Merriman or *LP* in placing this letter in 1535.
The suggestion of 1536 rests on the assumption that St. Claire was amenable to Rich's pressure in that year because Rich was both knight of
the shire of Essex and also the chief officer of the Augmentations, to
which St. Claire addressed himself in requests for land and favors. It
is interesting in that connection to note that St. Claire preferred to seek
the favor of Thomas Mildmay, am auditor of the court: *LP, Addenda*,
I, ii, 1663 and also 1554–1555.

No signature; a copy of the original, apparently in the hand of one of the clerks kept by Rich. At least it does not appear to be a hand of Cromwell's secretariat. Addressed: "To my loving friend Master Rich." Endorsed: Fol. 31*d*; minute of a letter.

8. To Mr. Claymond[1] and Dr. London[2]

PRO SP1/92/236–7   May [1535]
LP, VIII, 790; 104   London

IN 1535 CROMWELL became chancellor of the University at Cambridge, an office which gave him constitutional rights to meddle in university affairs. In the same year, he also became Henry VIII's vicegerent in spiritual affairs, through which office he could exercise general supervision over the University at Oxford as well. The universities were ecclesiastical bodies in law, and Cromwell's new power reminds us that the great statutes of 1533 to 1535 weighed as heavily upon them as upon any other institutions in the kingdom. They had formerly acknowledged the joint power of the pope and king. Now, they rested on the sole jurisdiction of the crown and its agents. This meant necessarily a profound change in the nature of the controls and influence that would be brought to bear on the many colleges composing the universities. The most important immediate consequence was this: that supreme power being vested in only one authority, which was close at hand and in Cromwell's person extraordinarily energetic, meant frequent intervention in academic and collegiate affairs. Thus the already ancient institutions began to feel the impact of the Reformation before the vast monastic establishment and even before the country as a whole. In the particular matter represented here, intervention in the choice of a new head of college, Cromwell's interests were probably more political than they were personal. Despite his statement about his "lover and friend," the man he recommended had already exhibited his loyalty to the new dispensa-

[1] John Claymond (1457?–1537), divine and president of Magdalen College Oxford, from 1504 to 1517, and from 1517 to 1537 president of Corpus Christi, where he established six scholarships for students in the "New Learning."
[2] Dr. John London (1486?–1543), another of Cromwell's Oxford supporters, was at the time warden of New College. He is most famous as a visitor of monasteries. As one of Gardiner's men after Cromwell's fall, he was convicted of perjury and died in prison.

tion in church and state as a strong supporter of the royal supremacy.

In my right hearty manner I commend me unto you. And where the President of Magdalene College,[3] aswell by his several letters as by mouth, of his mere motion at sundry times, which, commending the qualities of my lover and friend master Thomas Marshall,[4] granted unto me that he would be contented to resign that his room to the same Master Marshall, alleging that he was a man very apt and meet for the same, promising further and nothing doubting but in that behalf he both could and would find the means to obtain the good wills and minds of the Fellows of the said College; nevertheless, now of late (to my no little marvel) the said President, when I desired him to accomplish his said promise, alleged for his excuse that the good wills of the said Fellows could not in that behalf be obtained. Wherefore, I heartily desire to pray you effectually in my name to solicit and entreat the said Fellows as by your wisdoms you shall think most convenient; that they, for my sake, etc., at this my desire will be contented to conform themselves upon the resignation of the said President to the admission of the said Master Marshall or else that contrary-wise at the least I may know by your writing in whom the matter sticks. In doing whereof you shall not only deserve both laud and praise in the furtherance of the said Master Marshall, whose

[3] The president of Magdalen College here referred to was Thomas Knolles. He was pressured to resign, after holding office from 1527.

[4] Thomas Marshall, abbot of St. John's in Colchester, a Benedictine abbey. This Thomas Marshall is of extraordinary interest. In 1535 he was reckoned a staunch supporter of the king. But Marshall, *alias* Beche, was one of the three Benedictine abbots (along with Glastonbury and Colchester) executed for treason in 1539 for refusing to surrender his house because it was contrary to God's law to do so. Interestingly enough, it was Sir John St. Claire to whom Cromwell owed the evidence collected against Marshall (*LP*, XIII, ii, 887: "I like not the man. I fear he has a cankered heart."). It is Knowles's view (*The Religious Orders in England,* vol. III) that Marshall was a thoroughgoing conservative in doctrine, despite his acceptance of the Supremacy. As early as 1534 Cromwell had information that his house contained disaffected monks, but he did not pursue it. He spoke with reverence of Fisher and More, sympathized with the northern insurgents, and deplored the suppressions of 1536. That Cromwell knew this and recommended him to be president at Magdalen is either hard to credit or fathomable only on the view that Cromwell was not the witch-hunter usually represented by historians. Only in 1539, when Marshall overtly opposed the surrender of his own house, did an indictment result.

advancement I heartily desire, but also I will not fail to reimburse your kindness in that I may do you pleasure. And thus heartily fare you well, from London, the [lacunae in mss] day of May.

A copy. Endorsed: "Minute, a copy of a letter sent to Mr. Doctor London and Mr. Claymond."

9. To Sir Piers Dutton[1]

PRO SP1/103/90–91   3 April 1536
LP, X, 618; 143   The Rolls House

THIS LETTER and the one concerning the apprehension of the Bishop of Llandaff reflect the business of the king's council and Cromwell equally. As we have already noted, Cromwell's domination of ordinary affairs of politics, patronage, and routine matters ordinarily before the council makes it hard to unravel the twisted threads of private and public business. The same concern for equity and process outside the legal jungle of the courts evident in the case of the forged will or that of poor Richard Godwyn appears here, side by side with the evidence of the helplessness of central administration without the cooperation of the governors of the counties. The people concerned are none of them very powerful, apart from the sheriff of Cheshire, with whom Cromwell's relations were not especially good. Indeed, Cheshire as a whole often proved difficult for Tudor governments to manage.

In my right hearty manner I commend me unto you. And where I am credibly informed that one John Offeley, about the space of a year past, received at Calais of one Humphrey Lightfoot, then factor unto a friend of mine named Edmond Rouse, four hundred pounds,[2] to be delivered over unto the said Ed-

---

[1] The address is missing, but we know that Sir Piers Dutton was sheriff of Cheshire from 1535 to 1536, for which see *LP*, IX, 1106 and X, 870. The Duttons were a leading Cheshire family vital in the Tudor administration of regions difficult to govern—the Welsh march counties.

[2] Nothing much is known about the figures in this case. There is a fairly prominent Cornish family with court connections by the name of Ross,

mond here in London, which sum of four hundred pounds the
said Offeley, contrary to the trust and confidence that he was
put in, as yet has not made delivery of, but employs and con-
verts the same unto his own use, to the great hurt and hinderance of my said friends. Being now advertised that the said
Offeley has merchandises and wares and goods at this present
time within the town of Westchester[3] and other places adjoining within the limits of your office and that the said Offeley
has also personal recourse thither, I require you and in the king's
name will and command you, that for redress to be had of the
said detestable wrong and due restitution to be made unto the
said Edward Rouse of his said money dishonestly and untruly
kept from him by the said Offeley, according to justice and
equity, you do immediately after the sight of these my letters
attach and arrest the person of the said Offeley. And, unless
the same Offeley shall incontinent thereupon without delay restore unto the said Edmund his said money with his reasonable
damages and expenses sustained by his untrue dealings or otherwise compound with the said Edmund, to keep the same Offeley
in your safe custody and to convey him hither to London so
shortly as you conveniently may, personally to answer before
me and others of the king's honorable council—wherefore he
ought not to do. And if you shall not apprehend the person
of the said Offeley, then to arrest his said goods and to put the
same under your safe-custody until the said Offeley shall either
fully restore unto my said friend his said money or otherwise
give sufficient caution to answer him in the same according to
the due order of the law; showing such earnest, hearty diligence
herein as my said friend may by your policy and friendship,
for my sake to be extended unto him, be conveyed to his said
debt without further suits or delays, if by any honest means
you shall so compass the same. And I shall thankfully remember
your doing herein at my desire in case you shall make request

---

Rouse, or Rowse, which might explain the friendship mentioned. John
Offeley may be the brother of the London merchant Hugh. Lightfoots were
active at Calais in the early sixteenth century in the wool trade.
[3] The name given to the town of Chester, the seat of the government of
the County Palatine, also simply Chester, not far from Liverpool.
[4] The Rolls House, a dwelling attached to the office of the Master of
the Rolls, located in Chancery Lane. Cromwell held the office for about
two years (October 1534 to July 1536), but apparently occupied the
house beyond his tenure of office.

unto me at any time hereafter. And thus fare you heartily well. From my house at the Rolls,[4] the third day of April 1536. Copy, clerk's hand. Endorsed: "Copy from Mr. Cromwell."

10. To Lord Chancellor Audley[1]

BM Cotton Mss. Vespasian Fxiii,
   pt. ii, fo. 191   11 November [1534]
LP, VII, 1415; 85   The Rolls

THE PRICES of consumer goods had for centuries been regulated by statutes and proclamations within the context of medieval ideas of regulated or "fair" prices. In the early months of 1534 it seems that a severe inflation in the prices of meat, wine, small grains, and other commodities had caused great complaint against merchants who were holding common necessities off the market and contributing in that way to an already dramatic situation, partly caused by naturally low supplies. Of the eleven proclamations issued in 1534 and now extant, six deal with such matters, specifically mentioning the great harm done to the commonwealth by rising prices and the sharp practices occasioned by them. The proclamation meant in this letter attempted to reverse the enhancement "at unreasonable prices" of all grains, for "reformation whereof" the subtle craft of merchants is to be stopped under pain of imprisonment, with the Lord Chancellor Audley to have authority to establish commissions and supervise their inquiries into prices. Cromwell called the shots, however, with regard to publication and actual enforcement.

After my right hearty commendations to your lordship. Forasmuch as it shall be necessary to have some copies of the proclamation[2] also printed this night, to the intent the same may be

[1] Audley was one of Cromwell's ready servants, despite the fact that as lord chancellor he held the highest office in the Tudor hierarchy of secular administration.

[2] The proclamation against hoarders of grain is the only one that fits the date given by Cromwell. Hughes and Larkin, *Tudor Royal Proclamations* (New Haven: Yale University Press, 1964), I, 221–2, print it. The fact that Berthelet was the printer and the date fits makes it difficult to quarrel with the assignment of this to 1534. But the clerk who wrote this letter for Cromwell endorsed it as from "My lord my master." And Wriothesley was not in the habit of referring to Cromwell in that way *before*

sent into sundry parts with the books of answers,[3] these shall be to desire and pray your lordship to send me by this bearer a true copy of the same. And I shall send for Bartelet[4] the printer and first swear him and then cause him to attend this night to the printing of the copies thereof accordingly. And thus most heartily fare you well. From the Rolls, the 11th day of November.

P.S. I require your lordship to cause the proclamations to be written and sealed with such expedition as you may take the pain to be here with them tomorrow by ten of the clock, when my lord of Norfolk[5] and I, with others, will tarry dinner til your coming. Your lordship's assured.

Wriothesley's hand; autograph signature. Addressed: "To my very good lord my Lord Chancellor deliver this with speed." Endorsed: "My lord my master to my lord chancellor."

11. To Sir Thomas Wyatt[1]

BM Harleian Mss. 282, fos. 211–12   12 October 1537
LP, XII, ii, 890; 223   Westminster

THIS LETTER requires very little by way of explanation. When Jane Seymour went to bed to bear her child, Henry VIII must have experienced the ultimate anxiety of which he was capable: that once again the security of the dynasty would be frustrated, whether through birth of a daughter or loss of a son. But it

---

his master became the Baron Cromwell and Lord Privy Seal. There is no document of 1536 which fits the circumstances, however.

[3] I have been unable to identify the "books of answers" here mentioned.

[4] Thomas Berthelet, who succeeded Pynson as the king's printer, once Pynson's apprentice and probably the "Thomas Bercula Typographers" of a 1520 edition of the *Vulgaria* of Whitinton. On his identity and career, see E. Gordon Duff, *The Printers, Stationers and Bookbinders of Westminster and London from 1476 to 1535* (Cambridge: Cambridge University Press, 1906), pp. 177–83.

[5] Thomas Howard II.

[1] Sir Thomas Wyatt (1503–1542), poet and diplomat and once in love with Anne Boleyn. A staunch friend of Cromwell, after whose fall he was arrested in 1541. Soon released, he was again arrested, this time for treasonable actions, and soon executed.

was to be his wife he lost, Queen Jane died shortly after performing the one task meant for all of Henry's queens. Cromwell's joyous trumpeting of the news of Prince Edward's life had in it nothing of sycophancy or servileness. Most Tudor men and women, no matter what their politics and religion, could have wished for nothing more than a stable succession and an answer and end to the questions begun many years before in the origins of the Divorce. We must remember that English history gave scant comfort to Henry VIII and his councilors when they contemplated the possibility of queens-regnant. They could not know that in the sixteenth century many of the most remarkable and successful rulers would be women, though Margaret of Hungary already exercised wise power in the Netherlands. The two Mary's, of England and Scotland, and Catherine de Medici, to say nothing of Elizabeth I, were yet hidden in the future, and only a son seemed to matter. That this particular son would be famous as the "pious Imp" under whose rule Protestantism flourished was also then obscure, even to those who knew his connections with the Seymours. For that family in 1537 was known neither for reform-mindedness nor friendship to Cromwell.

After my right hearty commendations. These shall be to advertise you that since the departure of Rougecroix,[2] which was dispatched to you in post on Wednesday last,[3] here be no more news occurrants but very good news, which for certain I have received this morning: that it has pleased almighty God of his goodness to send unto the Queen's grace deliverance of a goodly prince,[4] to the great comfort, rejoice and consolation of the king's majesty and of all us his most humble and loving and obedient subjects. Whereof we have very great cause to thank our most benign and gracious Creator, who after so long expectation has exalted our prayer and desires. I have written this letter, having the opportunity of this present courier, to the intent that you shall advertise the Emperor thereof. I think that with convenient diligence the king's highness will write unto him and to other princes of the same, to make them participant of his great joy and comfort, whereof I shall move him tomorrow

[2] The Red Cross Herald, a frequent messenger between Henry VIII and Wyatt: *LP,* XII, ii, 228; 870.

[3] *LP,* XII, ii, 869. According to this letter, Wyatt is to tell Charles V of Henry's willingness to mediate the Valois-Habsburg conflicts.

[4] Prince Edward Tudor, later King Edward VI, born 12 October 1537.

at my being with his grace. Thus fare you heartily well. From St. James besides Westminister, this 12th of October, the 29th year of his most prosperous reigning. Your assured loving friend.

Sadler's hand; autograph signature. Addressed: "A mon tresbon et asseur amy Monsr Wyatt conseiller et ambassador du Roy d'Angleterre resident en la Cour tde l'Emperor." Endorsed: "My LPS in October by see of a courrier late after the date." And, "My LPS in October dd long after the date by the Sea of the news of the prince" (same hand as the main endorsement).

12. To the Magistrates of Canterbury[1]

BM Additional Mss. 32638, fo. 83   18 May [1536]
Not in *LP*; 148   The Rolls

THE GROWTH of Parliament and its new vitality in the business of the monarchy created certain difficulties for the crown, not the least of them the management of legislation in an age inclined to see the ultimate activity of the polity in the making of law by the crown, lords, and commons. At times the three acted together easily. But it was also at times true that fate failed to provide agreement. And for that reason the intensified life of Parliament led to a new or at least an intensified effort to manage representative assemblies in England. Simple packing, dictation, and coercion were not especially valuable techniques of management. Naturally, the chief battleground would be the House of Commons, and here again the Reformation Parliament had a great effect on things. Its long duration and important business made it imperative that the crown have some initiative and reliable members well placed in the process of legislation. Thus management worked through control of elections and influence over the elected house. While there is some evidence for both aspects of control, during the 1530's we find a minister of the crown devoting himself to these matters in an entirely self-conscious way. Cromwell's own entry into Parliament in 1529 had been through private patronage, and an object lesson was thereby given him. By 1536 we have at least one clear case among surviving records, a case in which Cromwell

[1] The mayor of Canterbury was John Alcock and the sheriff, one Mr. Hobbes.

intervenes decisively in the municipal election of the arch-episcopal city of Canterbury. Here direct compulsion was used, and Cromwell's critics have had a field day with it as embodying his spiteful attitude toward subjects' liberties. But in 1537 Cromwell extended his favor to one of the rejected members in a dispute with the magistrates, only to be told that the man in question had presumed to arrange his own election in 1536! This seems to indicate that some quite local affairs were vital in the matters touched in this letter, although we do not know their exact nature and Cromwell's whole role in electioneering.

In my hearty wise I recommend me unto you. These shall be for as much as the king's pleasure and commandment is that Robert Darknoll and John Briggs[2] shall be elect and chosen citizen or burgesses* for that City, by reason whereof my lord chancellor[3] and I by our letters written unto you advertised you thereof.[4] And you, the same little or nothing regarding, but rather condemning, have chosen others at your own wills and minds, contrary to the king's pleasure and commandment in that behalf, where at the king's highness does not a little marvel.

Wherefore in avoiding of further displeasure that might thereby ensue, I require you on the king's behalf, that notwithstanding the said election, you proceed to another and elect those other according to the tenor of the former letters to you directed for that purpose, without failing so to do, as the king's trust and expectation is mine.[5] And as you intend to avoid his highness' displeasure at your peril, and if any person will obstinately gainsay the same, I require you to advertise me thereof, that I may order him as the king's pleasure shall be in that case to

2 Nothing can be added about Darknoll and Briggs.
3 Sir Thomas Audley.
4 This letter is not in *LP*. But the events may be reconstructed from documents published in Elton, *The Tudor Constitution*, pp. 289–90. When the first order arrived, John Starkey, chamberlain and alderman, and Christopher Levyns, common clerk of the City, had been elected (John Hobbes, Sheriff, to Cromwell, 12 May 1536, PRO SP1/103/276–7). In Hobbes' letter it is clear that Cromwell had written before the twelfth, naming Darknoll and Briggs. Hobbes alleges he had not received that before the election was held on the eleventh. Cromwell's letter printed here then reaffirmed the king's wishes on the eighteenth, to which Hobbes made answer on the twentieth (SP1/104/39), stating that he had reassembled the commonalty of the City, ninety-seven in number, and with "one voice and without any contradiction have elected and chosen" the men named in Cromwell's letter.
5 See *LP*, X, 929.

command. Thus fare you well. At the Rolls, the 17th day of May.[6] Your loving friend.

Addressed: "To my right loving friends the Mayor, Sheriffs and councillors of the City of Canterbury and to every of them."

13. To Sir Edmund Knyvett[1]

PRO SP1/146/274–5   5 April [1539]
LP, XIV, i, 706; 303   London

IN 1539 WE have ample evidence displaying Cromwell hard at work in the cause of exerting the influence he and other royal councilors might command in the counties then facing elections, in the interest of preparing what he himself called "a tractable parliament." As Dr. Elton wisely remarked, "here we find nothing remotely improper, but only the full managerial skills of the old parliamentary system" at work. The effects of these machinations are not easily estimated. Certainly the Commons elected in 1539 were not men under Cromwell's thumb, or they would not have passed into law the Six Articles, which generally may be viewed as signaling the end of his dominance of politics. Not even Cromwell's careful management packed the house in the royal, let alone his own, interest. And in at least this one case Cromwell obviously put forward the king's interest rather than his own, with the result that a man sympathetic to the Duke of Norfolk had the place Knyvett sought.

After my right hearty commendations. Having received your letters of the second of this present,[2] I perceive by the same

---

[6] The letter bears a signature supposedly Cromwell's. But both the signature and the hand are the common work of the keeper of this little book, the memorandum book of one T. Beale, of Barham, Kent. The autograph entries at fos. 3 and 81 testify to this fact. Thus we have here a copy of Cromwell's of the eighteenth.

[1] Sir Edmund Knyvett (d. 1546), sergeant-porter to Henry VIII, and sheriff of Norfolk and Suffolk at various times.

[2] PRO SPI/146/237–8, Knyvett to Cromwell, 2 April 1539, in which Cromwell's friend stated that he would be ready with all his tenants to "cry so loud" at the election as to drown voices expressed for other candidates. He knows of common rumors that the king favors Southwell and Wyndham.

your gentle affection towards me with your desire to know mine advice touching the knights of the shire of Norfolk, the election of whom shall be the 14th of this month at Norwich. For answer whereunto, like as for the one part I do right heartily thank you, and shall be glad to consider your good will as occasion and convenient opportunity will serve me, so, for the other part, touching the knights of the shire, I have thought meet to signify unto you that of truth the king's majesty is well inclined to have Mr. Southwell[3] and Mr. Wyndham[4] elected and chosen to supply those rooms at this parliament. Whereunto my advice shall be that you shall conform yourself, not for that I do think either of them more able for the office than yourself, but because they being also convenient for the same, and partly minded by his highness, I would all my friends—in the number whereof I do accept you—should in all things apply themselves to satisfy his grace as appertains. Thus fare you heartily well. From London this Easter day. Your assured friend.

Wriothesley's hand, with autograph signature. Addressed: "To my loving friend Edmund Knyvett of Barham Castle Esq."[5] Endorsed: "My lord and master to Edmond Knyvett."

14. To Bishop Gardiner

PRO SP1/69/41–2   [January 1532]
LP, V, 723; 28   [Westminster]

UPON WOLSEY's fall Stephen Gardiner (1483?–1555) rose rapidly in Henry VIII's service. He acted as secretary of state to Henry, performed important ambassadorial functions, was named to fill the bishopric of Winchester vacated by Wolsey, and in general was the heir-apparent as chief minister. He was a champion of the Divorce and instrumental in securing opinions from Cambridge divines and professors favorable to Henry VIII. A brilliant student and fellow of Trinity Hall, Cambridge, Gardiner

---

[3] Sir Richard Southwell (1504–1564), courtier and official in Augmentations.
[4] Sir Edmund Wyndham, a dependent of the Duke of Norfolk (*LP*, XIV, ii, 572). The election ended in a riot and the return of Southwell and Wyndham, for which see *LP*, XIV, i, 800 and 808.
[5] Six miles ESE of Canterbury, Kent.

was trained in civil and canon law before becoming Wolsey's private secretary, from which circumstance he had a close friendship and working relationship with Cromwell. In the strain of the circumstances surrounding the fall of their common patron and master, Cromwell and Gardiner drifted apart to some extent, but there was no open rift. In fact Cromwell was closely enough connected with Gardiner down to 1534 for us to say that they were in some sense joint holders of the Wolsey legacy in administration, though they were clearly on opposite sides of some issues; for example, that rampant anticlericalism of the Reformation Parliament which figured in the annates issue here mentioned and in the Submission of the Clergy. With regard to the Act of Annates, we do not see Gardiner's hand, but Cromwell had a very active role in preparing the protest against clerical authority that led to the Submission of the Clergy a little later in 1532. In the struggle to avoid clerical suicide, the Bishop of Winchester wrote the first strong drafts of the *Answer of the Ordinaries,* aided by Lord Chancellor Thomas More, with the result that he soon was in his diocese, perhaps in disfavor. While Parliament languidly debated the matter of annates, by which the pope would be stripped of great revenues arising out of English bishoprics, Gardiner was in France and obviously anxious about the course of events in London.

My lord, after mine humble and most hearty recommendations, these shall be to advertise your lordship how that I have received your gentle letters to me delivered by the hands of Mr. Wriothesley.[1] And where I do perceive by my kinsman, this bearer, that you much desire to have news from hence, I assure you that here be none but such as you have undoubtedly by a multitude of your friends (which are far more secret and nearer the knowledge of the same than I am) be to your lordship already related and known. But yet to advertise of some part that I know, as this day was read in the higher house a bill touching the annates of bishoprics;[2] to what end or effect it

---

[1] Thomas Wriothesley (1505–1550) was a member of Cromwell's household and in effect the manager of the secretariat of the king during Cromwell's ministry. He was afterward made secretary of state and knighted (1540), from which eminence he rose higher, to an earldom and the chancellorship of England.

[2] Annates were in fact the first fruits, or the entire revenue of one year, paid to the pope by bishops and other beneficed clergy upon their appointment or transfer. The first Act of Annates imposed a conditional restraint on such payments as a weapon in the king's campaign against Clement VII. This income was unconditionally given to the crown by the second statute of that name, passed in 1534.

will succeed, surely I know not. And as yesterday, because I know your lordship not to be furnished of all things necessary for your being there, I moved the king's highness aswell for the money to be defrayed in and about the furniture of your purpose and affairs as also for your return hither, saying that upon mine own conjecture your lordship was weary of being there.[3] Whereunto his highness answered me that you were not so weary of your being there but he was as sorry, saying by these words expressly: his absence is the lack of my right hand, for I am now so much pestered with business and have nobody to rid nor dispatch the same.

So your lordship may well know that your absence is not to you so much painful and grievous as your presence here should be pleasant and comfortable to the king's highness and all other your poor friends. Beseeching therefore your lordship to find some means on your part, as much as in you is, that your return hither may be shortly, which is long looked and wished for, as our Lord knows, etc.

Draft, with some corrections in Cromwell's hand. Address and endorsement lacking.

15. To Henry VIII

PRO SP1/80/51–2   [Early July 1533]
LP, VI, 1369; 65   London

IT SEEMS clear that this letter, so closely related to the one placed before it by Merriman and the *LP* editors, must be of earlier date than Cromwell's letter of 23 July 1533, in which the two Friars Observant are mentioned as secretly resorting to Catherine at Buckden. When he wrote this letter, Cromwell did not yet know the identities of the friars in question, while Payne and Cornelius had already been revealed and arrested by late July. We do know that Catherine was forced to move from Ampthill to Buckden, Huntingdonshire, in July 1533. We further know that the earliest reports of suspicious friars communicating with the queen place the meetings at Buckden. But we have

---

[3] Gardiner was ambassador to France from 29 December 1531 to 7 March 1532. This letter is certainly of January 1532, the time of the introduction of the bill concerning annates.

no firm date for the entire affair, and this letter and the one following may well be placed later in 1533. Another circumstance that encourages an early guess, not a later one, is that Friar John Lawrence's activities in behalf of the government, including delations against the monks of Greenwich, were mostly late in 1532 and early in 1533. What we do know for certain is that by mid-November a commission composed of Cromwell, Cranmer, and Hugh Latimer sat at Lambeth Palace, unwinding the threads of the story of the queen's involvement with the frairs and the Nun of Kent.

Please it your royal majesty to be advertised how, that repairing homewards one of my lord chancellor's[1] servants met with me and delivered me your warrants signed with the hand of the Princess Dowager,[2] which warrants I do send to your grace here enclosed. What your pleasure shall be to have done therein being once known, I shall right gladly accomplish. I have also since my repair to London spoken with Friar Lawrence[3] who has since his repair to London heard diverse things touching the Holy Maid[4] which he will declare to your highness and to such others, as he shows me. Also, that there be two strange friars of the order of the Observants[5] lately repaired into this realm, which two friars have explored here for all such books, sentences and determinations as hath passed touching your highness' matrimony, which they intend with other privy practices to convey with them to Friar Peto[6] who, as I am credibly informed, sent them into this your realm. The said two friars, as

[1] Sir Thomas Audley, Baron Audley of Walden (1488–1544), one of Cromwell's close associates and a "political" chancellor, as opposed to those we think of as great judges or reformers.

[2] Catherine of Aragon. The warrants would seem to be those concerned with her style of address, which she signed only after striking out the "Princess Dowager" phrasing, thus negating the effect so greatly desired by Henry VIII.

[3] Friar Lawrence was a firm upholder of the Divorce. He was one of two Greenwich friars, the other being Richard Lyst, who were responsible for much mischief-making for their fellow monks in 1532–1533. Cromwell encouraged both of them to preach and work in favor of the king's actions. Lawrence applied for a dispensation from his vows.

[4] Elizabeth Barton, see the following letter.

[5] One other argument in favor of a July date is the fact that Hugh Payne wrote to the Franciscan provincial-in-exile, Peto, and was answered on 13 July 1533 (*LP*, VI, 836).

[6] William Peto died in 1557, after a long career in service of his church, having attained the rank of cardinal.

I am ascertained, have brought with them privy letters to deliver and have now gone to the said dowager. In my poor opinion it shall be right well done that they might be sent for by some trusty person, howbeit it were best that they first should be suffered to speak with her and such other of her's as would peradventure deliver to them any thing whereby their further practices might be perceived and so their cankered* intents might be thereby discovered.

I am also informed that there is a merchant of London[7] which does practice with them in these premises. I shall go very wary to have knowledge therein. If it be true, he is worthy to suffer to make others beware in time. He is of good substance. I will this day go about to know the truth. These things will be met withal in time and the sooner the better. I trust your Highness will by this bearer advertise me in writing what shall be your pleasure touching aswell the said false friars as also touching of the said Dowager's warrants. I have also sent to your grace one acquittance to be assigned for the twenty-four thousand crowns due to your Highness for the residue of the Emperor's debt[8] and also a warrant to your chancellor for the sealing of the same, which warrants and acquittances it may please your majesty to assign* and to send the same by this bearer, to the intent Robert Fowler[9] may be dispatched. The rest of the acquitances for your ordinance, pensions and sails [have] been already signed and sealed. And thus the Holy Trinity, to whom I shall continually pray to preserve your Highness in long life and most prosperous health, and the same the virtue with honor all your queens.

No signature; holograph draft, much corrected. Endorsed: "Two

[7] No identification possible.

[8] At the Treaty of Cambrai (1529), Wolsey obtained an increase in the pensions paid to Henry VIII by Francis I by persuading the French king to assume the debts of Charles V to Henry VIII. He did so as part of a consideration whereby the emperor released the two sons of Francis I long held as hostages. These imperial obligations were various loans made to Charles, plus the debt of £100,000 owed by Maximilian to Henry VII, and an advance on the security of items pawned by Maximilian with Henry VII. There were other elements as well. Between 1529 and 1531 no payments were made; but between 1531 and 1534 payments were resumed, only to be canceled again when the internal upheaval in England provided Francis with diplomatic trumps.

[9] Robert Fowler was undertreasurer of Calais; he was also a key administrator in more loosely defined roles in that port whose problems so preoccupied Cromwell from 1532 to 1540.

minutes of my master's letters with my lord chancellor," rather enigmatic in the light of the texts.

16. To Henry VIII

PRO SP1/78/26–7   23 July [1533]
LP, VI, 887; 52   London

THE CIRCUMSTANCES of this letter have to do mainly with the growing fear of intrigue and conspiracy which haunted Henry VIII in the wake of his divorce from Catherine of Aragon. Once it had been decided to allow Cranmer to hear the case and give sentence, the king's councilors were anxious about the reaction at home and abroad. In that atmosphere, prophecies against Anne Boleyn and the king's new hopes for a male heir were associated with various magic practices. As the summer of 1533 wore on, Cromwell began to investigate the sayings of a nun of Kent, Elizabeth Barton, a former servant girl who now spoke with angels and claimed divine inspiration for her continued trancelike states. She predicted dire consequences for the kingdom as a result of the course then being pursued. When professors of theology spoke with the Devil in Germany and kings plotted alterations in the constitution of their countries as a result of interviews with God, her ramblings were sufficient to cause men to claim her a "Holy Maid." Cromwell had no interest in bringing to the stake a mad girl. But he did want to guard the security of the crown and its wearer; and in the Holy Maid's mutterings he detected the germ of treason. Catherine's partisans, among them the two friars about whom Cromwell writes, were indiscreet enough to consort with the Nun of Kent. Cromwell appears to suggest torture, but there is no reason to believe that racking took place. Nor, indeed, is there anything to support the notion of a politically motivated witch-hunt such as the one described by the biographer of Catherine of Aragon (Mattingly, *Catherine of Aragon*) London: Jonathan Cape, 1942) pp. 166–74.

Please it your highness to be advertised that upon mine arrival at London I received certain letters out of the North directed unto your grace from the Lord Dacre,[1] which I have

---

[1] William, Lord Dacre of Gillesland, warden of the West Marches between England and Scotland. The letters are in *LP*, VI, 750 and 876.

sent unto your majesty here enclosed, with also certain letters
and news sent unto me from my Lord Deputy of Calais.[2] And
touching the Friars Observants[3] that were with the the princess
dowager:[4] being subtly conveyed from thence, [they] were first
espied at Ware[5] by such espials as I laid for that purpose, and
having good weight laid upon them were thence dogged to
London. And there (not withstanding many wiles and cauteles*
by them invented to escape) were taken and detained til my
coming home. So, as upon my arrival here, I called them before me and upon examination of them could gather nothing
of any moment or great importance. But entering into further
communication, found the one of them a very seditious person
and so committed them unto ward, where they now do remain,
til your gracious pleasure known. Immediately afterwards repaired unto me the Warden of the Grey Friars of Greenwich,[6]
who seems very desirous to have the punition of the said two
friars, being named Hugh Payne[7] and Cornelius,[8] and made
great intercession unto me to have them delivered unto him;
showing unto me further that the minister and general commissary of this province of England[9] had made out certain com-

[2] See letter 45, note 4, Cromwell to Fitz-James, 24 September 1532. The
letters are in *LP*, VI, 839.
[3] The Grey Friars, or Friars Observant, were differentiated from the other
Franciscan conventuals by their insistence that they alone exactly observed
the primitive rule of St. Francis. By 1532 they were openly in opposition
to the Divorce and the entire course of the Reformation Parliament, and
in 1534 were suppressed because of their refusal to disavow papal
supremacy.
[4] Catherine of Aragon greatly favored the Grey Friars, especially their
house at Greenwich.
[5] Ware, in Hertfordshire, about one mile NNE of Hertford.
[6] Thomas Sydynham, warden of the Grey Friars of Greenwich; see *LP*,
VI, 705.
[7] Hugh Payne and Cornelius were not racked by Cromwell. They were
in fact allowed their liberty after close questioning. But Payne was
arrested again in July 1534 for persuading people to adhere to the doctrine
of papal supremacy (*LP*, VII, 939). On this episode, see Hutton, *The
Franciscans in England* (London: n.p. 1926), pp. 243–4.
[8] Cornelius is not mentioned again in the records.
[9] The "minister and general commissary of this province of England" was
the Observant Friar Willian Peto. He had been arrested for refusing to
relieve the warden of Greenwich, John Elstow, of his office, when the
latter had preached openly against the king around Easter of 1532. Peto
was imprisoned for his refusal, along with Elstow. They were shortly
afterward released, however, and escaped to Antwerp, where under the
emperor's protection they campaigned vigorously against the Divorce and
Reformation. They were in regular touch with the Greenwich congrega-

mandments unto the said friars, willing them by virtue of obedience to repair unto him at Richmond,[10] to the intent they would have the correction of them accordingly, which commandments being contained in certain minutes of paper[11] I have sent to your grace here enclosed.

It seems assuredly that the said minister is a right honest and discreet person and feign would have presented and taken the said friars, if he could by any means. Beseeching your grace that I may know your gracious pleasure, whether I shall keep and detain them in ward and bring them with me at my repair to the court, or whether your grace will have them sent immediately to any other place or what other direction to be taken therein, as shall and may stand with your high pleasure. It is undoubted that they have intended and would confess some great matter, if they might be examined as they ought to be, that is to say by pains. For I perceive the said Hugh Payne to be a subtle fellow and much given to sedition.

I have also sent unto my lord of Canterbury,[12] according to your gracious commandment, touching the dissimuled holiness and superstitious demeanours of the hypocrite Nun.[13] And [I] have declared your gracious pleasure unto the Staple,[14] whom in manner I do find agreeable to all things according to your grace's demands; saving only they as yet require longer days for the payment of the sum of ten thousand pounds by them granted[15]

---

tion, which fact alone shows that the activities Cromwell watched were real enough and under foreign sponsorship, and not some tricked-up device of his own against either Catherine or the Friars.

[10] Richmond, in Surrey, about ten miles WSW of London.

[11] A rough draft, or something to be further elaborated.

[12] Thomas Cranmer.

[13] Elizabeth Barton (1506?-1534), a domestic servant at Aldington, Kent, prophesied that the king would die in the month after his new marriage. She was repeatedly examined and finally put to death for treason.

[14] The Staple here must mean the corporation of the Merchants of the Staple at Calais, where the continental monopoly in the handling of wool-trading was established under Edward III. In 1466 Edward IV renewed their monopoly in exchange for their agreement to finance the administration of the port. This act of retainer was the basic agreement between the crown and the Staplers, and was renewed in 1475, 1485, and 1515. By 1528 the company was in grave trouble and unable to meet its contracted obligation, while the king for his part reneged on loans owing to them. From 1527 to 1533 the act of retainer was in suspension, and in 1533 it was abolished, for the king confiscated all Stapler property in Calais, including their inn or house mentioned here.

[15] This sum must be one of the specifically contracted debts then outstanding, particularly the £10,022/4/8 payable to the treasurer of Calais for the maintenance of the garrisons there.

and firmly required that your highness will grant them their
house for a reasonable sum of money yearly, which I do stick
with them in. And as tomorrow they will give me a resolute
answer in the whole. And thus I shall daily pray unto almighty
God for the prosperous conservation of your royal majesty in
long life and good health felicitiously to endure. At London,
the 23rd day of July. Your highness' most humble subject.

Clerk's hand; autograph signature. Addressed: "To the King's
royal majesty."

17. To Bishop John Fisher

BM Cotton Mss. Cleopatra Eiv, fos. 101–4   February [1534]
LP, VII, 238; 68

LITTLE NEED be said of the matter of the Nun of Kent or of the
role played by Fisher in that affair. This letter is sufficiently
explicit on the grievances against Fisher and on a number of
points touched in the correspondence between Fisher and the
king in royal efforts to save Fisher from himself. I think, however, that two other general matters of context may well be
mentioned here.

The first of these is the matter of Cromwell's alleged hounding
of More and Fisher. From this letter it seems clear that Cromwell
played the same role with regard to the bishop as he did in
More's case. He performed the functions of a Tudor minister,
surely, and to the letter of the law, as he here reminds Fisher.
But it also seems that he did for Fisher what he did for More:
gave good counsel that was finally not heeded. And that good
counsel was not that either man sell his soul for purposes dear
to Cromwell. More wrote to Margaret Roper, his beloved
daughter, from the Tower, to tell her that Cromwell had cau-
tioned him *against* giving his reasons for opposing the king,
even under royal license of immunity: "In that good warning he
showed my especial tender friend," said More, just before relating how, when he finally refused the oath, Cromwell "said
and sware a great oath, that he had liever that his own son
. . . had lost his head, than that I should have refused the oath."
More at least knew Cromwell's regard for him and, we might
add, for Fisher. While both were in the Tower, Cromwell's
friend and agent Anthony Bonvisi regularly sent them supplies,

even delicacies. And we must also recall that it was the king who ordered Cromwell to tell Cranmer not to allow a modified form of the oath to More and Fisher.

The other matter of general importance is the context of the prosecution of Fisher. Many historians have seen it as one manifestation of Cromwell's avidness for hunting witches. This myth about the personality and ministry of Thomas Cromwell stems largely from the Nun of Kent affair and holds that Cromwell used witch-hunts and prophetic witches as a mask for political persecutions. But the study of more than sixty cases of witchcraft in the 1530's shows that Cromwell had little to do with the punishment of witches, except in so far as they practiced necromancy and prophetic missions menacing to the monarchy. While it seems clear that he shared contemporary beliefs about the spirit world, he seems to have made a careful distinction between "good" and "bad" witches, the latter being those who spoke against the king. It was only after his death (1542) that an act of Parliament made witchcraft a felony punishable by death, without regard to the character of the necromantic activity involved.[1]

My lord, in my right hearty wise I commend me to your lordship, giving you to understand that I have received your letters[2] dated at Rochester[3] the 18th of this month. In which you declare what craft and cunning you have to persuade and to set a good countenance upon an ill matter. Drawing some scriptures to your purpose, which well-weighed according to the places whereof they be taken, make not so much for your purpose as you allege them for. And where in the first leaf of your letters you write that you doubt nothing, neither before God nor before the world, if need shall that require, so to declare yourself, whatsoever has been said of you; that you have not deserved such heavy words or terrible threats as have been sent from me unto you by your brother.[4]

How you can declare yourself affore God and the world when need shall require I cannot tell. But I think verily that

---

[1] The matters related here depend on a seminar paper done by Miss Sharon Gordon, "Thomas Cromwell and the Witch-Hunting Conspiracy," in my Tudor seminar at U.C.L.A.

[2] At the end of January, Fisher wrote to Cromwell twice, in the first asking to be spared from court because of illness, and in the second, stating that he did not want to declare his conscience concerning the Divorce because he feared Henry VIII's wrath; *LP*, VII, 116 and 136.

[3] Rochester, Kent, about eight miles NNW of Maidstone.

[4] Fisher's brother was named Robert; *LP*, VIII, 856, 858, 888.

your declaration made by these letters is far insufficient to prove
that you have deserved no heavy words in this behalf. And to
say plainly, I sent you no heavy words but words of great comfort, willing your brother to show you how benign and merciful
the Prince was, and that I thought it expedient for you to write
unto his highness and to recognize your offence and desire his
pardon, which his Grace would not deny you now in your
age and sickness. Which my counsel, I wish you had followed
rather than to have written these letters to me, excusing yourself
as though there were no manner of default in you. But my lord,
if it were in an other man's case than your own, and out of the
matter which you favor, I doubt not but that you would think
him that should have done as you have done not only worthy
heavy words but heavy deeds.

For where you labor to excuse yourself of hearing, believing
and concealing of the nun's false and feigned revelations[5] and
of your manifold sending of your chaplain unto her, by a certain intent which you pretend yourself to have had; to know
by communing with her or by sending your chaplain to her,
whether her revelations were of God or no, alleging diverse
scriptures, that you were bound to prove them and not to reject
them afore they were proved. My Lord, whether you have used
a due mean to try her and her revelations or no, it appears by
the process of your own letters. For where you write that you
conceived a great opinion of the holiness of the woman for many
considerations rehearsed in your letters, comprised in six articles,
whereof the first is ground upon the bruit* and fame of her;
the second upon her entering into religion after her trances
and disfiguration; the third upon rehearsal that her ghostly
father[6] being learned and religious should testify that she was
a maid of great holiness; the fourth upon the report that diverse
other virtuous priests, men of good learning and reputation,
should so testify of her, with which ghostly fathers and priests
you never spake, as you confess in your letters; the fifth upon
the praise of my late Lord of Canterbury,[7] which showed you
(as you write) that she had many great visions; the sixth upon
this saying of the prophet Amos: *non faciet dominus deus ver-*

---

[5] On 27 February Fisher confessed to a meeting with the Nun of Kent
and remarked that she intended no evil against the king. He also wrote
in her behalf to the Lords of Parliament; *LP*, VII, 239–40.

[6] The Nun of Kent's father confessor.

[7] William Warham (1450–1532), archbishop of Canterbury.

bum, nisi revelaverit secretum suum ad servos suos prophetas[8]
by which considerations you were induced to the desire to know
the very certainty of the matter; whether the revelations which
were pretended to be showed to her from God were true revelations or not? Your lordship in all the sense of your letters show
not that you made no further trial upon the truth of her and
her revelation, but only in communing with her and sending
your chaplain to her with idle questions as of the three Mary
Magdalens, by which your communing and sending you tried
out nothing of her falsehood, neither (as it is credibly supposed)
intended to do, as you might have done many ways more easily
than with communing with her or sending to her. For little
credence was to be given to her affirming her own feigned
revelations to be from God.

For if credence should be given to every lewd person as
would affirm himself to have revelations from God, what readier
way were there to subvert all commonwealths and good orders
in the world?

Verily my Lord, if you had intended to try out the truth of
her revelations, you would have taken another way with you.
First, you would not have been contented with the vain voices
of the people making bruits of her trances and disfiguration.
But, like a wise, discreet, circumspect prelate, you should have
examined (as other have) such sad and credible persons as
were present at her trances and disfigurations; not one or two,
but a good number, by whose testimony you should have proved
whether the bruits of her trances and disfigurations were true
or not. And likewise, you should have tried by what craft and
persuasion she was made a religious woman. And, if you had
been so desirous as you pretend, to inquire out the truth or
falsehood of this woman and of her revelations, it is to be supposed you would have spoken with her good religious and well
learned ghostly father (as you call him) before this time: and
also with the virtuous and well learned priests (as they were
esteemed), of whose reports you were informed by them which
heard them speak. You would also have been minded to see the
book of her revelations which was offered you, of which you
might have had more trial of her and her revelations than a

---

[8] Amos 3:7. "Surely the Lord God will do nothing but he revealeth his
secrets unto his servants the prophets" (*King James* version.) In the Latin
Cromwell had in mind, apparently quoting from memory, the text reads,
"*Quia non facit Dominus Deus verbum . . .*"

hundred communications with her or as many sendings of your
chaplain unto her. As for the late Lord of Canterbury's saying
unto you that she had many great visions, it ought to move
you never a deal to give credence unto her or her revelations.
For the said lord knew no more certainty of her or her revelations than you did by her own report. And as touching the saying of Amos the Prophet, I think the same moved you but a
little to hearken to her, for since the consummation and the end
of the Old Testament and since the passion of Christ, God has
done many great and notable things in the world, whereof he
showed nothing to his prophets that has come to the knowledge
of men. My lord, all these things moved you not to give credence
unto her, but only the very matter whereupon she made her
false prophecies; to which matter you were so affected (as you
be noted to be on all matters which you once enter into) that
nothing could come amiss that made for that purpose.

And here I appeal your conscience and instantly desire you
to answer: whether if she had showed you as many revelations
of the confirmation of the king's grace's marriage which he now
enjoys as she did to the contrary, you would have given as much
credence to her as you have done and would have let the trial
of her and of her revelations to overpass these many years,
where you dwelled not from her but twenty miles, in the same
shire, where her trances and disfigurings and prophecies in her
trances were surmised and counterfeyed.* And if perchance you
will say (as it is not unlike but you will say, minded as you
were wont to be) that the matters be not like; for the law of
God in your opinion stands with the one and not with the other,
surely my Lord, I suppose this had been no great cause more
to reject the one than the other. For you know by histories of
the *Bible* that God may by his revelation dispense with his own
law, as with the Israelites spoiling the Egyptians, and with
Jacob to have four wives, and such other.[9]

Think you my Lord that any indifferent man considering the
quality of the matter and your affection, and also the negligent
passing over of such lawful trials as you might have had of
the said nun and her revelations, is so dull that he can not
perceive and discern that your communing and often sending to
the said nun was rather to hear and know more of her revelations than to try out the truth or falsehood of these same? And

[9] Exodus 11 and Genesis 29 and 30.

in this behalf I suppose it will be hard for you to purge yourself before God and the world, but that you have been in great fault, hearing, believing and concealing such things as tended to the destruction of the Prince. And that her revelations were bent and proposed to that end, it has been duly proved affore as great assembly and counsel of the lords of this realm as has been seen many years heretofore out of parliament. And what the said lords deemed them worthy to suffer, which had believed and concealed these false revelations, be more terrible than any threats spoken by me to your brother.

And where you go about to defend that you be not to be blamed for concealing her revelations concerning the king's grace, because you thought it not necessary to rehearse them to his highness, for seven causes following in your letters; affore I show you my mind concerning these causes, I suppose that, albeit you per case thought it not necessary to be showed to the Prince by you, yet that your thinking shall not be your trial, but the law must define whether you ought to utter it or not.

And as to the first of the said seven causes. Albeit she told you that she had showed her revelations concerning the king's grace to the king herself, yet her saying or others discharged not you, but that you were bound by your fidelity to show to the king's grace that which seemed to concern his grace and his reign so nighly. For how knew you that she showed these revelations to the king's grace but by her own saying, to which you should have given no such credence as to forebear the utterance of so great matters concerning a king's wealth. And why should you so sinisterly judge the Prince, that if you had showed these same unto him, he would have thought that you had brought that tale unto him more for the strengthening and confirmation of your opinion than for any other thing else? Verily my Lord, whatsoever your judgment be, I see daily such benignity and excellent humanity in his Grace that I doubt not but his highness would have accepted it in good part, if you had showed the same revelations unto him, as you were bounden to do by your fidelity.

To the second cause. Albeit she showed you not that any prince or temporal lord should put the king's grace in danger of his crown, yet there were ways enough by which her said revelations might have put the king's grace in danger, as the foresaid counsel of lords have substantially and duly considered.

And, therefore, albeit she showed you not the means whereby the danger should ensue to the king's grace, yet you were nevertheless bounden to show him of the danger.

To the third. Think you my Lord, that if any person would come unto you and show you that the king's destruction were conspired against a certain time, and would further show you that he were sent from his master to show the same to the king and will further say unto you that he would go straight to the king, were it not yet your duty to certify the king's grace of the relation, but also to inquire whether the said person had done his aforesaid message or no? Yes, verily. And so you were bound, though the nun showed you it were her message from God, to be declared by her to the king's grace.

To the fourth. Here you translate the temporal duty that you owe to your Prince to the spiritual duty of such as be bound to declare the word of God to the people and to show unto them the peril and punishment of sin in an other world, the concealment whereof pertains to the judgment of God. But the concealment of this matter pertains to other judges of this realm.

To the fifth. There could be no blame be arrested to you, if you had showed the nun's relations to the king's Grace, albeit they were afterwards found false. For no man ought to be blamed doing his duty. And if a man would show you secretly that there were a great mischief intended against the Prince, were you to be blamed if you showed him of it, albeit it were a feigned tale and the said mischief were never imagined?

To the sixth. Concerning an imagination of Master Pacy.[10] It was known that he was beside himself; and therefore they were not blamed that made no report thereof. But it was not like in this case. For you took not this nun for a mad woman. For if you had, you would not have given unto her so great credence as you did.

To the final and seventh cause. Where you lay unto the charge of our sovereign, that he has unkindly entreated you with grievous words and terrible letters for showing his grace truth in his great matter, whereby you were discomforted to show unto him the nun's revelations; I believe that I know the king's goodness and natural gentleness so well, that his grace would not

---

[10] Richard Pace (1482?–1536), diplomatist, dean of St. Paul's, agent in Rome, and secretary of state to Henry VIII. He became quite insane before his death and had "fearful visions" touching the "King's Great Matter"; *LP*, VII, 1559.

so unkindly handle you, as you unkindly write of him, unless you gave him other causes than be expressed in your letters. And whatsoever the king's Grace has said or written to you heretofore, yet that notwithstanding, you were nevertheless bounden to utter to him these pernicious revelations.

Finally, where you desire for the passion of Christ that you be no more quickened in this matter, for if you be put to that straight, you will not lose your soul but you will speak as your conscience leads you, with many more words of great courage: my Lord, if you had taken my counsel sent unto you by your brother and followed the same, submitting yourself by your letters to the king's Grace for your offenses in this behalf, I would have trusted that you should never be quickened in this matter more. But now, where you take upon you to defend the whole matter, as you were in no default, I cannot so far promise you. And surely my Lord, if the matter come to trial, your own confession by these letters, besides the witnesses which be against you, will be sufficient to condemn you. Wherefore my Lord, I will eftsoons advise you that, laying apart all such excuses as you have alleged in your letters, which in mine opinion be of small effect, as I have declared, you beseech the king's Grace by your letters to be your gracious lord and to remit unto you your negligent oversight and offence committed against his highness in this behalf. And I dare undertake that his highness shall benignly accept you into his gracious favor, all matters of displeasure past affore this time forgotten and forgiven.

As touching the speaking of your conscience: it is thought that you have written and spoken as much as you can—and many things against your own conscience (as some right probably believe). And men report that at the last Convocation you spake many things which you could not right well defend.[11] And therefore it is not greatly feared what you can say or write in this matter, howsoever you be quickened or straightened. And if you be taken . . .[12]

A draft in a clerk's hand; much corrected in Cromwell's hand, but unsigned.

---

[11] In the Convocation of 1533 it was moved that the popes could not dispense with the impediment that barred marriage between a man and his brother's widow. Fisher voted against the measure.
[12] The draft breaks off at this point.

18. To Archbishop Cranmer

PRO SP1/83/98–9   April [1534]
LP, VII, 500; 71

THE ACT of Succession laid it down that every person subject
to Henry VIII should take an oath, when required, to uphold
the provisions of the Act. Those refusing to swear were to be
guilty of misprision of treason and punished by imprisonment
at the king's pleasure. The statute did not, however, stipulate
the actual form of the oath, although it was clearly the case
that a personal act to support the establishment succession, ex-
cluding Catherine of Aragon's daughter Mary, was intended.
Every person of authority was to administer the oath to his
inferiors, down to the justices of the peace in the shires. At
the summit of the system sat Cranmer, Audley (lord chancellor),
and the dukes of Norfolk and Suffolk, who on 30 March 1534
were appointed commissioners to organize the swearing of the
oath. Cranmer and his colleagues at first drafted an oath which
required the people to swear they gave no allegiance to a foreign
authority (the pope). But in that, they clearly acted beyond
the powers conferred in the Act. It contained neither the form
of the oath nor any clause enabling commissioners to imprison
those refusing to swear to anything but the succession to the
crown of England. Parliament remedied this defect in November
of 1534, when it was enacted that the oath drafted by the
commissioners was the oath intended by the first statute. But
even this *ex post facto* law was not relevant to the fate of More
and Fisher. On 13 April 1534, Cranmer sat at Lambeth, along
with Cromwell and the abbot of Westminster, to receive the
oaths of the London clergy. More and Fisher were also summoned to take the oath on that day. More refused, after a subtle
exchange of arguments with Cranmer. What he did concede was
that he would swear to the Succession if he were allowed to
draft the form of the oath he would take. Fisher did likewise.
They went free, only to be arrested four days later. Then
Cranmer intervened on their behalf in a famous letter to Cromwell, reminding Cromwell that More and Fisher had agreed to
swear an oath to the Act itself, taking exception only to the
preamble. Why could they not swear an oath, setting aside the
preamble, he asked. Cranmer was confident that an oath from
Fisher and More, even one based on compromise, would induce

everyone in the kingdom to follow suit. Cromwell's undated reply follows here.

My Lord, after my humble commendations. It may please your grace to be advertised that I have received your letters and showed the same to the king's highness who, perceiving your mind and opinion is that it were good that the bishop of Rochester[1] and Mr. More[2] should be sworn to the Act of the King's Succession and not to the preamble of the same,[3] thinks that if their oath should be so taken it were an occasion to all men to refuse the whole, or at least the like. For, in case they be sworn to the succession and not to the preamble, it is to be thought that it might be taken not only as a confirmation of the Bishop of Rome's authority but also as a reprobation of the king's second marriage. Wherefore, to the intent that no such things should be brought into the heads of the people by the example of the said bishop of Rochester and Mr. More, the king's Highness in no wise wills but that they shall be sworn to the preamble as to the Act of Succession. *For the conducing whereof, to effect in every manner of ways, the king's highness has special trust and expectation in your grace's approved wisdom and dexterity.*[4] Wherefore, his grace specially trusts that you will in no wise suppose or attempt [to] move him to the contrary. For as his highness supposes that that manner of swearing, if it should be suffered, may presently be an utter destruction to his holy cause and also to the effect of the law made for the same.[5]

Draft, much corrected in Cromwell's hand.

[1] John Fisher (1459–1535), bishop of Rochester, executed in 1535 for refusing to swear to the Succession.
[2] Thomas More (1478–1535), formerly lord chancellor, executed in 1535 for the same cause.
[3] The preamble of the first Act of Succession (25 Henry VIII, c. 22)· stated, among other things, that danger to England must ensue if any had doubts about the Bishop of Rome's usurped authority, since a disputed succession would provide him with an opportunity to interfere in England's internal affairs. The body of the act, which alone makes some thing the law of the land, as opposed to preambles of statutes which are *obiter dicta* often expressing the motives of policy, had to do only with the status of Catherine of Aragon, Anne Boleyn, and their daughters.
[4] Italics in manuscript.
[5] The date must certainly be about 17 to 21 April 1534. We know that Cranmer's plea to Cromwell was written on 17 April. And Cromwell must have written his answer to Cranmer in time for the archbishop to

19. To Sir John Wallop[1]

PRO SP1/95/155–62   23 August [1535]
LP, IX, 157; 113   Thornbury

WE SEE here mirrored several major concerns of Cromwell and
his king in the summer of 1535. Francis I had hoped to cement
an alliance with Clement VII, the aged Medici pope, by arrang-
ing a marriage between the future Henry II and the niece of
Clement, Catherine de Medici. Conferences toward that end
had been conducted in 1533 at Marseilles and the marriage concluded in October of that year. Henry VIII and Francis also
contemplated a marriage alliance, which, if coupled with some
agreement with the German Protestants, would complete the
isolation of Charles V and nullify any imperial threat to either
England or France, and also to Rome, if Clement should suddenly look more favorably on Henry VIII. Melanchthon was to
be the chief agent on the Protestant side. For a variety of reasons these efforts did not amount to much. But one of the most
important of these was the reaction of Rome to the execution of
Fisher and More. A shock of horror ran through Europe. In
England the press and pulpit were marshaled to explain the
heinous treasons for which they died. Bishop Gardiner wrote
an elaborate justification of English policy. Efforts were made
to undermine French claims that Francis I had tried to protect Bishop Fisher. But in France numerous pamphlets telling
the tale of More's death were printed and freely circulated,
which was strongly resented by Henry VIII. Even more out-
rageous to English minds were remarks that traitors should
merely be exiled, though exile was the natural concomitant of
disagreement in an age devoid of a concept of loyal opposition.
That would but provide a vast breeding ground of treason
abroad, beyond the king's reach. With the apparent end of
efforts at a threefold alliance, suspicion and recrimination were
the natural idiom. And off in Rome Clement's successor, Paul
III, readied his bull *Christiani nominis opprobrium* (August

---

consider it in his examination of Fisher, who was again asked to swear
the oath on 21 April.
[1] Sir John Wallop (d. 1551), soldier and diplomat, captain of Calais,
and ambassador in France from 1532–1537.

1535), in which an act depriving Henry of his kingdom was considered, though three more years were to pass before its publication. When it finally appeared, deprivation was dropped and only excommunication was pronounced. While Francis achieved the papal blessing and the Medici alliance, Henry waited the autumn of 1535 with nothing accomplished on the diplomatic front and the threat of a holy war hanging over his head.

Sir, after my most hearty commendations. These shall be to advertise you that the seventeenth day of this month I received from you a packet of letters which undelayedly I delivered unto the king's highness and conferred with his Grace the effects both of your letters and all others within the said packet being directed aswell to his highness as to me. And after his highness had with me perused the whole contents thoroughly of your said letters, perceiving not only the likelihood of the not repairing into France of Philip Melanchthon,[2] but also your communications had with the French king upon your demand made of the king's highness' pensions,[3] with also your diverse answers and replications made in that behalf, for the which his majesty gives unto you his hearty and condign* thanks; you shall understand that his highness commanded me to make you answer in this wise following.

First, as touching the king's money. His highness doubts not but seeing both the French king and also the Great Master[4] have promised you it shall be dispatched. You will as the case shall require not cease to call upon them till it be dispatched. And further considering that the said French king upon your said demand of the said pensions so suddenly fell into communication with you, aswell of his friendship and humanity showed to the king's highness, alleging that he at all times has answered for the king's highness, specially being last at Mar-

[2] Philipp Melanchthon (1497–1560), friend and disciple of Martin Luther and a leader of Protestant reform in the second generation. He advised Henry VIII to take a second wife. In 1535 attempts were made to bring him to England, or at least to keep him from going to France.

[3] On 27 December 1525, Francis I agreed to pay Henry VIII a pension of 100,000 crowns a year for life, if the English would break their alliance with Charles V. On 30 April 1527, a further pension of 50,000 crowns was granted in exchange for English renunciation of claims to France.

[4] Anne de Montmorency (1493–1567), Count Beaumont and grand master of France.

seilles with Pope Clement with other kings,[5] as in your said
letter appears, as also concerning the executions lately done here
within this realm;[6] the king's highness marvels not a little there
at and thinks it good that as of yourself you take some occasion
at convenient time and opportunity to renovate the said communication, both with the French king or, at the least, with
the Great Master. Saying unto them that, where the said French
king alleges that he has at all times answered for the king's
highness in his cause and specially to the said Pope Clement at
Marseilles, affirming his proceedings to be just and upright
concerning the matrimony, as you do write, in that the king's
highness proceedings in all his affairs within this realm being
of such equity and justice of themselves as they need not any
defence or assistance against Pope Clement or any other foreign
power, having God's word and laws only sufficient to defend
him. Yet in that the said French king has as he says answered at all times on the king's part, then he has done nothing
but the part of a brother in justifying and verifying the truth
and so continuing shall do as appertains to a prince of honor—
which the king's highness doubts not he has, and will do only
in respect to the verity and truth, besides the amity betwixt
them both justly requiring the same.

And concerning the executions done within this realm. You
shall say to the said French king that the same were not so
marvellous extreme as he alleges. For touching Mr. More and
the Bishop of Rochester with such others as were executed here,
their treasons, conspiracies and practices secretly practiced,
aswell within the realm as without, to move and stir dissension
and to sow sedition within the realm, intending thereby not
only the destruction of the king but also the whole subversion
of his highness' realm, being explained and declared and so
manifestly proved afore them that they could not avoid nor
deny it; and they therefore openly detected and lawfully convicted, adjudged and condemned of high treason by the due
order of the laws of this realm, as shall and may well appear
to all the world that they having such malice rooted in their
hearts against their Prince and sovereign and the total destruction of the commonwealth of this realm, were well worthy if

[5] Even after the Divorce and the marriage of Henry to Anne Boleyn,
Francis I offered to mediate the papal-royal conflicts. Henry assured
Francis it was not necessary, but the French king was intent on his own
pursuits, especially the Medici alliance.
[6] Fisher was executed late in June 1535. More died 7 July 1535.

they had a thousand lives to have suffered ten times a more terrible death and execution than any of them did suffer.

And touching such words as the said French king spake unto you concerning how Mr. More died and what he said to his daughter going to his judgment and also what exhortations he should give unto the king's subjects to be true and obedient to his grace (assuring you that there was no such thing), whereof the Great Master promised you a double at length.[7] In that the king's pleasure is that you shall not only procure the said double and send it hither, but also say unto the said French king that the king's highness can not otherwise take it but very unkindly that the said French king or any of his council, at whose hands he has so much merited and to whom he hath ministered so many great benefits, pleasures and commodities, should so lightly give ear, faith and credence to any such vain bruits* and fleeing tales, not having first knowledge and advertisement from the king's highness here and his council of the verity and truth; affirming it to be the office of a friend hearing any such tales of so noble a Prince, rather to have compressed the bruiters thereof to silence, or at the least not permitted them to have divulged the same until such time as the king's majesty, being so dear a friend, had been advertised thereof and the truth known before he should so lightly believe and allege any such report. Which ingrate and unkind demeanor of the said French king used in this behalf argues plainly not to remain in his breast such integrity of heart and sincere amity towards the king's highness and his proceedings as his highness always heretofore has expected and looked for. Which thing you may propone* and allege unto the said French king and the Great Master, or to one of them, with such modesty and soberness as you think they may perceive that the king's highness has good and just cause in this part somewhat to take their light credence unkindly.

And where as the said French king says that touching such laws as the king's highness has made he will not meddle with all, alleging it not to be meet that one Prince should desire another to change his laws, saying that his be too old to be changed; to that, you shall say that such laws as the king's highness has made here be not made without substantial grounds by great and mature advice, counsel and deliberation of the

[7] The "double" must be a copy of one or more of the pamphlets circulating in France. There were also anonymous poems or elegies on More published in France.

whole policy of this realm and are indeed no new laws but of great antiquity and many years passed were made and executed within this realm as now they be renovate and renewed only in respect to the common weale of the same. And it is not a little to his highness' marvel that the said French king ever would counsel or advise him, if in case here after any such like offenders should happen to be in this realm, that he should rather banish them than in such wise execute them. And specially considering that the said French king himself, in communing with you at that time, not only confessed the extreme executions and great bruyllie* of late done in his realm, but also that he now intends to withdraw the same and to revoke and call home again such as be out of his realm, the king's highness therefore the more strangely takes his said advice and counsel; supposing it to be neither the office of a friend nor of a brother that he would determine himself to call home into his realm again his subjects being out of the same for speaking against the Bishop of Rome's usurped authority and counsel the king's highness to banish his traitors into strange parts, where they might have good occasion, time, place and opportunity to work their feats of treason and conspiracy the better against the king's highness and this his realm. In which part you shall somewhat engrieve* the matter after such sort as it may well appear to the said French king that not only the king's highness might take those his counsels and communications strangely and unkindly, thinking the same not to proceed of mere amity and friendship, but also using such policy and austerity in proponing the same with the said French king and the Great Master, taking such time and opportunity as may best serve for the same, as they may well perceive the king's highness proceedings here within this realm, both concerning the said executions and all other things, to be only grounded upon justice and the equity of his laws, which be no new laws but ancient laws made and established of many years past within this realm and now renovate and renewed as is aforesaid for the better order, weale and surety of the same. And you may further say that if the French king and his council well consider, as they ought to do, that it were more better to advance the punishment of traitors and rebels for their offences than to punish such as do speak against the usurped authority of the Bishop of Rome, who daily go about to suppress and subdue kings and princes of their authority given to them by God's word.

All such matters the king's pleasure is that you shall take time and occasion, as you talking again with the French king or the Great Master may declare your mind as before is prescribed unto you, adding thereunto such reasons after your accustomed dexterity and discretion as you shall think most expedient and to serve best for the king's purpose, defence of his proceedings, and the proof of the French king's ingratitude showed in this behalf; not doubting in your wisdom, good industry and discrete circumspection for the ordering and well handling of the same accordingly.

And touching Melanchthon. Considering there is no likelihood of his repair into France, as I have well perceived by your letters, the king's highness therefore hath appointed Christopher Mont[8] undelayedly to take his journey where Melanchthon is and, if he can, to prevent Mons. de Langie[9] in such wise as the said Melanchthon's repair into France may be stayed and diverted into England, not doubting but the same shall take effect accordingly. And as to Mr. Heynes,[10] the king's pleasure is that he shall go to Paris, there to learn and decipher the opinions of the learned men and their inclinations and affections, aswell touching the king's highness' proceedings as to the Bishop of Rome, his usurped power and authority, after such sort as the king's said highness has now written to him by his gracious letters addressed both to him and the said Christopher Mont, directing them what they shall do in all things committed to their charge at this time, as I doubt not they will put thereunto their devoirs* for the accomplishment of the king's pleasure, as appertains.

And thus making an end, praying you to use your discretion in the proponing of the premisses to the French king and the Great Master, or the one or both of them; using the same as a medicine and after such sorts that as near as you can it be not much displeasantly taken, advertising the king's highness from time to time of the successes thereof and of all other occurants

[8] Christopher Mont (d. 1572), Henry VIII's agent in Germany, had entered Cromwell's service in 1531 and had been sent often to Protestant courts after 1533. His purpose was to prevent German reformers from accepting the mediation of Francis I. Bishop Foxe of Hereford was soon afterward dispatched to aid Mont. Whether these acts were of Cromwell's design, and whether they constituted a plan for an evangelical alliance (*foedus evangelicum*), is now impossible to discover.

[9] Guillaume du Bellay, Sieur de Langey (1491–1543), author and diplomat, variously French ambassador to England, Rome, and the German Protestants.

[10] Simon Heynes (d. 1552), president of Queen's College, Cambridge, and ambassador to France in a joint commission with Gardiner.

as the case shall require. I shall for this time bid you most heartily farewell, etc. Thornbury,[11] the 23rd day of August.

Copy in unknown hand; other copies at Longleat, Bath Mss.

20. To the Privy Council[1]

PRO SP1/86/58[2]   17 October [1534]
LP, VII, 1271; 83   London

LETTERS RELATING to the apprehension and detention of men suspected of treason are frequent in Cromwell's correspondence. In the past they have been glossed to show that he was bent on erecting a despotism, or at the very least intent on the arbitrary use of authority to stifle dissent on the course upon which England was launched. But we must remember the circumstances of the autumn of 1534 if we are to put such letters in context. The disaffection which was evident in the Nun of Kent affair and the secret wanderings of Observants was not perfectly suppressed. England lived in fear of an invasion from the Continent to overthrow the "Turk" who ruled and was considered more of a threat to Christendom than the real Turk on the Danube. Royal proclamations to enforce the Supremacy and Succession were being cried up and down the land. More and Fisher were jailed in the Tower. Ireland was engulfed in the rebellion of the Geraldine Earl of Kildare, the maximum danger of which coincided with the month of this letter— October 1534. Kildare's agents applied to Charles V for aid. Open resistance abroad was coupled with preaching at home against the king's reformation. Since May 1534 a rash of prophesies sounding dangerously like the tocsin of rebellion sounded about London and in the West Country. England was in reality

---

[11] Thornbury, Gloucester, twenty-one miles SSW of Gloucester.

[1] The privy council was an organized board of about twenty members, most of them officers of state or household officials of the king, which, moved about with the sovereign and met as required. It concerned itself with traditional council duties, especially advising on foreign policy, but it also attended in detail to executive and administrative matters. It did not achieve final institutional form and records of its own until about 1540, but from the early 1530's it conformed to this description to a high degree. Dr. G. R. Elton has attributed the change in the council to Cromwell's reforms in government.

[2] The manuscript of this letter is no longer bound in the volume to which it belongs. On 16 July 1956 it was transferred to Wall Case II, item 3, PRO Museum, where it is still exhibited.

a nation at war, the sort of war hard for contemporaries to understand, but perhaps more familiar to a generation nurtured on the idea of ideological conflict.

My Lords, after my most hearty, affectuous commendations. This present bearer, my Lord of York's servant,[3] is arrived now to me with letters both to me and to the king's highness. I have remitted him further to deliver his majesty's letters. And because he can fully instruct your lordships and inform you of many things, I pray you to hear him favorably and to give him full credence. For you shall hear of him sundry notable things and especially against him that was apprehended on Sunday last, whom I take to be a very evil disposed person and the which, if he be examined according to the said bearer's relation, you shall know things greatly to be marked and noted.[4]

Therefore, I beseech you to have this matter recommended, and that the said person so apprehended be not put to death till we may know the whole and profound bottom of his cankered heart. I pray you to send to me advertisements how you shall find him and acknowledge of the very matter and also of any such things as I can do here anything for the furtherance of any the king's matters, for I shall spare no diligence. Thus Our Blessed Creator have you in his tuition and keeping. From the Rolls this 17th of October. Your lordship's assured friend,

Autograph final salutation and signature; rest in clerk's hand.

21. To Sir Gregory da Casale[1]

PRO SP1/82/240–3   10 April [1535]
LP, VII, 268; 101

POPE CLEMENT VII died on 23 September 1534 and, after a stormy conclave the cardinals elected Cardinal Farnese, who took the name Paul III. Of all Italian cardinals he was the man most likely to work toward healing the schism. In the Curia

---

[3] Dr. Edward Lee (1482?–1544), archbishop of York.
[4] It has not been possible to identify this particular man or the nature of his heresy, treason, or other crime.
[1] Sir Gregory da Casale or Casalis was a naturalized Englishman who had been one of the English resident ambassadors in Rome since 1527.

debates on the Divorce he had urged Henry's side of the case. He had a reputation as a proponent of general reform, and was an admirer of Erasmus and critic of abuses of monastic life. More to the point, after the final sentence of curial censure of Henry VIII had passed, he urged the reconsideration of that step. His opinions were well known, as was the fact that he was elected with French influence, which expressed a hope for re-union in Christendom. He had announced his intention to call a general council, perhaps under the auspices of Francis I, who was negotiating with the Protestants of Germany and in league with Henry VIII. All of this raised the hope that some new determination of the king's "Great Matter" might yet be made. This throws some light on the fact that a policy of re-conciliation still seemed possible during Cromwell's ministry, unless we see the elaborate correspondence between England, France, and Rome as a blind to cover the accelerating tempo of reform activity within England. While Casale and Cromwell were exchanging letters about a papal-royal compromise, with the first advance to be made on the Roman side, the winter of 1534–1535 had been spent in getting new parliamentary elabora-tions of the Supremacy and in commissioning Cromwell to make a general visitation of the church and to get a new valuation of all benefices in England. Indeed, in April there was an order to arrest all supporters of the pope's jurisdiction in England. It is therefore hard to avoid the conclusion that renewed diplomatic efforts cannot be taken to mean an abandonment of results already achieved, or even a willingness to negotiate seriously.

After my right hearty commendations. Since your departure I have received sundry of your letters, whereof the last bear date at Rome the 20th day of February. And whatsoever you have signified unto me by your said letters aswell as the public occurents there, as of the king's highness private affairs, I have always intimated and declared the same to the king's majesty, who right thankfully and acceptably takes and esteems your diligence in writing. And now, having perused and read both your letters addressed to his majesty and also to me, his highness has specially noted in the same amongst other that the Bishop of Rome,[2] speaking to you, showed himself very propence* and desirous to gratify his said highness; and that he had sent for out of Etruria two lawyers[3] being singularly well learned, in whose doctrine and good judgment he has great trust and con-

[2] Paul III.
[3] *LP*, VIII, 251, identifies them as Reynaldo Petratius and Decius.

fidence, whose sentences and opinions do stand wholly with the king's highness' cause; affirming (as you write), that the said Bishop of Rome of his duty and office ought to approbate and confirm this present matrimony, albeit it depended upon the validity of the dispensation made by Julius.[4] So as notwithstanding that the king's majesty, having his said cause sufficiently defined and being in that behalf resolutely determined and grounded, as upon the foundation of verity and truth, has discharged his conscience therein like a good, vertuous and Catholic prince afore God and the world; yet his majesty does in such sense interpret your letters that (as appears by the same) the said Bishop of Rome begins now somewhat to savor and feel the justice and equity of the said cause and partly to stand with the king's majesty in the same.

Wherefore, if the said Bishop of Rome does indeed bear so friendly and sincere good mind and will towards the king's highness as you do write, or rather if he love the truth as it becomes a very good man to do, setting apart all hatred and affection, it is his part to show the same now to the universal world in this most just and righteous cause by his own public testimony and approbation and of his own free will, without any suit or intercession of the king's majesty; only adhering to the truth and neglecting all other respects to pronounce the invalidity of the first matrimony and the validity of the second according to the sentences, judgments and definitions of the said two learned men. Which, as you write the said Bishop of Rome called and sent for unto him for that purpose, if the said Bishop of Rome will, surely he shall do [a] thing worthy [of] his office and merit of God and the world and to the king's highness' very thankful and acceptable pleasure and also to himself and his See much more profit and good than now needs to [be] express. And you for your part in this matter, as of yourself you can anything profit or prevail by your good policy and dexterity towards the conducing of the said Bishop of Rome to that conformity (as you write in your said letters), you shall then undoubtedly answer to the king's highness' expectation. And the same, proceding of the benevolence of the said Bishop of Rome and the zeal that he has to the due exercise of his office and duty, shall be the more great and acceptable a great

[4] Pope Julius II had granted to Henry VIII a dispensation to marry his brother Arthur's widow. At the same time he had also issued a brief for the same purpose, unknown to the English, which was in Spanish hands. The original bull was dated 26 December 1503.

deal to the king's highness and the whole world, seeing that the mere verity and the respect that he has to God and his own conscience shall move him thereunto, without any mortal man's procurement.[5]

This letter is an English draft of the Latin one in *LP*, VIII, 523; it appears to be in Thomas Wriothesley's hand. Endorsements: "A minute of certain letters responding to one at Rome." "A minute of a letter to intimate to the Pope the king's desire to have him in agreement to the divorce and to allow the second marriage."

22. To an Unknown Agent[1]

PRO SP1/103/88   3 April [1536]
LP, X, 617(1); 141   London

In October 1535 Catherine of Aragon, in failing health, had been moved from Buckden to Kimbolton. The change seemed to revive her spirits, while in Rome the new pope championed her cause. But, as Froude remarked, "the repose was but the stillness of evening as night is hastening down." The royal officers were not welcome in her household. She lived wholly among her own friends and people. Her only connection with king and court was in the person of the imperial ambassador, Chapuys, and it was through him that Henry VIII learned of the death of Catherine on 7 January 1536. The king ordered the court into mourning. The dead queen was buried at Peterborough, which was soon established as a new bishopric. The aura of her household and staff was one of secrecy and mystery. Her confessor, the Bishop of Llandaff, busied himself with various

---

[5] Elton, in "King or Minister" (see bibliography), has argued most strenuously to show that after Cromwell became the king's chief councilor the policy of a diplomatic settlement was at an end. It would seem that the effectiveness of that case must turn on what we think about the negotiations of the English with Paul III in 1535. If we take them as a serious effort to settle differences, rather than as an effort to buy time to consolidate reforms already in effect, we may well question that part of Elton's interpretation of Cromwell's purpose.

[1] Since this draft bears no endorsement, no identification of the receipient can be certain. But it is likely that Cromwell was writing to Sir William Petre, master in Chancery, administrator and prominent civilian lawyer, appointed executor of Catherine's estate.

affairs of his late mistress, often getting in the way of Sir William Petre, to whom Cromwell had given the execution of Catherine's will. On 3 March 1536 a French observer, Antoine de Castelnau, reported that Llandaff had been arrested while about to embark for Spain in sailor's dress. The bishop claimed he was going on a pilgrimage, but was rumored to have illegally sent out of the kingdom about £25,000 worth of gold and other valuables. On 7 March Chapuys reported that Llandaff had been put in the Tower, after an effort at escape was foiled. Early in the summer, Cromwell decided to release him, upon urgent requests from the agents of Charles V, and on 22 September Llandaff was at liberty.

I commend me unto you and have received your letter dated at Carew[2] the 26th day of March, by the which I have well perceived your diligence and good policy used in ensearching* the untruth of my Lady Catherine's priest,[3] which, as I perceive, had conveyed such plate, evidence and other things contained in your letters; which letter I showed unto the king's highness who, for your diligence, good policy and good acquittal in that behalf, gives you right great praise and also allows your deeds. And his gracious pleasure is that you, calling to your search discrete and worshipful men, as you shall think most meet for that purpose, shall cause the said priest to be straightly examined of such other things as he has counseled and caused to be embezzled; and after examination, to put him in surety to appear before the king's council to answer such things as shall be further on the king's behalf laid unto his charge.

And as to all such stuff as you shall think in any wise meet to be carried, leave it not in no wise behind you, but cause it to be brought up if you suppose it may be worth the carriage; and if not, to make the most thereof you can. Also, hearken that you do lack of the number of your ships. I pray you make diligent inquiry for them and all other the goods that you shall suppose to be embezzled or concealed and know who have been the doers or maintainers thereof. And in any wise devise you

---

[2] Carew or Carey, Pembrokeshire, about four miles east of Pembroke.
[3] Jorge de Athequa, Bishop of Llandaff, who had come into the Queen's service at the time of the Divorce as one of the counsel allowed her. He was described by Mattingly, *Catherine of Aragon*, p. 201, as "a good, simple, timid soul." He gave spiritual counsel as her chaplain until her death. The implications of his release are hard to read, though it may be that nothing collusive could be proved against him. For the relevant documents, see *LP*, X, 410, 429 and XI, 80, 479.

that the things may be brought hither surely and so trussed as they do take none moisture nor other harm. And specially have you good eye to the evidence, plate and principal household stuff. And I trust at your return you shall not repent of your journey. I heartily thank you on my part. And thus having respect always that all things may be substantially done and furnished, as shortly as you conveniently may, I trust you will repair homeward, whereof I would be glad. But in any wise I pray you examine well the priest. And thus fare you well. At London, the third day of April.

Draft in Cromwell's hand, much corrected.

23. To Sir William Fitzwilliam[1]

PRO SP1/155/162–3
LP, XIV, ii, 726; 329

24 December [1539]
London

GREAT MATTERS of state were involved in the arrival of Anne of Cleves. And matters of great moment presented themselves in any concealment of treason. Both the hoped-for Cleves marriage and the detection and execution of men guilty of treason were aspects of the Cromwellian program of the 1530's. So, too, was the "new order" innocently mentioned in this letter. What is meant is the reform of the king's household designed by Cromwell. As early as 31 July 1539 Cromwell was busy with a scheme to reshape the royal household, which on its business side had the work of a department of state, while doubling as the entourage or court of a king on its ceremonial side. To streamline both aspects and reduce expenditures for the household was perhaps an objective incompatible with the establishment of the new guard of pensioners who were maintained by the king. Contemporaries were more struck by the reforms of the royal chamber than by most others, especially the degree to which Henry VIII seemed to emulate French court practices. But from Cromwell's point of view the significance was otherwise. By reducing the authority of household financial officers, he wove more closely the web of his own control in the financial courts he instituted, and he worked through his dependents. At the same time, the new pensioners were a crucial element in the personal politics of high court life. A memorandum survives in

[1] The Earl of Southampton (d. 1542), also lord high admiral of England, 1536–1540. He headed the party entertaining Anne of Cleves at Calais.

which a list of "spears," or gentelmen-pensioner, applicants appears. Cromwell's friends on that list are four in number. Fitzwilliam (Earl of Southampton), Norfolk, and Suffolk, the king's brother-in-law, are down for one each. These figures fairly illustrate Cromwell as a politician vying for control in the difficult times of 1539–1540 and using the new household reforms as a stratagem in that struggle.

My very good lord, with my most hearty and effectual commendations. Having the king's majesty seen and perused your letters of the 21st of this present which arrived here this afternoon, his highness has commanded me for answer to the first part of the same to signify that albeit his grace does very much desire the good arrival of my lady's grace,[2] of your lordship and the rest of his servants there in England, yet seeing the wind does let and stay you therein, his highness takes your demore* in good part as reason requires and prays you heartily so to cheer my lady and her train as they may think the time as short as the tediousness of it will suffer.

For the second part, touching the priests, his grace would you should cause them both to be executed, if the laws and justice will condemn them both,[3] and if not, then to proceed to the execution of Richardson[4] and to award such punishment to the other[5] for the concealment as your wisdom shall think expedient for the example of others. His majesty will neither make store of them nor bestow two pennies for their conveyance hither, unless you shall see further cause than is yet apparent, not doubting but your good lordship will cause them to be substantially examined before the execution. I trust there be no more there of this rank sort; a few of these might breed as great a sedition as was so much written of.

[2] Anne of Cleves (1515–1557), Henry VIII's fourth queen. She was selected by Cromwell and arrived at Calais 12 December 1539, but because of bad weather was not able to reach England until early January 1540. The marriage took place at Greenwich on 6 January; a few months later it was annulled by act of Parliament.

[3] The conditional "if" is important in the correction of the picture of Cromwell arbitrarily murdering priests and other Englishmen. As Cromwell was never tired of pointing out, he never condemned men, only the laws of the land did that.

[4] William Richardson, formerly of the religious establishment of Calais. Richardson had gossiped that he could not accept the king as head of the church.

[5] William Peterson, parson of Bonningue, and formerly commissary of Calais, had some papist leanings, according to depositions taken at the time. But his chief offense was his concealment of knowledge of Richardson's denial of the royal supremacy: *LP*, XV, 37.

This day his majesty moves to Greenwich[6] and there begins to enter his new order; and amongst the rest, as many of the gentlemen pensioners as be here give their attendance with their axes upon him.[7] Our Lord send his majesty long life and good health to enjoy his most noble devises in their perfection. I send your lordship again the bill of Richardson's hands and so pray God to send you with all your charge health and a propitious and merry wind to bring you nearer unto us. From London the . . . [breaks off]

Draft, Wriothesley's hand.

24. To Lord Stourton[1]

PRO SP1/157/224v   15 February [1540]
LP, XV, 252(ii); 337

IN THE late winter of 1540, Cromwell's hold on power was rendered insecure by the king's distate for the new queen from Cleves. Beyond matrimonial problems, however, there arose matters more central to the concepts of reform for which Cromwell worked. Not the least of these was the increasing tension in the country caused by the retreat of the Six Articles and the concomitant "Tudor reaction." The power of the faction led by Norfolk and Gardiner seemed to wax daily, and those who knew the signs thought Cromwell to be finished. But the Lord Privy Seal went about the business of government as

[6] We know that Henry moved to Greenwich, his favorite palace, for the celebration of Christmas, from which we can date the letter. The palace lies three miles ESE of London Bridge.

[7] John Husee, Lord Lisle's loose-tongued agent, reported on 22 December that the household *was to be altered*. He then reported that the new measures were to go into effect on Christmas Eve, when the king removed to his birthplace, Greenwich; *LP*, XV, 719, 745–6. The new order unfolded slowly and in fact was not completely set forth when Cromwell fell in July 1540. The gentelmen pensioners were first mentioned in the abortive plans of 1537–1538 and represented a revival of the "spears" of Henry VII's day, still intact in 1509, but apparently disbanded between 1509 and 1537.

[1] I conjecture this addressee on the basis of the fact that Lord Stourton was active in affairs in Wales and the marches, while the letter printed here is written on the back of one from Stourton to Cromwell, SP1/155 /224r, which is printed in *LP*, XV, 252(i).

briskly as ever. And he continued to show both that zeal for justice and insistence on loyalty within the law that characterized his handling of the issues arising out of the royal supremacy. Far from a despotic manipulation of power, Cromwell's ministry characteristically relied on the law to unveil traitors—or false informers—in an age dependent on the sometimes ugly business of informing for profit.

After my right hearty commendations unto your lordship. Whereas I am enformed that Sir Richard Smith,[2] parson of Langham in the county of Pembroke, is accused and laid in prison by the bailiff[3] there for certain words spoken sounding to be treason against the king's majesty, these shall be to require you with convenient celerity [to] send as well for the said parson as other his accusors, and upon examination had and due proofs, and the said Smith found guilty therein, he to remain in prison to such a time as the king's pleasure shall be known therein. And in case his said accusors can make no due proof of the same, that then, you taking sufficient sureties of the said parson *per bondes* for his appearance at all times when he shall be called for by the king's highness of any of his honorable council, you suffer him to go at liberty.

Draft; Wriothesley's hand.

25. To Sir Thomas Butler[1]

PRO SP1/110/22–3   30 October [1536]
LP, XI, 919; 167   Windsor

THE FIFTEEN months stretching between the execution of More and the outbreak of that great crisis of the reign of Henry VIII called the Pilgrimage of Grace stand in the mind of a historian as perhaps the most trying months in the history of the Tudor dynasty. The deaths of More, Catherine of Aragon, Anne Boleyn,

---

[2] Sir Richard Smith (alias Rawlyns) was vicar of Llangan, Pembrokeshire, in 1540 (*Valor Ecclesisasticus,* IV, 410), and appeared elsewhere in state papers; *LP*, XV, 52.
[3] Thomas Webbe.
[1] Butler commanded a company of 368 men under the Earl of Derby during the first phase of the Pilgrimage.

and the saintly Carthusians must ultimately bear different
legends. So must the Visitation and Dissolution, Cromwell's
elevation to an unchallenged power in church and state, and
the spreading discontent of many northerners with Henry VIII's
reformation and the minister who led it. Nowhere were feelings
of opposition and loss stronger than in the Tudor North. There
religious discontent was a motive to rebellion, though the majority of rebels were drawn from men disadvantaged by the
transfer of land and the withdrawal of monastic patronage or
hospitality. There monks found willing ears in old lords who
scarcely understood the fact that the Reformation was only beginning but who well enough grasped that it was somehow
inimical to them. Certain northern lords, Darcy and Hussey
especially, had been telling Chapuys for years that England was
ready to revolt against Henry VIII. Toward the end of the
summer rumors spread wildly in the North that heavy taxes
would be imposed on Christian rites, that all cattle would be
marked for the king's use, that all churches within five miles
of another were marked for destruction. Malice and mendacity
coupled with discontent in an array whose structure has to this
day defied complete analysis. And by 3 October, at Caistor in
Lincolnshire, the pilgrims began their march, to be followed in
short order by those of Yorkshire under Robert Aske. A crucial
question, perhaps the fate of the monarchy, turned on the loyalty
of local gentry and their tenantry, to whom Cromwell and the
king had good reason to be thankful when they answered the
king's call and not those voices urging revolution.

Master Butler, after my right hearty commendations. Having
received your letters sent unto me by your servant with other
instructions sent also by the same, I have not only declared
your diligence and approved truth therein expressed to the
king's highness, who gives unto you for the same his right
hearty thanks, but also do myself much rejoice, both to hear
of the towardness of my lord of Derby[2] and to perceive the
loyalty of all your other gentlemen and others the king's good
subjects in those parts. The sequel of which truth shall not be
more acceptable to his majesty than beneficial to yourselves, as
a thing preserving that policy without the which they that have
most gotten by their honest industry should be in the worst
case. I have procured such letters of thanks as you desired and
the same sent unto you by the bearer. And thus desiring you

[2] Sir Edward Stanley, third earl of Derby (1508–1572), a signer of
Henry VIII's petition of divorce to Clement VII, and prominent in the
suppression of the rebellion in 1536–37.

to be vigilant now in this quesy time I bid you well to fare as I would myself. From Windsor, the penultimate of October.[3] Your assured friend.

Wriothesley's hand; autograph signature. Addressed: "To my loving friend Sir Thomas Butler knight give this in haste."

26. To the Duke of Norfolk[1]

PRO SP1/120/165–6   22 May [1537]
LP, XII, i, 1257; 188

ANY DETAILED retelling of the Pilgrimage of Grace is beyond the scope of this note. From October through January 1536–1537 the Pilgrimage convulsed the North. The Duke of Norfolk headed the suppression of it in Yorkshire, after a period of prolonged negotiations with the rebels at Doncaster. After the last phases of active rebellion had been put down in Cumberland and in Yorkshire, Norfolk exercised what men of the time called his "hanging commission," in which over two hundred of the rebels, among them many leaders, were put to death for their role in the abortive revolution. Among them were men like Sir Francis Bigod, who for some time had had the reputation of being a special friend of Cromwell, but who in critical phases played a strong role against the crown in behalf of causes not all of a piece with those of feudal aristocrats of the Percy clan. The bewildering complexity of causes contributing to the upheaval defy simplistic attempts either at enumeration or understanding. It is clear, however, that Norfolk saw in the loosening of social bonds and the execution of many old leaders of northern society a chance to carve out a power base for himself in the North. This effect Cromwell actively opposed in a campaign that embittered Norfolk and advanced new reasons for the Duke's dislike of Cromwell. We see a trace of Cromwell's interruption of Norfolk's efforts in this letter, along with much of the routine business of establishing again that civil order

---

[3] A fragment of a similar letter addressed to Sir Ralph Eure survives in SP1/111/23, in which Eure is an instrument of rejoicing at a "time when a fearful rebellion hurts the land. . . ."

[1] Thomas Howard (1473–1554), earl of Surrey and duke of Norfolk. Howard was primarily a soldier. He did, however act as the fixed center of aristocratic opposition to the two great bourgeois ministers of Henry VIII, Wolsey and Cromwell.

which loomed so large in the ideas of Cromwell and the reformers, to whom the Pilgrimage could only be a perverse
resistance to necessary change.

Please it your grace to be advertised that the king's highness,
having received your letters[2] dated at Burlington[3] the 18th day
of this month; whereby his grace perceives your order taken for
the same Burlington and the house of Jervaise.[4] His highness
giving unto you always his most hearty thanks, has commanded
me to advertise you of his gracious pleasure, both touching the
effects of the same your letters and also to the matters comprised in your letters to me with certain effects delivered unto
me by Leonard Beckwith.[5] And as touching your said order,
surely the king's highness likes it very well.

And albeit that he doubts not but the persons whom you have
appointed will do everything to the very best, yet nevertheless
for as much as by act of parliament all lands attained must pass
by the hands of the king's General Surveyors, and certain things
by the order of the law, both in finding of offices and other
things is to be observed,[6] you shall understand that the king's
highness at this time does send down certain of his counsel to
take perfect order in that matter; aswell touching the finding of
offices as also to make certain and perfect books of all things
belonging to the same. Not for that they shall attempt to annul
or infringe anything that shall be done by you nor by the
persons appointed by your lordship, but that they all together
may so confer that anything may be perfectly and duly done
to the king's honor and reasonable profit; his grace thinking that

[2] On 18 May 1537 Norfolk sent to Beckwith instructions concerning the
suppression of Bridlington and Jervaulx (see footnotes 3 and 4 ff.); *LP*,
XII, i, 1214.
[3] Bridlington or Burlington Abbey, a house of Augustinian friars whose
abbot and prior sent a contingent to aid the Pilgrims. William Wood, the
prior, was executed 2 June 1537.
[4] Jervaise (Gervies) was the Cistercian abbey of Jervaulx in north
Yorkshire. The abbot, Adam Sedbergh, was hanged on 2 June 1537,
for sending aid to the rebels. Since the abbey itself had been fortified,
it was blown up by government troops, and the monks were turned out.
[5] Leonard Beckwith was a Yorkshire man prominent in the administration of Augmentations business in the shire, where he was receiver of the
revenues of the court.
[6] By 27 Henry VIII, c. 62, the office of general surveyor was made a
permanent part of the administration of the crown lands, but in essence
subordinated general surveyors to the Augmentations in matters of newly
acquired lands.

afore the same shall be directly and perfectly accomplished, considering the time of the year now and that the farmers commonly enter not but about Michaelmas,[7] it should not be for his grace's profit to make any grant of any part of the said lands until the said time and also that the same may be well surveyed. At which time his highness will not only have such a respect both unto the poor men inhabiting about Burlington and Jervaise, but also forsee for some substantial person meet and necessary to stay the country and keep hospitality to dwell in the principal part of the monastery, for whom his highness is minded to follow much your lordship's advice and counsel and both require you to advertise him fully of your opinions touching the same.

And as touching the depositions taken of certain women anempst* the cutting down and burial of the traitors in Westmoreland and Cumberland.[8] Surely, having regard and respect to the evil example and perverse minds of the offenders, which is thought came not only of womens' heads, but some men were the principal procurers, the king's highness thinks verily that if the said depositions had been earnestly taken, the plainness of that matter might have been easily known. And therefore considering that such a misbehavior is not to be passed over without some convenient punishment, his highness requires you, according to your high wisdom and his trust, by all means possible, to try and search out the principal doers and occasioners of the same; which, once done and they apprehended, punishment shall be devised for them according to the qualities of their offenses.

And as to the haven,[9] whereof your lordship writes, the king's highness, upon such considerations as be mentioned in your said letters, is contented that if twenty pounds, according to the saying of Beckwith, will amend it, that you shall cause the same to be done this summer in all haste possible, remitting nevertheless the further expense to your wisdom.

---

[7] The meaning here is that the king's revenue farmers will not enter or go into the lands in question to assert crown rights until 29 September 1537.

[8] In February 1537 a rising of common tenants in Cumberland and Westmoreland under Captain Poverty took place. Norfolk, who saw the difficulty of moving against the rebels with common law since they would not testify against one another, exercised a commission of martial law at Carlisle, under his powers as king's lieutenant in the North.

[9] This refers to the haven or port of Burlington or Bridlington.

As for the shrine,[10] the king's highness, to the intent that his people should not be seduced in the offering of their money, his grace would have taken down; which, and all other plate and jewels appertaining to his highness, except such as you desire to have for your money (which his highness is content with) his pleasure is shall be sent up hither with all speed; being also contended that you, according to your desire, shall have such vestments and ornaments of the church not being meet for his highness' use—the same being appraised for your reasonable money as shall appertain. And also that the corn and cattle, especially such as be meet to be sold, his highness thinks to be best uttered* now, remitting the discretion and order thereof unto you. And also the lands likewise at this time of the year, being both sown and of other nature, his highness doubts not but that you will substantially order the same as shall be for his highness' profit. And the pleasure of his highness is that the due debts of the said houses, well provided without covin,* shall be contented of the goods of the same.

And as to the lead and all other things wherein you be willing to know the king's pleasure, your lordship shall understand that upon the view and survey thereof now at this time by your grace and his commissioners to be eftsoon* sent unto his highness in all things, he will upon the sight of the same determine his further pleasure.

The king's highness also desires your lordship that you will make due search of all such lands, offices, farms, fees* and all other things as were in the possession of the Lord Darcy,[11] Sir Robert Constable,[12] Sir Francis Bigod,[13] Sir John Bulmer,[14]

[10] Norfolk soon sent gold from the shrine to Henry VIII; *LP*, XII, ii, 34, 35, 92.

[11] Thomas Darcy (1467–1537), Baron Darcy, statesman, administrator of the Council of the North, and rebel leader who delivered Pomfret Castle to the Pilgrims; he was first pardoned and then beheaded for further complicity in rebellion in 1537.

[12] Sir Robert Constable (1478–1537), an ardent Romanist and insurgent leader, executed in 1537.

[13] Sir Francis Bigod (1508–1537), an advanced reformer and an agent of Cromwell in reformation of the Yorkshire clergy and monastic establishments. His career as a radical Protestant is well documented. That he should have been executed in connection with the allegedly Catholic risings is comprehensible if we remember that his motives for antigovernment activity were primarily tied up with family loyalties and the vast economic problems afflicting the heir of an ancient fortune.

[14] Sir John Bulmer, uncle of Sir Francis Bigod, who refused to join in the 16 January 1537 rising led by Bigod, but who was implicated in the Pilgrimage and later executed.

Sir Stephen Hamerton,[15] Sir Thomas Percy,[16] Nicholas Tempest[17] and all the persons of those parts lately attainted here and to certify the same to his grace, to the intent the same may confer them to the persons worthy accordingly; and likewise to cause a perfect inventory of their goods, lands and possessions to be made and sent up with convenient speed as shall appertain.

As touching news, there be none here but that there is lately coming hither two ambassadors from the Emperor out of Spain— the one of them named being of a good house and near unto the Emperor.[18] As yet I cannot certify your grace of their purpose, because they have not had access to the king's highness. When I shall know, I shall make your grace participate thereof. Where I. . . .

Draft in Richard Derby's[19] hand; much corrected by T. Cromwell. Endorsed: "Copy of my lord's letters to my lord of Norfolk 22 May."

27. To Bishop Tunstal and the Council of the North[1]

PRO SP1/126/62–5   2 November 1537
LP, XII, ii, 1016; 227   Westminster

IN THE north of England and in the west, hard against the Scottish and Welsh borderlands, the powers of the crown had been for centuries but weakly exercised. Special problems of government provoked special means of dealing with them. More

[15] Sir Stephen Hamerton, leader of a family known for its conservatism and staunch Catholic views well into the late sixteenth century, a leader of the Pilgrimage, executed in 1537.
[16] Sir Thomas Percy, the brother of Henry Percy, earl of Northumberland, also an active rebel executed for treason in 1537.
[17] Nicholas Tempest, brother of Sir Thomas, also implicated in the Pilgrimage and executed in 1537.
[18] In early May 1537, Don Diego Hurtado de Mendoza arrived in company with Don Jorge de Ourton, sent from Charles V to discover the state of the North, to learn of Henry VIII's relations with Francis I, and to urge an Anglo-imperial alliance.
[19] One of the signet clerks and a member of Cromwell's household.
[1] Cuthbert Tunstal, president of the Council.

specifically with regard to the Tudor North, a system of march lordships and wardens maintained the area as a permanent defensive center against the Scots, linking the shires of Northcumberland, Cumberland, and Westmoreland under great local feudatories—the Percies, Nevilles, and Dacres. While in the western marches the Welsh connections of the Tudors helped subdue the area, in the North traditional Yorkist sentiment and resentment of religious reforms mixed with deep agrarian unrest to make Tudor power there feeble against the "true kings" of the Percy clan and its allies. Even before the Pilgrimage of Grace, however, Edward IV and his successors had built on Richard of Gloucester's council an instrument of government. When Richard became king as Richard III this development was reinforced by royal power, a strength lacking in the first Tudor, who had neither great estates in the North nor administrative experience there. Indeed, until at least 1522 it was not possible for the Tudors to govern the North effectively. But by 1525 Wolsey had established a council, staffed largely by lawyers and ruled by Henry VIII's bastard son Richmond, exercising a far-ranging criminal and civil jurisdiction that moved into Yorkshire and other parts of the turbulent society there. From 1525 to 1530 the council's fortunes varied, and then were bankrupted by an inability to contain the power of the great lords. By 1535 a policy of breaking the power of the Percies was in effect; and in the Pilgrimage the king and Cromwell found the lever to overturn the remnants of feudal power. Cromwell in fact designed a permanent council and attendant institutions under a lord president, aided by judges, lawyers, revenue administrators, and secretaries, responsible for the whole North and in theory at least controlled from the center. Under its commission it had common law powers and could deal with treason and felony, as well as equity powers centered in the council sitting as a court of conscience. It also possessed a Star Chamber competence in riots and administrative matters, though in all matters it was watched closely by the privy council and by the jealous local powers.

After my right hearty commendations to your lordships. These shall be to advertise the same that the king's majesty, having aswell received your letters[2] of the fifteenth of the last month addressed from you and certain others of his council there to his highness, has seen and perused the letters which with the same your lordship sent unto me. His grace's pleasure is that I should make sure answer unto your said letters as ensues.

First, his highness takes your proceedings for this beginning

2 See *LP*, XII, ii, 914.

in very good part and specially gives unto you his right hearty thanks for your letters written to Sir Reynold Carnaby.[3]

Second, his majesty is well content that you shall use the signet[4] being in the custody of you, Master Uvedale,[5] the stamp whereof his grace likes very well for that it has notable differences from all other his grace's signets and is also well graven, as it was judged by the print, which with the carriage was nevertheless somewhat pressed out. .

Third, as concerning the pledges* of Tynedale[6] and Reddisdale.[7] As his majesty refers the bestowing of them to your wisdom, so his grace thinks the matter thereof of no such importance as should require his highness' letters to Newcastle[8] or to any other place or person without the limits of your commission.* Having his majesty given unto you such ample commission as he thinks shall not need any supplement, unless the matter were of greater difficulty than the keeping of those pledges is, whom it is thought you may easily keep in sundry places, having order taken for your allowance for their charges without such fears as should cause you to put them to such straightness as might be called an imprisonment.

Fourth, the names of Darcy,[9] Constable[10] and others shall be withdrawn out of all commissions.

Fifth, his grace is content that Mr. Fairfax[11] shall enjoy a place in his council there, with twenty pounds fee, to come and go at his liberty; for which purpose your lordship shall receive a new commission herewith, wherein he is inserted.

Sixth, you shall herewith receive a commission for the levying of men in case of need, which commission his majesty's pleasure is shall remain with you my lord of Durham only for a sheet anchor if that extremity should chance; which his grace thinks cannot happen, if you will earnestly punish evil disposed persons in time convenient.

[3] Sir Reginald Carnaby, keeper of Tynedale, an active crown agent in Northumberland and Yorkshire after the suppression of the Pilgrimage of Grace.

[4] The king's signet seal authorized for the Council of the North as the official warrant signifying royal business.

[5] John Woodall or Uvedale, secretary to the council in 1537; *LP*, XII, ii, 100–2.

[6] In Northumberland, on the banks of the Tyne.

[7] In Northumberland, on the banks of the Rede.

[8] Newcastle-on-Tyne, Northumberland.

[9] Thomas Darcy, a leader of the Pilgrimage.

[10] Sir Robert Constable, who also rebelled in 1536–1537.

[11] Thomas Fairfax, sergeant-at-law, for whom Tunstal had made a special request as a commissioner, *LP*, II, ii, 1076–77, and also 915.

Seventh, as touching the children of Sir Thomas Percy[12] remaining in the custody of Sir Thomas Tempest.[13] If you think not that place sure for them, his majesty's pleasure is that you shall bestow them in such other places further within the heart of those arts as you shall think expedient, the charges of whose diet shall be defrayed accordingly.

Finally, touching the books of decrees. You shall receive it by the next messenger who shall also bring unto you the warrants for your diets and the fees of the rest of the council, with the pensioners of the Marches[14] which, if our heavy chance should not have happened,[15] should have been dispatched unto you before this time. From Westminster, second November, Anno regni regis Henry VIII. xxix.

Draft, Wriothesley's hand; corrected by Cromwell, with the last line and signature by Cromwell. Endorsed: "Copy of my lord's letter to the President and Council of the North."

28. To John Doraunt[1]

PRO SP1/126/221   4 December 1537
LP, XII, ii, 1167; 230   Chelsea

THE TUDOR policy of building their power in the North we have already touched upon. One of the chief limitations of that plan was that power in the North was historically local power based

---

[12] Upon the arrest of Sir Thomas Percy, his children were put under the care of Tempest (*LP*, XII, ii, 229). But on 15 October Tunstal wrote that Tempest felt they should not be in close proximity to the river Tyne, where Tempest lived.

[13] Sir Thomas Tempest, a royal agent in the North. In 1537 a letter from him to Cromwell rehearses his services in the Pilgrimage, commissions for maintaining the peace with the Scots, various Border commissions, and so on; for which, see *LP*, XII, ii, 152.

[14] Either certain captains in the march area or some English dependents among the Scottish gentry and aristocracy.

[15] Doubtless this refers to the death of Queen Jane Seymour in the course of a postpartal illness following the birth of Edward VI early in October 1537.

[1] John Doraunt, a very obscure official, was escheator in the county in which Hussey's principal estates lay. It was his job under the law to "find a true office" of the lands, that is, to hold an inquiry concerning any matters that entitled the crown to the possessions of lands, goods, or

on large estates and a numerous rent roll, from which tenants could be drawn when a show of force became necessary. In this regard the Pilgrimage was a boon to Tudor government. Many of the rebels were great landholders in the various northern shires (among them Lord John Hussey), and either their conviction at common law or their attainder for treason presented an opportunity to the crowd to take into its own hands the lands of "attainted persons." But first an "office" or systematic evaluation of such property had to be made by one of the king's agents called an escheator, an official whose special job it was to determine the royal interest in various categories of land held in wardship or other circumstances. As new lands were acquired, primarily in the 1530's by acts of attainder (apart of course from the suppression of the monasteries), they were governed as proprietary additions to the crown lands, in accordance with the old principle that the scattered lands of the monarchy really constituted a single vast estate. When the Court of Augmentations was reformed in 1547 it had two dozen or more such groupings, among them lands once belonging to the Hussey family, the Nevilles, Darcies, Hamertons, Bulmers, and Constables, as well as the Percy lands and many others not taken as a result of the Pilgrimage.

After my right hearty commendations. You shall receive hereinclosed the form of the office of Hussey, which the king's pleasure is that immediately upon the sight hereof you shall cause to be found in a due order and course of the law, without alteration of any word in the same, of all the manors, lands, tenements, et cetera, which the said Hussey late attainted of high treason had and was seised of in possession or reversion within the limits of your office at the time of his attainder.[2] Not failing to finish this matter with all diligence and like circumspection and dexterity as you tender his majesty's pleasure. Thus fare you heartily well, from the Nete,[3] this fourth day of December, the 29th year of his grace's most noble reign. Your loving friend.

---

even chattels of an attainted person. The inquiry was made by virtue of the power of the escheator's office or on occasion by a special writ or order. The facts were determined very quickly before a jury of indefinite number (not always twelve), and then a "return" was filed in exchequer.
[2] Sir John Hussey, employed before 1533 as chamberlain to Princess Mary, an opponent of religious reform and a militant searcher-out of heretics as early as 1529.
[3] The Nete, likely the Neathouse, a small royal residence in the London suburb of Chelsea, not far from the celebrated bridge and market garden.

Unknown clerk's hand; autograph signature. Addressed: "To my loving friend John Doraunt of Ketismer[4] the king's escheator in his grace's counties of Northampton and Rutland." Endorsed: "My lord privy seal."

29. To Reginald Pole[1]

BM Cotton Mss. Cleopatra Eiv, fo. 371   April [1535]
LP, VIII, 220; 133   London

CONCERNING CARDINAL POLE

FEW ITEMS in the correspondence of Thomas Cromwell reflect more pertinently the traumatic impact of the Reformation in England than those letters which touch the affairs of Reginald Pole. The future cardinal and Roman reformer was a cousin of the English king, being descended from Edward IV's brother George Plantagenet, duke of Clarence. A brilliant youth, Pole seemed destined for a career in the church and in scholarship from an early age. After frequent excursions among the devout monks of the charterhouse at Sheen, Pole went to Magdalen College, Oxford, which we know as a center of reform and humanist activity in the early sixteenth century. Though he was not in holy orders he received the income of a number of ecclesiastical benefices from his royal cousin, along with money grants as a royal exhibitioner to study in Italian universities from 1521 to 1526, where he won the approval of celebrated French and Italian humanists. To them he appeared a prodigy of English learning, *non anglus sed angelus* (not English but an angel). The poet Bembo and the great Latin and Greek scholars Flaminio and Buonamici joined Erasmus in singing his praises. Erasmus said more than once that he esteemed Pole above all others. His return to England in 1526 almost coincided with the first phase of the king's "Great Matter," into which he was relentlessly drawn because of his noble connections and reputation for learning in scriptural studies and philosophy. For a time he evaded the Divorce crisis. But escape it entirely he could not, and in 1529–1530 Henry urged upon him a mission to the Sorbonne to obtain a judgment favorable to the wish

[4] Ketismer? Most likely Cottesmore, Rutland, about 18 miles NW of Leicester.
[1] For most questions of fact and bibliography about Pole see Constant, *The Reformation in England,* I, 256–84.

to put Queen Catherine away. By July 1530 Pole was back among his friends at Sheen, after Paris responded favorably. The king then offered him a choice of Winchester or Wolsey's see at York, a move conveyed by Norfolk with a hint that the king would not tolerate a man in either office opposed to the Divorce.

Pole, despite heavy pressure from his family, refused the king's offers. In an interview and a letter now lost he made it abundantly clear that he saw in the royal course a great error and sin. His fall from the king's grace was not absolute. But by 1532 he was sincerely unable to continue in England and obtained license to go back to Italy to continue his studies. Henry VIII retained in force the various allowances and benefices, even though for a time Pole was in the famous papal enclave at Avignon studying theology. Soon Padua and Venice called, however, and he made his way to Italy, there to resume his friendship with Bembo and also to cultivate new friendships with a remarkable group of reform-minded priests and bishops (among them Cosimo Gherio, Gasparo Contarini, and Ludovico Beccadelli) vital in the later Counter Reformation Catholic reforms.

At Padua, Pole gathered a household famed throughout Europe for its hospitality and intellectual attainments. Beccadelli was Pole's secretary in a group that also included Richard Morison and Thomas Starkey.

Distance proved no protector against the king's needs. Henry wished desperately to have his cousin's approval of his novel headship of the church in England, a mission assigned to Starkey, who was by 1534 a chaplain in Henry VIII's entourage and a useful ambassador to Pole in Padua. Pole promised his answer in reply to a letter communicated through Starkey from Cromwell (April 1535). His work came only in May 1536, however, and the book on church unity was not such a book as the king or Cromwell had hoped it would be. There Pole announced without qualification that "No temporal prince can be supreme head of the Church in his own country." After supporting papal power by scripture, tradition, and history, Pole dealt at length with what he thought to be Henry's unfortunate passion, one that had led the king astray and caused the deaths of famous and saintly men. After some hesitation, Pole sent the book to the English court by the hand of his servant Michael Throgmorton (Throckmorton).

Throgmorton left Venice with a letter for Henry VIII on 27 May 1536, with Pole's assurance that the book contained his truthful opinion in reply to such questions as had been addressed to him from Henry, Cromwell, and Starkey. Pole had few illusions that his arguments would succeed where others had

not and confided to Contarini that he had no hope of seeing
England again, that he would go back only after Henry VIII
was converted to Roman allegiance again. On the same day
(8 June 1536) he wrote to Tunstal, the bishop of Durham, that
his prayers were all that God would give the king one drop of
grace to shed one tear of pure penance. Whatever Henry's
reaction was, he urged Starkey and Tunstal to refute Pole's
views and to attempt the conversion of his cousin! Pole's friends
advised him against any return to England; going back to England, Beccadelli wrote, could end only by making Pole an open
rebel.

In July Paul III summoned Pole to Rome to take part in the
drafting of reform proposals, along with Ghiberti, Contarini, and
Caraffa, as members of the famous *Consilium de emendenda
ecclesia,* which was to prepare the agenda for a council Paul
III called for 1536 at Mantua. Paul III there informed
Pole (who was still a layman) of his intention to make
him a cardinal. Pole begged him to postpone the honor, not
because it was wrong to advance laymen—e.g., Bembo and
Contarini—to the cardinalate, but because of the impact such a
move would have on his relatives among the aristocracy in
England. While Paul yielded for a time, in December 1536
Pole was given the tonsure and the red hat. In February of
1537, while the northern pilgrims convulsed the country, Pole
was named legate for England, a move about as sensitive as
Paul III's offering the red hat to Fisher in April 1535. It was
an open secret that Pole had a mission to spread disaffection
among English Catholics and to tempt either Charles V or
Francis, or both of them, to lend arms for a papal deposition
of Henry VIII.

By the time Pole reached the Low Countries all hopes of
the Pilgrims had been crushed, and with them any movement
of imperial or French sentiment toward Pole's attempt to advertise a papal deposition of the English king. By July 1537
Paul III had called Pole back to Rome. Cromwell's final efforts
to move Pole back into the English camp had not been any
more successful than had Pole's to convert the English to Roman
obedience. But the king's minister revealed in his very extensive
correspondence with Pole's agents and friends a very great respect for Pole and a heavy sadness over his abandonment of his
country and its Reformation. The spent tries are evident in
the letter to Throgmorton, while the last glimmering traces of
hope appear in the instructions to Wilson and Heath. This correspondence throws fresh light on the traditional views of Cromwell and his regard for Pole, views gathered primarily from
Pole's retrospective accounts of his relations with Cromwell and
colored throughout by the tragic events that were to overtake
his family in 1538.

The cardinal's younger brother was committed to the Tower in August 1538. Whether to escape death himself or because he really had loyalties to the crown which transcended family affection, Sir Geoffrey Pole gave information against the family of Courtenay, marquis of Exeter, who had already argued with Cromwell in council sessions about matters of religion and the whole problem of the northern uprisings. Exeter was descended from Edward IV and like Pole was a grandnephew of the Yorkist king. The leaders of other old Yorkist families were linked in treasonable correspondence with Cardinal Pole by Sir Geoffrey, among them the Nevilles and the Montagues. The chief men of the group were all tried and executed, while Exeter's wife and the mother of Pole, the countess of Salisbury, were lodged in the Tower. That this was Cromwell's revenge on Pole may well be disputed. But that the apparent triumph of reform was also the triumph over the Pilgrims and the remnants of the Yorkist line cannot be controverted. Perhaps this explains why Pole, who in 1537 still spoke of Cromwell as his good friend among Henry VIII's councilors, was to remember Cromwell in later years with disgust and contempt.

Sir, after my most hearty commendation. This shall be in few and short words to require you, according to the calling that our Lord Jesus Christ has called and indained* you, that is to say as well with the gift of good letters and understanding as with the most excellent gift of judgment in the same, you will endeavor yourself to make answer unto such things as be contained in Master Starkey's letter[2] to you written at this time by the king our master's own sovereign express commandment and that the same answer may be of such gravity as the light and truth thereof may be to the honor of God and the satisfaction of his highness. Whereof, I assure you, I would be as glad as any parent or friend you have living, not doubting in your approved wisdom and judgment, but that you will extend the

[2] Thomas Starkey (1499–1538), author and royal household chaplain. His *Exhortation to Christian Unity* (1535) is one of the main treaties against papal supremacy. The *Dialogue* in which Pole and Lupset are speakers supposedly represents Pole's view of the events in England, while Starkey was also actively soliciting Pole's views directly. The letter mentioned could be one of two: either 15 February 1535, when he wrote to Pole to explain the internal history of reformation and ask Pole's support (*LP*, VIII, 218); or an undated letter in which Starkey set out his own views of the Divorce and subsequent statutes and asks Pole's approval for the Divorce (*LP*, VIII, 219). Pole responded to the prodding in 1535, but did not send his considered opinion for another year (*LP*, X, 974-5).

gifts given unto you in such wise, as leaving all your respects
and affection would so insearch your conscience and judgment
for the truth, as you would both discharge yourself against God
and your Prince. In doing whereof, you should assuredly do
the thing much to the increase of your merit and fame. Wherein
as he that is your assured friend to his little power, I require
you to have indifferent consideration and so to order yourself
therein as the expectation of your friends, with the judgment of
all men that know you, may be satisfied in that behalf. And
thus Our Lord send you no worse to fare that I would you did.
At London.

Copy, in Thomas Starkey's hand, on the flyleaf of a letter from
Starkey to Edumund Harvel. Addressed: "To my singular friend
Master Edmund Harvel merchant at Venice." The reason for
attributing this to Cromwell lies in Starkey's correspondence as
well as the Cromwellian style of this letter.

30. To Master Wilson[1] and Doctor Heath[2]

PRO SP1/124/145–52					September [1537]
LP, XII, ii, 620; 217

A remembrance to Mr. Doctor Wilson and Mr. Heath, chap-
lains to the king's majesty, for the better direction of themselves in their voyage into Flanders, and the advancement of
the purpose of their journey thither.

First, whereas Michael Throgmorton,[3] servant to Reginald
Pole,[4] which Pole against his duty of allegiance and in the plain,
open and manifest contempt of the king's majesty, his natural

[1] Nicholas Wilson (d. 1548), a conservative divine who at first refused
the oath of supremacy but relented and took it in 1537. In 1540–1541
he was imprisoned in the Tower for aiding men refusing the oath.
[2] Nicholas Heath (1501?–1578), archbishop of York and later lord chancellor of England, a diplomat and administrative bishop.
[3] Michael Throgmorton (d. 1558) had arranged to enter Pole's service
some time before 1536, perhaps pretending to be a spy for the king.
His letters home were favorable to the future cardinal, whose loyal
servant he became.
[4] Pole's dates are 1500 to 1558.

and most benign sovereign lord that of his own goodness from his mother's pap nourished him, not without his great expense and charge, in vertuous discipline and good letters, has lately given himself into the hands of his highness' mortal and sworn enemy the Bishop of Rome and taken upon him the most miserably and ingrately that has been seen or heard of: to become both a sycophant in writing and a most unkind deviser and worker of things most detestable and traitorous against his said sovereign lord that has done so much for him and besides erected the family whereof he is come, being so depressed, and worthily for their treasons heretofore against their Prince and country committed, overwhelmed and cast down and of less than nothing, has given them investiture of honor and with the same possessions accordingly; did of late with a pretence of a certain loyalty towards the king's highness write unto me the lord privy seal his letters from Leige,[5] bearing date the twentieth of August last past, in the which, amongst other things that the same Throgmorton did set forth concerning the purposes of the Bishop of Rome. He did also insert that the said Master Wilson should in his opinion be a meet instrument to stay the said Pole whom, it appears, the said Throgmorton takes to be of no such judgment as might not well be stayed in his folly by men of right learning and gravity; were it not that his foolish, willful will being glorious in itself and thereby glad to win to it such as will flatter him in his fantasy to his own destruction, if he repent not shortly, must for his recovery, if there be any recovery in him, have such persons to set forth his said folly afore his face; as he may be no less unable to defend the same by any color of learning against them than ashamed, if he be not more than past shame to stand in argument against men of such learning and gravity as the said Wilson and Heath be.

Having communicated the effect of the said Throgmorton's letters to the king's said majesty and there with made most humble suit unto his highness to grant license unto the said

---

[5] Throgmorton's justification of his conduct was that both he and Pole were loyal to Henry, though they would not deny important differences of opinion; *LP*, XII, ii, 552. Pole, as legate *a latere*, was dispatched in early 1537 to France (March) and The Netherlands (April) in efforts to get secular support for a papal move against Henry. Francis refused to see the legate and harried his efforts, which caused Pole to flee to Cambrai, where he was similarly ushered out of the emperor's dominions by the regent of the Netherlands. He was given some shelter by Erhard van der Marck, bishop of Liège, where Throgmorton apparently accompanied him.

Master Wilson to repair to the said Pole, being here at hand in the confines of Flanders, I found a gratuitious inclination in him to condescend to my desire, which as I followed with humble petition, so the same brought me forth the perfect accomplishment of my suit. Such was the great clemency of his majesty that he could not but show himself willing to have recovered that he had made something of nothing, when he sees it in such jeopardy of utter destruction. How much evil soever it has deserved of him for the great benefits it received, so as finally his grace licensed me not only to send the said Wilson and Heath to the said Pole, but also to instruct them for the better achievement of that purpose with such advice of some others of his highness' council as were thought meet for their learning and judgment to consult upon the same. Whereupon joining to me the reverend fathers in God the Bishop of Durham and London,[6] men of no less estimation for their virtues than for their excellent learning, like as they have both in the declaration of their sentences in the points of learning to the said Wilson and Heath in their letters therein conveyed and directed to the said Pole sufficiently done their parts; and as well for their instruction and for the full reconciliation of the said Pole, if he will well perpend* and weigh their writing and confirm himself to ensue and follow the same. So far the rest it pleased his majesty to appoint to instruct the said Mr. Wilson and Mr. Heath and form following.

First, that addressing themselves in journey towards the place where the said Pole does lie, which is at [blank in ms.], they shall [have] with them this remembrance with the letters written from the said bishops, a sermon lately made by the Bishop of York,[7] an oration set forth by the Bishop of Winchester,[8] a book of

[6] Cuthbert Tunstal (1474–1559), bishop of Durham, after a career in London as bishop and master of the rolls. He remained conservative in doctrine but gave obedience to the political implications of reform. The bishop of London meant is John Stokesley (1475–1539), who was, like Tunstal, strongly in favor of the divorce proceedings and the Supremacy but against religious innovations.

[7] Edward Lee (1482?–1544), archbishop of York. While anxious to avoid the royal displeasure, he was opposed to the party of the New Learning and inclined to Roman usages. In a letter of 1 July 1535, Lee claimed to have written a little book explaining the pope's lack of jurisdiction in England, which he had sent to curates who were too poorly educated to sustain the case for themselves; *LP*, VIII, 936.

[8] Stephen Gardiner (1483?–1555), bishop of Winchester. The work is *De vera obedientia*, an oration maintaining the supremacy of the secular power over the pope's.

certain things lately determined here by the whole clergy[9] [blank in ms]. . . .

And at their arrival there they shall plainly and in a frank sort declare unto the said Pole his miserable state and condition and on the other side and great clemency and benignity that is in the Prince, which has suffered them for his reconciliation to resort unto him with the great appearance they have that his majesty will yet take him to mercy and besides put him in the state of an honest man, if he would return home from his folly, acknowledge his fault and desire forgiveness for it. Advising him as much as they may to weigh and consider in what state he stands, what grace he may now find if he will conform himself to it and what the end is like to be if he persist in his madness. In the declaration of which parts and the reasoning of the points of learning which they shall allege for his conversion, they shall in no wise call him by any other name than by the title of Mr. Pole, nor in their gestures give him any preeminence. But they shall fashion both their words and gestures of such sort as he may perceive that they have him in the less estimation for his vain title and unadvised proceedings to the same. And if they shall perceive him repentent for his foolish madness and glad to seek for the remission of the same, they shall then advise him for a testimony thereof both to submit himself to the king's majesty by his letters and to send unto the same continently the minute of his fantastic book,[10] putting himself also in order to repair hither with diligence in his person to make like submission as shall be first signified in his letters. And if he shall put any danger in his coming hither without a further assurance, the said Mr. Wilson and Mr. Heath shall in that case advertise me with diligence what he shall therein desire. And I shall be an humble suitor to the king's majesty to declare his clemency in such wise towards him as he shall not need I trust to fear anything in that behalf.

Draft memorandum, Wriothesley's hand. Endorsed: "Mr. Wilson remembrance for Pole."

[9] *The Institution of a Christian Man* or *The Bishop's Book,* primarily an exposition of the Apostles' Creed, the sacraments, Lord's Prayer, Ave Maria, and the Decalogue, compiled by a committee of bishops and divines in 1537.
[10] This is the *Pro ecclesiasticae unitatis defensione* or *De defensione ecclesiae,* in which Pole censured Henry VIII.

31. To Michael Throgmorton[1]

PRO SP1/125/87–9   September [1537]
LP, XII, ii, 795; 218

. . . I thought that the singular goodness of the king's highness
unto you and the great and singular clemency showed to that
detestable traitor your master in promising him not only forgiveness but also forgetting of his most shameful ingratitude,
unnaturalness, conspiracy against his honor, of whom he has
received no more but even as much and all that he has; I thought,
I say, that either this princely goodness might have brought
that desperate rebel from his so sturdy malice, blindness,
pervicacie,* or else have encouraged you to be his highness'
true and faithful subject.

But I now remember myself too late. I might better have
judged that so dishonest a master could have but even such a
servant as you are. No, no, loyalty and treason dwell seldom
together. There can be no faithful subject so long abide the
sight of a traitor so heinous to his Prince. You could not all this
season have been a spy for the king, but at some time your
countenance should have declared your heart to be loyal toward
your prince and utterly bent against his [Pole's] traitorous
dealings.[2] No, you and your master have both declared how
little fear of God rests in you, which led by vain promise of
promotion, thus against his laws work treason toward your
natural prince and country; to serve an enemy of God, an
enemy of all honesty; an enemy of right religion; a defender of
inquity, of pride, a merchant and occupier of all deceit and of
twenty things that no honest man's pen can well touch, much
less utter and put forth. You think you do good service there

---

[1] See footnotes 3 and 5 to letter 30.
[2] It is this phrase which supports the notion that Cromwell had planted
Throgmorton in Pole's household in order to keep a check on Pole's
doings. If so, it is Cromwell who was duped, for Throgmorton was then
in reality hiding from him Pole's mission while trying to convince him
that the cardinal was ripe for reconciliation. Both of the main tones of
this letter are explicable on that reading: hurt and real sadness about
Throgmorton's role.

to the king's highness; for asmuch as you now see things, that
being absent, you should not have seen, such verily as might
have done great damage, if you had not seen them. You have
bleared mine eye once. Your credit shall never more serve you
so far to deceive me the second time.

I took you as you are and do think it much light for you to
forge letters which by words not long sought for have deceived
me. Your part was to do as your sovereign lord the king had
commanded you. Your praise was to be sought in obeying his
highness' pleasure and not in serving your foolish fantasy, although you have thought this way to have done his grace better
service. But now, to stick unto a rebel, to follow a traitor, to
serve a friend of his, which mortally hates your sovereign lord,
to love him whom God cannot but hate; what folly is it to excuse such mad lewdness! Your good master, lately entered into
the religion that has been the ruin of all religion, cannot, you
say, but be the king's high friend. He will (as you write)
declare unto the world why the king takes him for a traitor. In
this thing he needs never to travail a deal. All princes (almost)
know how well he has deserved this name. Yea, the king's highness is much beholden unto some of them, of whom his grace
has learned the goodly enterprise that this silly cardinal went
about.[3] Now, if those who have made him thus mad, can also
persuade him to print his detestable book,[4] where one lie leaps
in every line in another's neck, he shall be then as much bound
to them for their good counsel as his family is bound to him
for his wise dealings. God, I doubt not, will send him as little
joy thereof as his friends and his kinfolk are like to take profit
of it. Pity it is that the folly of one brain-sick Pole, or to say
better, of one witless fool[5] should be the ruin of so great a family.
Let him reign and follow ambition as fast as he can, these that
little have offended (saving that he is of their kin), were not the
great mercy and benignity of the prince, should and might feel
what it is to have such a traitor to their kinsman.

Let his goodly book, the fruit of his whole study, come abroad:
Is there any man, but he may well accuse our Prince of too
much clemency and much marvel that no way is found to take
away the author of such treachery? Surely, when answer shall
be made to his heady malice, I think there shall be very few,

[3] The missions to Francis I and Charles V.
[4] The *Pro defensione*.
[5] In Cromwell's autograph and that of this letter, Pole is spelled Poole,
to rhyme with fool.

but they will think (as I do) he has as he deserves, if he be
brought to most shameful death. Let him not think but though
he can lie largely, there be some with us that can say truth of
him. His praise shall be great, when men shall see the king's
highness' benefits towards him, the advancement of his family
from nothing at all to that they now be in, and then shall look
upon his good heart, his grateful mind, his desire to serve the
king's honor. Let his lewd work go forth. After that, let princes
judge whether the king can take the author of so famous a
libel to be his true subject. Let the king's high benefits and
(which is more to be esteemed) his singular benevolences
showed unto him of a child come and make their plea. Can
you, or he, think any ground safe for him to stand in? Has he
not just cause to fear, lest every honest man should offer himself
to avenge this so enormous unkindness. Shall he not think every
honest man to be his foe—to be mistrusted? Shall not his detestable acts, written in his conscience, ever more bring him to
perpetual sorrow, vex him, and so vex him, that nowhere he
shall be quiet. And you know that whensoever the king will,
his highness may bring it easily to pass: that he shall think of
himself scarce sure of his life, although he went tied at his
master's girdle. There may be found means enough in Italy,
to rid a traitorous subject. Surely let him not think but where
justice can take no place by process of law at home, she may
be enforced to seek new means abroad.

Amongst all your praty* news, these are very pleasant: that
the wily Bishop of Rome intends to make a lamentation to the
world and to desire every man to pray that his old gains may
return home again. Men will well think he has cause, or at the
least good time to lament, not that the king of England has
pulled his realm out of thraldom, but that a great part of the
world is like to do the same. Many a man weeps for less. We
blame him not, if he lament. Howbeit, doubt you not, he shall
find some man with us that shall bid him to be a better man,
though they bid him not be of better cheer. If your good master
take upon him to make this lamentation (as indeed I think there
is no man alive that has better cause to wail than he has), assure
you him that he shall lack no consolation. Paul popes jollily,[6]
that will desire the world to pray for the king's apairment*
This hypocrisy comes even as it should do and stand in place
meet for it. The world knows right well what other wiles he has

---

[6] Pope Paul plays at being pope in the old manner.

practiced these three years. They shall laugh well to see his holiness come to prayer, because he cannot bring to pass that he most desires. He that the last day went about to set all princes in his grace's top,[7] writing letters almost to all princes for the bringing of this to pass, shall he not now be thought holy, that thus suddenly casts away his weapon and falls to his beads.

God hears (as Peter said) the prayers of the just sinners. If they be heard at any time, it be when they pray for good things. He may not pray so fast that we may return to error, to the defense of tyranny, ungodliness, untruths—as we shall pray unto God that his grace long may continue towards our most virtuous Prince, us subjects and servants to both. We trust our prayers shall be heard. And that hyprocite shall (after this day) never reign over us.

Of the general council I need say nothing.[8] Every man well perceives the difference between a frank, a holy, a godly, a general council, and an assembly of ambitious manciples, of men sworn to pope's lust and gains. The first shall never be, as long as the popes shall rather seek their own glory than God's honor. There may be (as there have been, too, too often) a company confederate against God, his laws, his glory. These may be gathered together, never better than now (the world being so occupied in every corner of it, as it is). A general council begins a day after the Greek Kalends.[9]

Michael, if you were either natural towards your country, or your family, you would not thus shame your kin. I pray God they bide but the shame of it. This I am sure of, though they

[7] To make war on the king.

[8] Francis I had supported the call for a general council, in which Henry had been his ally before 1535 when an appeal from the pope to a general council held out some help of rallying the French, English, and German Protestants in a common cause against pope and emperor. But in 1536 the resumption of war between Charles and Francis gave Henry VIII the diplomatic freedom he badly needed. So long as Habsburg and Valois fought, he could stand outside of such alliance systems, using Francis as a lever to force Charles to behave and also playing on the hopes of a Protestant coalition. When Paul III announced the Council of Mantua (convoked in 1537, with the reform commission sitting from 1536), Henry obtained a vote from Convocation refusing any English representation there and imposing a dictim that a true general council could rest only on a kind of *liberum veto* of the European sovereigns as to time and place and conditions of meeting.

[9] Since the Greek calendar had no kalends in reckoning time, this is a broad jest.

by and by suffer no loss of goods, yet the least suspicious shall be enough to undo the greatest of them. Wherefore, if you will yet turn to your country, to show yourself sorry for that you have foolishly done, I dare assure you, you shall find the king's highness much more ready to seek commendation of clemency than of justice at your faults. Turn in time: you have tarried almost too long. If you come not now, you may perchance be as evilly dealt with in Rome itself as you have deserved to be in England. I can no more but desire God that your master and you may acknowledge your detestable faults and be good witnesses of the king's high mercy. You may turn; if you so do, I doubt not but the king's highness will show the world that he desires nothing more than the saving of his subjects. If you continue in your malice and perverse blindness, doubt you not but your ends shall be as of all traitors for the most part is. I have done what I may to save you. I must I think do what I can to see you condignly punished. God send you both to fare as you deserve; that is, shortly to come to your allegiance or else to a shameful death.

Though this extensive fragment in Stephen Vaughan's hand lacks address or endorsements, it is clearly not a copy or draft. Folios 87 and 88 show traces of the application of a seal.

32. To Lord Leonard Grey[1]

PRO SP60/5/128   13 December [1537]
LP, XII, ii, 1207; 233   Oatlands

IT was during the ministry of Thomas Cromwell that the most remarkable strides were taken in the integration of the various outlying and march regions composing the dominions of England into the central realm. The Calais Act of 1534 and 1536 restrained local jurisdictions and extended that of the crown. In Wales, the great statute of 1536, which finally incorporated Wales into the English shire system for administrative purposes, completed the work of earlier reforms. We have already noticed

---

[1] Lord Leonard Grey (d. 1541), the fifth son of the Marquis of Dorset and hence descended from the Yorkist king, Edward IV, Viscount Grane of Ireland, a diplomat, and administrator, convicted of treason by attainder and executed on Tower Hill.

the systematic extension of counciliar government to the North and the Welsh marches. But Ireland even more than Wales needed the application of the doctrine of empire which Cromwell had spelled out in various preambles to statutes between 1533 and 1536. Irish affairs had been sacrificed to the continental policy of the Wolsey era, along with other matters we might comprehend within the terms of the British question. And in 1528 the outbreak of war with Charles V saw the first arrival of Spanish emissaries at the courts of Irish chiefs. In the autumn of 1534 the whole of Ireland outside the Pale around Dublin revolted. A year later Sir William Skeffington, who led the suppression, died, to be followed in office by Lord Leonard Grey. The new deputy failed to overcome Irish factionalism, and it ruled even in his council, where the allies of his brother-in-law, the Geraldine Earl of Kildare, were under deep suspicion as a result of the revolt. It was in such circumstances that Cromwell formed a commission to thoroughly survey Ireland, its land, peoples, government, and problems in 1537, with an eye toward imposing English forms of land tenure, language, and religious policies. The tension of Cromwell's letter to Grey anticipates the later charge of treason against Deputy Grey.

After my right hearty commendations to your lordship. Whereas by the bearer your servant I received certain letters[2] from you, the contents whereof requiring now answer to be at the least speedily dispatched, I willed him to remain here till a further opportunity of writing thither occur. And the same being now happened by the advertisement of O'Connor[3] now enterprising, it was thought meet that a post should be dispatched with diligence, which part he should have furnished if it had not been his chance to have been absent. Now being desirous to return unto you, I thought convenient as well to write this for his exercise in his long abide, as to advertise you eftsoons to handle that matter O'Connor with such a dexterity as he may be hanged upon the terrible example of all such traitors. The expulsion of him was taken very well. But the permission of him to have such a scope to work mischief at his

---

[2] *LP*, XII, ii, 724, in which Grey complains that Bernard (or Brian) O'Connor, Lord of Offaly (1490–1560?), acted more the role of a rascal than that of the governor of a country.

[3] When Grey invaded O'Connor's district in 1537, in alliance with the Desmonds against the Ormonde forces, he appointed Cahir O'Connor, the brother of Brian, Lord of Offaly. Brian was on bad terms with Cahir and ousted him by force, a circumstance which led Cromwell to warn Grey about his misgovernment of that affair.

pleasure, as knowing he must need be remaining in despair of restitution, was neither wisdom nor yet good precedent. Redoub* it my lord in the just punishment of his traitor's carcas and let his treason be a warning to you and to all that shall have to do for the king's majesty, there never to trust traitors after, but to use them without tract,* after their demerits. And thus fare you heartily well, from Oatlands,[4] the thirteenth day of December. Your lordship's assured.

Clerk's hand; signature suspect, perhaps in same hand as that of the letter, but certainly not Cromwell's. Probably a copy of the one sent, however, rather than a forgery. Addressed: "To my lord deputy."

33. To Sir Thomas Wyatt

BM Harleian Mss. 282,
    folios 159[1] and 167–70[2]   11 February [1538]
LP, XIII, i, 255; 238   Westminster

DESPITE THE optimism surrounding the birth of Edward, Prince of Wales, Tudor statesmen turned with alarm to the European scene. The French and Scots had just concluded the second of two marriages, this one to last, uniting James V and Marie de Guise. The child of that union born in 1542 would, as Mary Queen of Scots, make more trouble for England than could have been guessed even by the greatest pessimist. The other evil omen was the sign of a rapprochement between the papacy and the empire. Such moves must seriously reduce Henry's ability to play off Francis against Charles V. It weakened England in the North, where lately the Pilgrimage had raged. And in the light of papal support, Francis I might divert his gaze from Milan, ever the bone of contention between France and the empire, and seek another Milan in the British Isles. But reasoned arguments tended to support the view that Charles V would no more willingly see France powerful in Britian than in Italy. Yet Englishmen eyed nervously the war between the Valois and Habsburgs. Francis had occupied Savoy and Pied-

[4] Oatlands, Surrey.
[1] Folio 159 is the original of the letter, in code.
[2] Folios 167 to 170 constitute the decipherment of this letter by one Francesco, Wyatt's clerk.

mont Italy; but Milan eluded him. Charles held Milan and Artois, but in Burgundy, Provence, and Languedoc his efforts proved very futile, and he too was wearying of the war. Besides, Lutheran princes were gaining in Germany and Suleiman had defeated the emperor's brother Ferdinand at Essek, in Hungary. In such circumstances, amid rumors of peace between Valois and Habsburg, it was Henry's and Cromwell's policy to play the honest broker between the two great powers, thereby short-circuiting a similar plan of Paul III. Meanwhile, against the Franco-Scottish alliance, Henry would tempt the Habsburgs with the offer of a dazzling triple marriage alliance of England, Portugal, and empire, confirming in the second generation what Henry VII and Ferdinand had first brought about in the late fifteenth century. The upshot of all of this was nothing. And, in the bargain, Paul III did mediate the Valois-Habsburg war and arranged the Treaty of Nice (June 1538) a few months after this letter was sent.

Master Wyatt, this shall be to advertise you that the king, having seen and perused your letters of the 18th of last month addressed to me, does thankfully accept the gratuity in the same declared towards him. And considering the matter of peace between the Emperor and the French king is not concluded;[3] for a declaration both of his zeal to the quiet in Christendom and of a just correspondence of kindness again towards the Emperor, if the same could be content to commit the marrying of the peace to his majesty with wise and reasonable order for the Duchy of Milan, refusing the Bishop of Rome to mean therein, who can be no mete arbiter for that purpose, as well for that he pretends for interest in part of Milan as in Parma and Placence;[4] as for that there is great likelihood that in the doing of it he will follow the steps of his predecessor,[5] who in such cases has ever used to work there in his own benefit and establishment, whatsoever should succeed of the rest; the king's majesty would I doubt not but go through out of hand

[3] On 11 January 1538 a six month truce was made between France and Charles V. England wanted to be a party to any peace and wished to prevent the papacy from being mediator. The pope, however, did eventually mediate and brought about a treaty on about 18 June 1538.
[4] Parma and Piacenza, both papal states, must be meant. Cromwell means that the pope might take Milan, which was then under Charles' control, as he had seized Parma and Piacenza on another occasion.
[5] Clement VII (1523–1534). I cn only guess that Cromwell meant that Paul III might regain these territories in the same way that Clement, who was a Medici, had regained Florence for his family.

with the marriage of my Lady Mary's grace[6] and couple his
son the prince[7] with the Emperor's daughter born or to be
born of years mete for him, with bonds yet he shall at the years
of consent take her to marriage, and further also join his other
daughter the Lady Elizabeth in marriage with one of King
Ferdinand's[8] sons, limiting such dates as should be mete for his
grace's daughters. And over and above this I am assured that the
king's majesty will give such aid to the Emperor in any expedition to be made against the Great Turk as shall be greatly to
his advantage.[9] So he will open his purpose therein and reason-
ably demand towards the same.

This I have thought convenient to write unto you, that you
may of yourself declare to the Emperor what likelihood you
have from me and other your friends here, that there shall
ensue a most firm knot between the king's majesty and him. And
advertise again how you shall find him disposed in that behalf.
Mr. Wyatt, I perceive your credence there is good. Keep it
well; it may turn to your commodity. Thus fare you heartily
well; from the Court being at Westminster, the 11th of February.
Your loving friend.

A letter in cipher, with the decoding in the hand of a clerk,
apparently of Wyatt's entourage, since it is in the same hand
as the endorsements. Addressed: "To my assured loving friend
Sir Thomas Wyatt knight, being the king's highness' ambassador
with the Emperor." Endorsed: "My LPS of the 11th of February; rec. by Francisco the 23rd of the same in Barcelona."

[6] Mary Tudor, Henry's daughter by Catherine of Aragon, who was intended for the Infant of Portugal in this idea.
[7] Edward, Prince of Wales.
[8] Ferdinand I (1503–1564), brother of Charles V, elected emperor in
1556.
[9] By a remarkable coincidence, on the day before Henry's minister wrote
suggesting a league against the Turk, Paul III concluded the Holy League
of Venice, Rome, and the empire, 10 February 1538. This pulled the
last tooth of the plan here set forward.

34. To Archbishop Cranmer[1]

BM Harleian Mss. 6148, folio 81   5 January [1534]
LP, VII, 19; 66   London

GIVEN THE difficult circumstances of the early 1530's for English politicians, especially the threat of intervention from abroad, Cromwell looked to the enemies of Charles V for allies. Apart from approaches to Francis I, efforts in the direction of the Lutheran powers of Germany seemed in order. In 1530–1531 they had banded together under the leadership of Philip of Hesse and the Elector of Saxony in self-defense against the emperor. Charles's many preoccupations with rebels in Spain and the Turkish threat might well prevent him from crushing the rebels of Germany, and that meant a military and diplomatic counter lay ready at hand for Cromwell's play. By 1533 he had already sent Stephen Vaughan to report on the Schmalkaldic League. It was obvious that politics and religion in Germany might combine with England's necessity. It was that fact which prompted the mission of which this letter is the opening move. Heath was to tell the Germans that Henry VIII was the sworn enemy of the Roman pontiff and would join with them in a new holy war to extirpate Rome's usurped power. The princes proved unreceptive, with the result that before the year was out England began negotiations with the city of Lübeck, which led Hanseatic cities in a war against the Danes, where a vacant throne lured their own ambitions. In exchange for help against the pope, England pledged its aid in the struggle in Scandinavia. That effort also failed when the Danes named the Duke of Holstein their king, as Christian III, thus ending the alleged Protestant purpose of the alliance. With a Lutheran in Denmark as king, Cromwell began to cast about for new allies in the summer of 1534, his agents urging the English king to join with Denmark in forming the nucleus of a new league of north European powers. But Henry VIII stubbornly resisted all efforts to force his hand in the direction of new allies flying the flag of Protestantism.

---

[1] The importance of Cranmer's household and cathedral chapter in Reformation administration and diplomacy has not been adequately studied. But the close working alliance of Cranmer and Cromwell seems evident here.

After my most hearty commendations. It may please your Grace to be advertised that the king's highness has commanded me to write unto your Grace, requiring the same with all convenient celerity to send up hither Mr. Heath,[3] who for his learning, good gravity and circumspection the king's highness intends to send unto the parties of Germany in Ambassade, to treat there with the princes of Germany aswell in the king's great cause of matrimony as in other causes pertaining to the wealth of this realm.

And for as much as your Grace knows the ground, very justness and equity of the king's said cause, his highness requires you so to instruct the said Mr. Heath in the same as he may be ripe and perfect in the knowledge of the whole circumstances of the same; and that for lack of instruction, when time shall come to propone* the matter, it appear not in him to be unperfect and remiss to do such service unto the king's majesty in that behalf, as shall be to his gracious trust and expectation, which his highness nothing at all doubts. Howbeit, your Grace's advertisement and good instruction directed unto the said Mr. Heath shall undoubtedly make him more ripe and perfect in the premisses, to do that thing that may be much to your honor and his prayer and merit; as knows our Lord, who send your Grace long life and good health. At London the 5th day of January. Your Grace's beadsman.*

P.S. The king's highness also intends to practice certain things in the said parts of Germany concerning the authority of the bishop of Rome.

Copy; in Crammer's receipt.

2 Nicholas Heath (1501?–1578), later lord chancellor and archbishop of York. See *LP*, VII, 21, for details of his mission in 1534.

35. To Bishop Gardiner[1] and Sir John Wallop[2]

BM Additional Mss. 25114, fos. 160–1   14 May [1536]
LP, X, 873; 147   The Rolls

CONCERNING BISHOP GARDINER

HISTORIANS OPERATE within the limits of the conventions they accept about the men and movements they study. So it is not surprising that Stephen Gardiner and Thomas Cromwell have come to be written of as polar opposites and antagonists in Reformation history. From 1536 until Cromwell's death in 1540 there is clear evidence of a growing estrangment between them. But it was not always so.

Their first direct contact came in Wolsey's service, almost certainly before 1528, when the first document attesting to a relationship is dated. Gardiner had gone on embassy to convince Clement VII about the justness of Wolsey's conversion of monastic endowments to use at his colleges. After his return from Venice, we begin to see him often in Cromwell's company. But in the events surrounding Wolsey's fall in 1529, Cromwell, or at least men in his household, expressed a clear distrust of the man one of them termed Wolsey's Judas. While Cromwell was still laboring at two removes from active political power, his clerical counterpart had become the king's principal secretary and seemed about to succeed Wolsey in Henry VIII's favor. The two men worked together in Cromwell's plan to gain favor at the court for Wolsey and themselves by distributing pensions and fees liberally.

By 1530, while both men measured their words carefully, some evidence of tension between them appears in letters written by their servants. Throughout 1530–1531, on the surface their relationship was cordial, and it would seem that beneath the surface the same was true. For when Gardiner was nominated to Winchester, which was the wealthiest see in England, Cromwell loaned him money toward the restitution of his temporalities (the act of investing a bishop with his income) just prior to

[1] Bishop of Winchester.
[2] Soldier and diplomat (d. 1551), also ambassador to France 1532–1537 and 1540.

Gardiner's departure for France on what was to prove the first
of a series of diplomatic missions for the king's secretary. It
was during Gardiner's absence that Cromwell first advanced in
the council. That does not mean he supplanted Gardiner. But
it does mean that in 1531 Cromwell began to have some influence over policies the fruit of which was to prove unpalatable
for the Bishop of Winchester. Nevertheless, even by 1533, when
Cromwell clearly had taken the place of chief influence away
from Gardiner, the letters of the two men reflect the fact that
each needed the other's help and confidence in advancing basic
self-interests and royal business.

What is clear from their correspondence and other letters of
the 1530's is that Cromwell did not seek to oust Gardiner from
the king's favor, though Gardiner himself believed that Cromwell had maneuvered him into a defensive position in most
important matters. Many years later, in a letter to Protector
Somerset, Gardiner was himself to project backward into the
1530's the still unrevealed bitter rivalry of the two. Again, however, on the surface both men pursued the same royal policies
with regard to the newly formulated Supremacy, the disposition
of More and Fisher, and a number of other issues. In some
routine patronage matters, Winchester revealed clearly that he
still regarded Cromwell as his special friend. But 1535 was also
to mark the first clear shift in their relationship. At least that
is the evidence of Chapuys, the imperial ambassador, who suspected that Cromwell practiced entrapment with the king's more
conservative bishops and councilors. Despite their cooperation in
the enforcement of the Supremacy and the preaching in behalf
of it by Gardiner, many suspected that Gardiner's being sent
to France again in September 1535 was a Cromwellian ploy to
get him away from court and so to minimize his influence.

During Gardiner's three-year stay in France much happened
in England to change the nature of political alignments and to
redefine the relationships between the king's two greatest men
of affairs. Catherine of Aragon died. Anne Boleyn fell for treason.
Jane Seymour became Henry VIII's third queen. The Dissolution moved ahead vigorously. The most formidable threat to
the dynasty was met and beaten in the Pilgrimage of Grace.
Convocation passed the Ten Articles and the destruction of
images and shrines began in earnest. The possibility of an agreement between Francis I and Charles V gave to all diplomatic
efforts, and especially to Gardiner's, a sense of urgency well communicated by the bishop.

The purpose of Gardiner's mission, which forms the chief
burden of letters sent by him to Cromwell, may be stated briefly.
He was to keep open the possibility of an alliance with France
against Charles V. He was also to play skillfully the role of de-

stroyer with regard to the French wish to see a general church council convoked. Given these tasks, Gardiner must have chafed severely under the pressure of the possibility of an alliance between the two greatest powers in Europe, a league which would threaten England with the choice of perhaps becoming an imperial satellite or a French dominion if the pope could persuade either or both kings to a holy war against the schismatic English king.

To this pressure was added the open expression of the king's feeling that English diplomatic failures rested with her ambassadors rather than with the policies given them to effect. So much was said also by Cromwell, who laid the blame squarely on what he called Gardiner's irritability and clumsiness. It is not surprising that relations between Cromwell and the Bishop of Winchester rapidly deteriorated after such remarks were passed between men equally jealous of their honor and position. Nor is it surprising that their letters express the growing spirit of hostility in greatly magnified disputes about relatively trivial matters: the Brian pension; Bonner's flippancy; Gardiner's taste for luxury at a time when English official pockets were pinched; or the more important question of whether Gardiner aided and abetted the Sorbonne decision to seize the Grafton-Coverdale Bible being set in Paris. Despite frequent protestations of grievances, Cromwell gave at least the appearance of civility and a desire to continue their friendship. And in that he was wise. For when he finally did alienate Gardiner completely, the Winchester-Norfolk affinity had all the powerful voices in chorus against Cromwell, whose success in pursuing various reforms depended to a large extent on his ability to keep any faction opposed to him and his program either weak or away from court. By 1539 he had failed on both counts.

Apart from any light these letters cast on the politics of the Tudor Reformation, they have an intrinsic interest for the history of that period. The announcement of the great errors of Anne Boleyn ended what for all practical purposes was a phase of the history of reform. So also we may consider the evidence that the King of England had abandoned the pretense of hoping to convoke a general council. This certainly signaled the beginning of a more radical reform temper in England, if for no other reason than that it now seemed clear neither popes nor general councils were thought fit vehicles for reformation of Christendom. This view implies another: that by 1536 Cromwell had the appearance of absolute power in the king's business, a charge apparently made by Gardiner with reference to the Brian pension granted out of Winchester episcopal revenues. While it is clear that Cromwell denied the facts alleged by Gardiner, it nevertheless seems true that the lord privy seal *did* so much

have the king's confidence that he exercised what in effect was
the royal will in many affairs. Obsequious and flattering to Henry
VIII though he might have been, Cromwell had by 1536 such
a hold over secular and ecclesiastical administration and in politics as to warrant the subsequent French charge that he was
an *alter rex* in England.

From another point of view, 1536 is the beginning of the important phase of doctrinal and devotional reform which marks
the critical period in the unfolding of Anglicanism. The constitutional revolution made between 1533 and 1536 by the great
statutes was nearly complete. And with the completion of it
Cromwell was free to turn the energies of the monarchy to other
works. The Dissolution and the Injunctions of 1536 were soon
followed by the campaign against superstitions, pilgrimages,
images, and the full apparatus of the sacramental system. Another element which promotes the notion that 1536 marks an end
and a beginning is, of course, the Pilgrimage of Grace, a movement clearly indicative of the fact that opposition to the Reformation was popular as well as distinguished, and also directed
as much against Cromwell and some other royal ministers as it
was against their reforms. So it was also that Cromwell and the
councilors about Henry VIII found 1536 to be a critical year in
relations between Scotland and England. If some agreement
with France proved hard to come by, it was imperative to have
an "English" party in Scotland, or so to practice in that country
as to ensure the good disposition of a kingdom never lacking in
reasons for border warfare and always ready to renew the "auld
alliance" with France against England. The conclusion of a marriage alliance between James V and Francis I late in 1536 was
another reverse for Gardiner and more than any other provoked
his fearful anger in response to criticism from home.

After my right hearty commendations. Albeit you shall at
this time receive none answer to your letters sent by Salisbury,[3]
being the same deferred til the arrival of the Bailiff of Troyes,[4]
yet the king's highness thought convenient that I should advertise you of a chance, as most detestably and abominably devised,
contrived, imagined, done and continued, so most happily and
graciously by the ordinance of God revealed, manifested and
notoriously known to all men. Whereof, though you have heard

---

[3] Nicholas Shaxton, for whom see Cromwell's letter to him (63 below).
[4] Jean de Dinteville (1504–1555), bailey de Troyes, governor of Charles,
duc d'Angoulême. Ambassador to England in 1531, 1533, and 1535–1536,
but disgraced in 1538 in a domestic intrigue. He arrived in London 17
May 1536.

I doubt not the rumors, yet I shall express unto you some part of the coming out and of the king's proceeding in the same.

The Queen's abomination,[5] both in incontinent living and other offenses towards the king's highness, was so rank and common that her ladies of the privy chamber and her chambers could not contain it within their breasts, but detesting the same had so often communications and conferences of it that, at last, it came so plainly to the ears of some of his grace's council that with their duty to his majesty they could not conceal it from him; but with great fear, as the case enforced, declared what they had heard unto his highness. Whereupon, in most strict sort, certain persons of the privy chamber and others of her side were examined,[6] in which examinations the matter appeared so evident, that besides that crime, with the accidents, there broke out a certain conspiracy of the king's death, which extended so far that all we that had the examination of it quaked at the danger his grace was in and on our knees gave Him laud and praise, that He had preserved him so long from it, and now manifested the most wretched and detestable determination of the same.

Thus were certain men committed to the Tower for this cause, that is Marks[7] and Norris[8] and her brother.[9] Then was she apprehended and conveyed to the same place. After her was sent thither for the crimes specified Sir Francis Weston;[10] Brereton[11] and Marks be already condemned to death, upon arraignment in Westminster Hall on Friday last. She and her brother shall be arraigned tomorrow and will undoubtedly go the same way. I write no particularities. The things be so abominable that I think the like was never heard. And therefore I doubt not but that this shall be sufficient for your instructions, to declare the truth, if you have occasion so to do.

[5] The adultery of Anne Boleyn.
[6] The examining commissioners included Norfolk, Suffolk, Cromwell, and leading peers and judges; they began to take testimony on 1 May.
[7] Mark Smeaton, a lutanist of the court, friend of the king, and recipient of much patronage, confessed to adultery and was executed 17 May 1536.
[8] Sir Henry Norris, courtier and friend of Henry VIII, often granted offices, lands, and annuities.
[9] Sir George Boleyn, Viscount Rochford, warden of the Cinque Ports from 1534, arraigned and executed for high treason and the crime of incest.
[10] Sir Francis Weston (1511–1536), gentleman of the privy chamber, executed for misconduct with the queen.
[11] William Brereton, gentleman of the privy chamber and chamberlain of the palatinate of Chester, executed for misconduct with the queen.

Your lordship shall get in two hundred pounds of the three hundred that were out amongst these men,[12] notwithstanding great suit has been made for the whole, which, though the king's highness might give in this case yet, his majesty doth not forget your service. And the third hundred pounds is bestowed of the Vicar of Hell,[13] upon whom, though it be some charge unto you, his highness trusts you will think it well bestowed. And thus fare you right heartily well, from the Rolls in haste, the 14 of May. Your loving assured friend.

P.S. And you Master Wallop shall not at this time be forgotten. But the certainty of that you shall have I cannot tell; but in the next letters you shall know it. And I assure you the king's highness takes both your services in as thankful part as yourselves could wish or devise.

Wriothesley's hand; autograph signature. Addressed: "To my assured loving friends my Lord of Winchester and John Wallop knight, the king's ambassadors in France, in haste, haste, post haste." Endorsed: Seventeenth- or early- eighteenth-century hand, "Touching the detection, apprehension, etc., of Queen Anne Bollen." In Thomas Wriothesley's hand, "From the Rolls in haste the 14th of May [1536]. Another, noncontemporary hand, "Cromwell to Winchester." A third hand, but the same as that which added [1536] to endorsement above.

---

[12] In 1529 Wolsey had given a pension of £200 to Sir George Boleyn and £100 to Norris out of the revenues of his see of Winchester. As bishop of Winchester, Gardiner had been obliged to continue the pensions in effect, which he resented and tried to reverse when the original grantees were executed in 1536.

[13] Sir Francis Brian (d. 1550), courtier and diplomat and a very important poet of the Wyatt-Surrey circle. He was Anne Boyeyn's cousin and Henry VIII's favorite companion. The name was bestowed on him either by Cromwell or Cranmer; both use it in naming Brian.

36. To Bishop Gardiner and Sir John Wallop

BM Additional Mss. 25114, fos. 162–5   8 June [1536]
LP, X, 1084; 149   The Rolls

After my right hearty commendations. These shall be to advertise you that for as much as the French king has lately directed hither to the king's highness the Bailiff of Troyes, who has entreated only two special points; the one concerning his grace's opinion and sentence touching the indiction of a general council, the other to attain knowledge of his grace's resolution concerning their desired aid and contribution to be given by his majesty towards the supportation and maintenance of his good brother the French king's war against the Emperor.[1] Like as his highness deliberating upon the same has made such answer as all parts considered was thought convenient, so, to the intent having knowledge of the same you should better prepare and arm yourselves, not only to maintain the wisdom and equity of them, but also to advance the same in such wise as may be for his grace's honor and the general quiet and repose of all Christendom, his highness has commanded me in such order, word for word, to signify the said answer unto you, as the same were conveyed and translated into French [to] be now delivered to the said Bailiff.

First, concerning the general council. Like as his majesty otherwise think but that a free Christian general council should be both expedient and necessary, both for the increase of the honor of God and the extirpation, abolition and extinguishment of such abuses, errors and enormities as have been long violently maintained, to the obfuscation of God's holy and indivisible truth and to the derogation of the powers and authorities of kings and

---

[1] On 30 April, Henry VIII had informed his ambassadors of French proposals by which Francis would make no peace with the emperor without consulting England; England would join France in a war against Milan in return for French defensive pledges against an imperial attack on England, with Henry VIII contributing 50,000 crowns to Francis I's war chest in the event of a Habsburg attack on France; *LP*, X, 760.

princes due unto them by the same; so his highness thinks it
shall be more than necessary for all princes specially, not only
to foresee that no council shall be indicted but in such places
as may be tote* indifferent and such as wherein all men that
may resort thither may frankly and freely speak and pronounce
their opinions and sentences in matters to be entreated in the
same; and thereupon to have such direction taken as may be
concordant to God's word and beneficial to the whole unity,
state and body of Christendom; but also that there may be an
order taken amongst Christian princes before as well for the
appointment of such a place as is specified. As for the manner
and printing of the indiction, and who shall be the minister
in the same, for his highness has so well and perfectly de-
ciphered the usurpations of the Bishop of Rome, chiefly attained
by a pretended supremacy* in such councils; that his grace has
certainly resolved neither to condescend to any council to be
by him indicted nor by any other potentates, unless the same
shall be before agreed upon in manner and form before expressed. As his majesty warily trusts his good brother the said
French king, whose wisdom his highness knows, to perpend and
weigh right wisely and prudently the premises, will for his part
do the semblable.

Concerning the contribution. Albeit the said French king shall
at all times find his majesty a most sure and faithful friend unto
him, yet forasmuch as his highness perceives at this time a certain inclination both in the Emperor and in his said good brother
to compromit* all such matters as depend in controversy between them in his highness' hands,[2] to be by him compounded
and determined; his grace thinking and certainly knowing and
considering that the appointment of any such contribution at
this present should make him an unmete arbiter and judge between them, which might be hinderance, let, stay and impeach-
ment to many good purposes and successes, not only to his said
good brother, but likewise to all Christendom, has thought it
requisite and necessary to put over the certain determination
of the said aids and contributions until such time as he shall
see an actual invasion of the Emperor in the dominions of his
good brother, or that the Emperor shall refuse, upon his media-
tions, to come to such conformity as shall appertain; trusting to
receive speedily such articles from his said good brother touch-

[2] From the early part of 1536 until the autumn of 1537, Henry VIII was
arbiter between France and Charles V, using his position to encourage
alternately one side and then the other to embroil them more.

nig his offers already made and the Emperor's demands, as whereupon he may entreat with the said Emperor and thoroughly feel his inclination and resolution in the same. And like as his highness trusting verily that his good brother, sending to him such articles, will in the same not only for the better conducing of his desires to effect, but also for that his assured friend shall have the entreaty of them, being one that will travail to make his bargain as good as he can devise and compass, declare and offer such things as may be honorable and reasonable, and rather commit more to his grace's fidelity and friendship in the conclusion thereof than he has already offered and committed to the Bishop of Rome or any other potentate or ambassador. So in case his highness shall not thereupon induce the Emperor by any means to harken to reason, his grace will not fail then to make such answer to his said good brother touching the contribution as it shall appear to all the world that his grace is his most perfect and entire friend.

Thus have I written unto you the king's answer to the said two articles proposed by the said Bailey of Troyes, which his grace doubts not but you will as well think reasonable and maintain with such reasons as shall be with his grace's honor, with entertainment of the amity and the advancement of the purpose contained in the same: that is to have the king the moderator between these two princes, which his grace will neither much seek not yet refuse, if it be put unto him. And as the Emperor's ambassador resident here has good hope that his majesty shall by his means condescend thereunto, so as the French king will do the semblable, even so has the Bailiff of Troyes and Mons. de Tarby[3] also, that their master will not fail gladly to come to the same purpose, which towardsness on both sides caused and compelled his majesty to stay in the granting of any contribution, for the respects expressed, till he shall know further certainties in this behalf.

Finally, his grace desires you also, Master Wallop, to travail of yourself in the furtherance of this matter with the Emperor's ambassador[4] and likewise with all others whom ye shall think may advance the same, which commission is to both of you indifferent. And you shall, my Lord of Winchester, understand that the king's highness was much offended with your recent

[3] Antoine de Castelnua, bishop of Tarbes (1510–1539), ambassador to England 1535–1537.

[4] Jan Hannaert, count of Lombeek and Liedekerke, imperial ambassador to the French court.

suit for the pension appointed to Mr. Brian, taking it half unkindly, that though his grace had no pretence of right in it, you
should labor so earnestly to defeat his earnest promise. And
therefore I shall friendly advise you by your next letters so
frankly and simply to grant the satisfaction of his pleasure
therein, as you may redoub that is passed and continue your
estimation with him, which may be as much worth to you as
that amounts to. And this I assure you I write more friendly to
you a great deal than you have held your peace with me in a
matter of a great deal less weight. And thus fare you heartily
well, from the Rolls, the 8th of June. Your lordship's assured.

Clerk's hand; autograph signature. Addressed: "To myne assured loving friends my Lord of Winchester and Sir John Wallop
knight, the king's ambassadors in France. In haste, poste haste,
hast." Endorsed: "From the Rolls, the 8th of June, Master Secretary." Another hand, much later: "Cromwell to Winchester in
France." A third hand, nearly contemporary: "About an indiction of a general council and a contribution to the French king
his wars against the Emperor, both proposed by the Bailiff of
Troyes to K. Henry and here resolved."

37. To Bishop Gardiner

BM Additional Mss. 25114, fos. 175–7   5 July [1536]
LP, XI, 29; 153   The Rolls

After my right hearty commendation to your lordship. I have
received your sundry letters, for the which I do right heartily
thank you. And amongst others, those of the 21st of last month,
written for your answer to a few words inserted in the end of
my letters a little before addressed unto you touching your contention for the annuity by the king's highness granted to Master
Brian upon the attainder of Norris; the cause of which you stay,
or I may still call it contention therein, appears in your said
letters not so friendly conceived, as I think my merits towards
you have deserved, being only your fantasy that I should rather
of my self than otherwise promote that matter. You, for so you
wot, when his majesty shall give me an express commandment,
and say my pleasure is you thou shall pay one hundred pounds

to such an use, etc., truly my lord, though my talent be not so precious as yours, yet I trust, with his help that gave me'it, to use it so as it shall do his office, without gathering such suspicions upon friendship.

I repeat that word again, because I meant friendly in the writing of it. Or the adhering so fast to the imagination thereof, that I should do nothing without express commandments at his request, whose only inclination should of consequence bow the affections of such men as we be, who have received all we have at his hands, and cause us rather kindly to give place, than so earnestly to contend as might percase neither prevail in nor suffer the thing to have that grace it might have had at the beginning. And yet would I as one that took myself in your own estimation for your friend desire you to think that I will not wade* in any private matter in the king our sovereign lord's name, unless I have his commandment so to do. As in my first letters written for the said, a minute I declared unto you I had, which of his great goodness it pleased his highness to avouch at this time unto you.

But now to your letters. Your gifts received of God be great; and so much the more cause you have to thank Him for them. Your other gifts, received of the king, be not small; and therefor your service to his majesty for the same is loyal and diligent. And so both for your discharge and the safeguard of your estimation it ought to be. Your wisdom his grace knows in the order of your things and therefor desired you not to do him pleasure, if you will exclude utterly right; for that you could not use it pleasantly yourself, but for that he thought yours and his had not been yet so divided but he might with a piece of prayer have done as much with you in such a matter as with a strict commandment. What your debts be, his grace knows not.[1] Nor I, for my part, have fully so much leisure that I cannot either take a just account of you, of all that you owe and received and paid, since you were Bishop of Winchester. I advised you not to enter gifts with your prince, whereby your creditors should think you went about to give away that wherewith you should content and pay them their duties. But I signified as a

---

[1] In 1532 Gardiner complained to Cromwell that he had £1,300 less a year out of Winchester than Foxe had received between 1501 and 1528 and owed twice as much as Foxe was worth when he died; *LP,* V, 1138. Cromwell had an interest in the debts of Gardiner, because Gardiner had borrowed from him at his installation as bishop of Winchester; *LP,* V, 886 and 1285(iv), and *LP,* VI, 841.

minister, though not worthy of credence, his grace's mind only in the best owing of one part of three parts of that which you never had before. And thereunto you made reciprocal agreement, that if the king had an interest in the bestowing of it, you trusted in consideration of your need and service he would bestow it upon you. And if the law would allot it unto you, you said you trusted his grace would permit unto you the use of your own. Which, when I perceived that his majesty took not in very good part nor determined upon that gentle dilemma to leave his determination imperfect, I wrote unto you friendly, advising you rather frankly and with an appearance of a good will to satisfy his grace, than so to contend in it as he might take it unkindly. And now, for that advice which I take to be friendly, you take great pain to make me believe that I have neither friendship in me nor honesty. Wherein how friendly you proved with me, but that you be much given to your own judgment, I durst make yourself the judge.

And now that I have again uttered all my choler* towards you, I remit your own matter to your own order and shall only wish that you may take that way that I would take and would have taken in this or a semblable case. Touching your great desire of news: In good faith I wrote as much and as plainly of the matters that chanced here as I could devise, unless I should have sent you the very confessions, which were so abominable that a great part of them were never given in evidence but clearly kept secret. That the king is married again I doubt not but you know.[2] And for your further satisfaction, like as all his nobles and council upon their knees moved him so to do, so has his grace I think chosen the virtuous lady and the veriest gentlewoman that lives and one that varies as much from the condition of the other as the day varies from the night.

My Lady Mary[3] is also a most obedient child to the king's highness and as conformable as any living subject can be. The late Princess, the Lady Elizabeth, is by parliament pronounced also illegitimate.[4] I trow I shall now please you, for more you cannot require of me than I can signify. I have delivered your

[2] Henry married Jane Seymour on 30 May 1536.

[3] Mary Tudor, daughter òf Catherine of Aragon, reconciled to Henry VIII after Anne Boleyn's execution upon acknowledging her bastardy and the royal supremacy.

[4] Elizabeth Tudor, later Queen Elizabeth I, the only child of Anne Boleyn and Henry VIII, declared illegitimate before Henry married Jane Seymour.

servant Peter Lark[5] money according to your desires, that is to say two-hundred and thirty-three pounds, six shillings and eight pence. I require your lordship by the next post to send unto me the copy of the treaty with the French king made last when Pommey was here.[6] And thus most heartily fare you well, from the Rolls, the 5th of July. Your lordship's assured friend.

Clerk's hand; autograph signature. Addressed: "To my very good lord my Lord of Winchester, the king's ambassador in France." Endorsed: "From the Rolls the 5th of July per Mr. Secretary." Later hand: "Cromwell to Winchester." Another later hand: "Q. Elizabeth illegitimate by Parliament."

38. To Bishop Gardiner

BM Additional Mss. 25114, fo. 191   23 July [1536]
LP, XI, 152; 156   Dover

After my right hearty commendations to your lordship. By this courrier you shall receive the king's highness' answer[1] to such letters[2] as you have lately dispatched unto him, the effect whereof I doubt not but you will consider and accomplish if you may, as shall appertain.

And for asmuch as by your last letter of the 12th of this month written to me I perceive that upon mine written before, touching the cause of Master Brian,[3] you were somewhat moved, gathering what you could and applying the same if not colericly I must needs think melancholily* to your purpose, with change of some of my words and sentences, to make your matter the more apparent, being yet friendly disputed. To the intent the matter thereof might have no further mention, being now come

---

[5] A number of the Lark family of Hampshire were in Gardiner's service.
[6] Giles de la Pommeraye, French ambassador to England in 1531–1532. The treaty meant is that uiting Henry VIII and Francis I against the Turks, 28 October 1532; *LP*, V 1481.
[1] Henry VIII urged Gardiner to prevent Francis I from consenting to a general council and thanked Gardiner for compliance in the Brian pension; *LP*, XI, 151.
[2] Gardiner's letter is not in *LP* but is summarized in the king's reply.
[3] See Merriman, 153, for Cromwell castigating Gardiner's reluctance to meet the king's desire about the pension.

to a good end, both for the king's highness' satisfaction and the remotion* of that whole matter from both our stomachs, who be now, as for mine own part I dare avouch, so I think for yours, clearly purged; like as I commenced the same friendly with you, that is to say that part wherein at the least appeared a contention, so now I require you for your part to finish friendly, that you have promised, as I doubt not but you will. And to wrap up the rest in the patent to be made of the same, for I am for my part ever the same man I was before; that is your assured friend. Though in this matter thinking myself a little touched, I wrote somewhat quickly and doubt not to find the semblable inclination towards me. And thus most heartily fare you well, from Dover, the 23rd of July. I require your lordship to make mine hearty commendation to Master Wallop. Your lordship's assured friend.

T. Wriothesley's hand; autograph signature.
Addressed: "To my good lord, my lord of Winchester, the king's ambassador in France." Endorsed: "From Dover the 23rd of July per the Lord Privy Seal." A later hand: "Cromwell to Winchester in France, touching Master Brian's matter."

39. To Bishop Gardiner and Sir John Wallop

BM Additional Mss. 25114, fos. 237–9   24 December [1536]
LP, XI, 1363; 174   The Rolls

After my right hearty commendations to your lordship and semblably to you Master Wallop. For as much as from your letters of the 23rd of the month lately addressed to the king's highness it appears to his grace, among other things, that there be diverse rumors as well in those parts of the late rebellion attempted in the North parts of this realm, and especially one that for mistrust which the nobles and gentlemen had in the commons they were enforced to appease the matter with certain conditions and articles.[1]

[1] The king had issued an inclusive pardon for all rebellious districts making submission to Norfolk or the Earl of Shrewsbury; *LP*, XI, 1267

To the intent you may know the certainty thereof and compare yourselfs, the better both to refute the same and to answer all men that would say anything to the contrary, his majesty's pleasure was I should signify the perfect truth of the appearing of that trouble and commotion unto you. Which is that first there is no thing more false than that the commons assembled for the king's part were so faint and unwilling that they would not have done their duties, if it had come to extremity. For you shall understand the very same brute* was here told to the king's majesty, whereupon his grace advertised the captains, and received answer that they had perused and tried their men and found no one but they durst affirm would do his duty, when the case should require. And I am assured both by advertisement made to the king and otherwise that the most part of the king's retinue in manner wept, when they were commanded to retire, considering the rebels were not more extremely punished. So that you may affirm it for certain truth, that unless the great wisdom of the king's highness, forseeing that the stroke of battle should but only have diminished his force and strength and been the occasion of infinite mischief, have given strict commandments to his lieutenants, as indeed he did, that they should in no wise adventure his honor in battle wherein he could have gotten nothing but destroyed his own numbers that be ready to serve him, there had been much extremity administered by the party of his grace upon the rebels, as it was to be feared the like was not seen in many years. And those that be indifferent may see both the great wisdom and clemency of the king's majesty, which did rather devise to preserve his own, with his honor, than jeopard the losing of his army, wherein though he could not have lost honor in the cutting off of those corrupt members, yet he should have wanted the use of them, which being healed and recovered as they be, may and will ever stand him in good stead.

Second. Whereas it is reported that the matter should be taken up with conditions and articles, it is truth that at the beginning the rebels made petition to have obtained certain articles. But in the end they went from all and remitted all to the king's highness' pleasure only, in most humble and reverent sort, desiring their pardon with the greatest repentance that

---

(9 December 1536). The pardon did not make concessions to rebel demands that no more abbeys be put down, that further taxation be halted, that Cromwell be surrendered to the people, and that heretical bishops be deposed.

could be devised; in so much as in their chief,[2] which sent their pardon, was for a parliament, for that they might have their pardon therein confirmed, they remitted the appointment of the same wholly to the king's majesty, without the requirement of time, place, or any thing touching that matter.[3]

And this discourse you may declare to all men for truth, for men may with truth not impugn the same. And now my Lord of Norfolk[4] shall go thither to Lynn,[5] there as the king's lieutenant for the administration of justice and shall have a council joined with him as was appointed to the Duke of Richmond[6] at his being in those parts.

You shall also receive herewith two letters[7] written from the king's highness in the favor of the Earl of Angus[8] and his family, for their restitution and recommunication to the king of Scots[9] favor and the recovery of their states in his realm; the one as directed to the French king, to desire him to join with the king's majesty in this suit, or desire that desire, for that the said earl and his family have been ever true and faithful to the King of Scots himself, upon like grounds and persuasions, which letters the king's highness directs you to present to both kings and prosecute the obtaining of the king's majesty's desire therein. As earnestly and effectively, none can supply this part better than you, my lord of Winchester, who has good experience of the honorable demeanor of the said earl and his family toward the said king of Scots, ever since their first coming into England,

[2] Robert Aske.

[3] This was unduly optimistic. The rebellion flared up again in new districts and was not finally ended until February 1537.

[4] Thomas Howard II.

[5] King's Lynn, Norfolk, 41 miles WNW of Norwich.

[6] Henry Fitzroy (1519–1536), the natural son of Elizabeth Blount and Henry VIII. He was president of the Council of the North from 1525 until his death.

[7] See *LP*, XI, 1351, for Henry VIII to James V, asking that his brother-in-law Angus, head of the Douglas clan and ex-husband of Margaret Tudor, be allowed to return to Scotland, whence he had been banished along with other "English" earls and nobles.

[8] Archibald Douglas (1489–1557), earl of Angus, privately married Margaret Tudor, mother of James V and widow of James IV. He acted as guardian for the young king until his exile in 1528. Along with his brother, Sir George Douglas, he was the natural leader of the pro-English Scots.

[9] James V, who was fully emerged from his minority and very much influenced by pro-French elements among the higher clergy of Scotland. The letters are sent to France because James V was known to be there for the marriage of a Valois princess, Magdalene.

and, as it is thought, even the cause of their departure out of Scotland, as his highness trusts you will set forth accordingly.

And whereas you my lord of Winchester were formerly declaring your need thereof, I have this day caused one hundred pounds to be paid to your servant Peter Lark, in whom I assure you there is no default for calling upon me. For I think him many times too importune. But the fault that is, if there be any, must be imputed to the time, and after Christmas I shall cause him to receive a greater sum, trusting you will be content with this in the mean season.

You shall further understand that the king's highness is confirmed that Mr. Pole's servant,[10] of whom you wrote, is detained at [lacuna in ms], whose deliverance his grace would you should in every wise in such sort follow that you may obtain the same, inquiring the matter of his detaindor* as much as your wisdom shall think convenient.

And finally, for as much as there has lately been a fray[11] here between certain of the inhabitants of Fleetstreet and the ambassador of France, upon an arrest wherein the ambassador's men were evil handled; in case there shall be any thing said unto you therein, the king's pleasure is you shall make answer that, like as the madness of men will in time use such follies as shall be displeasant to themselves and also to others, so his grace has caused that matter to be examined with much dexterity and has determined to have the same so punished as it shall be an example to others, to use themselves in the like cases hereafter. And thus heartily fare you well, from the Rolls, the 24th of December. Your worship's assured friend.

P.S. Mr. Pole's servant's name is Throgmorton.

Clerk's hand; autograph signature. Addressed: "To my very good lord my lord of Winchester and to my loving friend Sir John Wallop knight, the king's ambassador-in France." Endorsed: Contemporary, "My LPS, from the Rolls, the 24th of December." Added in a later hand, "1536" added

---

[10] See the letters relative to Cardinal Pole. Throgmorton arrived in France 11 December 1536 and was to bear the papal censure of Henry VIII to England. On the way to Calais, he was taken by imperialist agents in Picardy; *LP*, XI, 1297, 1379.

[11] On 6 December 1536 Charles de Castelnau, brother of Antoine, the bishop of Tarbes and French ambassador, was set upon along with other members of the French staff. One of his servants was killed; *LP*, XI, 1334.

40. To Bishop Gardiner

BM Additional Mss. 25114, fo. 292   24 April 1538
LP, XIII, i, 832; 255   Stepney

After my right hearty commendations to your lordship. Because the repetition of such contentious matters as have been written between us should be but displeasant and noisome* to both parties, I shall lay the same apart for an entire end to it forever that fashion of writing.[1] Only advertise yourself that, howsoever you have taken me, I have reckoned myself your friend, when the time and occasion had served and have not written any more to you in any matter than the king's highness has before the sending of it perused further. And therefore I thought myself the more touched, that for my gentleness I should receive such unkind answer. But as I have now given place to your courage, so I shall put these matters in oblivion that have thus passed between us. And so fare you heartily well, from Stepney,[2] the 24th of April, at night. Your lordship's assured.

Clerk's hand: autograph signature Addressed: "To my very good lord my Lord of Winchester, the king's ambassador in the Court of France." Endorsed: From Stepney the 24th of April A. 30R. Cromwell to Winchester, a letter of reconciliation. In a later hand, probably that of Cotton, the antiquarian: The Lord Privy Seal

[1] Gardiner had stated that Cromwell was behind his being forced to give the pension to Brian in 1536 and the cession of estates at Esher to the king in 1537. This set of real or imagined hurts took on new life in 1538, when Cromwell did put the blame on Gardiner for the failure of English diplomacy to avert either the imperial-French alliance or the Franco-Scots pact of 1536–1537. He felt that Cromwell was responsible for his recall in July 1538; see James A. Muller, *Stephen Gardiner and the Tudor Reaction* (London: S.P.C.K., 1926), p. 74.
[2] Stepney, now in the East End of London, but then a very fashionable suburb, along with Hackney, where noblemen and very wealthy commoners had homes.

41. To the Lords of the King's Council

PRO SP1/161/173–4
LP, XV, 910; 351

24 July [1540]
The Tower

CROMWELL WROTE this letter in defense of his actions in one matter from the Tower, where he had been lodged from the time of his arrest on 10 June 1540. The charges against him were of the most serious nature, for mixed in with some complaints of a general sort were several specifications of treason and heresy. The Rochepot affair is at first glance a piece of backbiting and vilification. It was the custom to demean a fallen minister, perhaps to justify in the minds of the articulate Londoners the spectacle of execution soon to be enacted for them. But the matter of the prize jurisdiction seems curiously linked to another closer to the center of Reformation history. A full and circumstantial telling of the connection between the Rochepot affair and the seizure and release of Grafton's Paris edition of the Great Bible indicates that Cromwell, through Marillac, the French resident ambassador, may have indeed expressed an interest in the Rochepot affair beyond the call of his ordinary duty. What that interest was is hard to pin down exactly. But it certainly was not an illicit taking of profit for his role in settling the matter. Rather it seems to be the case that Cromwell enticed the constable of France, Anne de Montmorency, the Sieur de Rochepot's brother: If Montmorency would arrange the release of the Bible, seized on order of the king after a lengthy urging by Sorbonne divines, Cromwell might intervene in the admiralty court to effect a release of the case from English jurisdiction. That would doubtless bring scant justice to the Hanse merchants concerned. But it would satisfy the French. And it would provide "the book of the greatest volume" ordered by the Injunctions of 1538 and finally ready for sale in April 1539. The Paris printing was released on Cromwell's urgent negotiation, while the French were still complaining about the Rochepot affair after Cromwell's death.

Please it your good lordships to understand that I have read the letter[1] sent to the king's majesty sent from the French king

[1] After Cromwell was arrested, Francis I wrote to Henry VIII to the effect that Cromwell had adjusted a dispute over some prizes taken by

touching Mons. de Rocheport,[2] in which it appears that [the]
French [king] suppose that by my means the said matter has
not been justly ordered and that I should have a great part of
the prize.

My lords, first, as I shall answer to God, I never bore favor in
the matter otherwise than to justice appertains. Which was
that [the] Esterlings,[3] which said they were being in league
with the French king robbed by his subjects, desiring that forasmuch as their goods were safe within the king's ports that
they might have justice here; whereupon the matter was committed to the hearing of the judges of the Admiralty. And there
the proctor of Monsieur de Rochepot agreed and consented to
the jurisdiction of the court. And so the French party as well
as the Esterlings contended upon the matter, whether it should
be tried in France or England. And thereupon, as I remember,
a sentence was given that the matter should be tried in England.
Whereupon the French party departed and after sent hither an
advocate of France who took himself to be satisfied with the
order taken and also departed.

And after the ambassador now present[4] here made suit to
the king, for to have the matter remitted to be determined in
France; at which time a consultation of learned men was had
before the king's honorable council had at Gilford.[5] And there
it was thought that the king's majesty might with his honor
remit the matter into France. But it was agreed on the king's
part that, if the French king would send his Commissary* till
a place indifferent, then his majesty would the like and what-

---

de Rochepot in a way that made his conduct seem prompted by a desire
for personal gain; see Merriman, *The Life and Letters*, I, 299.
2 Francois de Montmorency, Sieur de Rochepot, governor of Picardy and
brother of the constable of France. The story is this: In August 1537 a
vessel captained by Hans Luben of Hamburg was taken by three ships
under de Rochepot's ensign. Luben and five of his men were kept aboard
the prize, along with a French crew intent on sailing into a French port
with the Esterlings. But a wind blew the ships apart from one another
and grounded the prize in an English port, Whitby. The French council
requested that the matter be sent to France for judgment. But Henry
asserted his imperial rights to judge the prize dispute on the grounds
that the ship and goods were in an English port and so not subject to any
foreign jurisdiction. Cromwell was, as he truly alleged, one of a group
of men commissioned to settle the matter between the contending parties.
3 Natives of eastern Germany, along the Baltic coast, but chiefly applied
to denizens of Hanse towns.
4 Claude de Marillac.
5 One of the king's favorite lodges, not far from London.

soever should be determined there should be performed. My lord of Norfolk,[6] my Lord Admiral,[7] my lord privy seal,[8] my lord of Durham[9] and my lord of Winchester[10] were at that council and my lord of London[11] was, at that time being the king's ambassador, fully instructed of the whole matter. But that ever I had any parts of the prize, or that I were promised any part thereof my lords, assure yourselves I was not, as God shall and may help me. And thus my good lords I pray the Eternal Redeemer to preserve you all in long life, good health, with long prosperity. At the Tower, the 24th day of July, with the trembling hand of your bedesman.*

Holograph; in a weak and trembling hand. Endorsed: "The French king's letter touching Mons. de Rocheport, which the Earl of Essex answered."

[6] Thomas Howard II.
[7] Sir William Fitzwilliam, earl of Southampton.
[8] Cromwell.
[9] Cuthbert Tunstal.
[10] Stephen Gardiner.
[11] Edmund Bonner (1500–1569), named bishop of London in 1539 after a turn as ambassador at the French court, in which service he helped negotiate the Rochepot case and the release of the Bibles.

II

Letters on the Commonweal:

Church and Religion

42. To Cardinal Wolsey

PRO SP1/47/166–7   2 April [1528]
LP, IV, 4135; 6   Oxford

THE BUILDING of Wolsey's college at Oxford out of the revenues
of suppressed religious houses was neither unprecedented nor
without parallels in contemporary Europe. In England certain
priories had been suppressed in the reign of Henry V, a time
of great criticism of the church and churchmen. At the end of
the century, Henry VII aided Windsor with the income of dissolved houses. In 1524 Bishop John Fisher obtained the decay-
ing nunneries of Bromehall and Higham, in Berkshire and Kent
respectively, for the purpose of aiding St. John's College at Cambridge. Where suppression was based on solid complaints against
violators of the regular monastic life, both the health of the
orders and other public purposes were well served. But Wolsey's
dissolutions between 1524 and 1529, under Cromwell's management, do not seem to have been the consequence of earlier
efforts of the cardinal at reform. Rather, the twenty-nine houses
of canons, monks, and nuns dissolved by his order over a five-
year period seem to have gone down to advance personal interests relating to his college at Oxford. St. Frideswide's, Oxford,
was the first of some score of houses whose revenues went to the
Oxford building program. The business of suppression Cromwell
had in hand, and in the course of it he became familiar with
every aspect of monastic life and finance. Throughout Europe,
reform-minded men and others simply ambitious had developed
the Erasmian idea of suppression in a general way. And in Denmark, Sweden, Switzerland, and the Germanies widespread dissolution of the monasteries was the rule. On the background of
this point, see Dom David Knowles, *The Religious Orders in
England, III, The Tudor Age* (Cambridge, 1959), pp. 157–72.

Please it your grace to be advertised how that I, according
to your most gracious commandment, have repaired unto the
late monastery of Wallingford,[1] where I found as well all the

---

[1] Wallingford, a Benedictine priory in Berkshire, was dependent upon
St. Albans. It was dissolved between 1525 and 1528, under Wolsey's
directives.

ornaments of the church as all other impliments of the household clearly conveyed away and nothing remaining, tarrying only
the evidences,* which I sorted and conveyed unto your college
at Oxford[2] and the same delivered unto your dean there.[3] And
afterward Mr. Croke[4] and I surveyed, amended and reformed
as well the letters patent* granted by the king his highness
unto your grace, as also your gifts and grants made unto your
said college, in such wise I trust that no default or omission is
left unreformed. I have also found offices* as well of the said
late monastery of Wallingford and of all the lands and tenements
belonging to the same within the counties of Oxford and Berkshire, as also of such omissions as were omitted within the
said counties belonging to Frideswide's[5] and Lyttlemore.[6] And
now I do repair unto the counties of Bucks and Bedford, for
offices to be found there, as well as such lands as appertain to
the said late monastery of Pray besides St. Albans.[7]

The buildings of your noble college most prosperously and
magnificently do arise in such wise that, to every man's judgment, the like thereof was never seen nor imagined, having consideration to the largeness, beauty, sumptuous, curious and most
substantial buildings of the same. Your chapel within the said
college is most devoutly and virtuously ordered and the ministers within the same not only diligent in the service of God
but also the service daily done within the same is so devout,
solemn and full of harmony that in mine opinion it has few
peers.

There is a benefice void within the diocese of St. Davies in
Wales,[8] which is of your gracious gift by means of the chancel-

[2] Cardinal College.

[3] John Higden was dean of Cardinal College; see *LP*, IV, 4074.

[4] John Croke, lawyer and writer (d. 1554). He was one of the six
clerks in chancery from 1522 to 1529, and after that was active in the
administration of chancery income as comptroller of the Hanaper.

[5] This house was an Augustinian foundation, properly called an abbey.
It had a net annual income of £220; only the Benedictine house of
Daventry, with £236 a year, was wealthier among houses suppressed
by Wolsey. But unlike Daventry, which had ten religious, St. Frideswide's
was clearly in decay, with only four inhabitants.

[6] Near Saunford in Oxfordshire, Lyttlemore was a Benedictine nunnery
granted to Wolsey and suppressed in 1525. It had perhaps five inhabitants
at the time and an income of £33 a year.

[7] St. Mary de Pré, commonly Pray Priory, was a Benedictine establishment in Hertfordshire which was annexed to St. Albans in 1528. It was
a nunnery with only three inhabitants at the time of dissolution (1528)
and with an income of £65 annually.

[8] The diocese of St. Davies (David) in Wales embraced Pembroke,
Cardigan, Carmarthen, and part of Glamorgan.

lorship of England.[9] If it may please your grace to give the same to Mr. Byrton,[10] he should be the more able to do your grace service. The name of the said benefice is called St. Florence. I assure your grace that Mr. Byrton is a right honest man and by common report right well learned and shall do your grace good service.

My business accomplished, I shall according to my duty repair unto your grace. Most humbly beseeching the Holy Trinity continually to preserve the prosperous estate of the same in long life and good health. At Oxford the second day of April. Your most humble servant.

Autograph signature: the letter is in a clerk's hand. Addressed: "To my Lord" in Cromwell's hand. Endorsements: There are two, the first very nearly contemporary, reading "Mr. Cromwell ii April 1528"; while the second seems also to be a Tudor hand, it glosses the letter as "To the Cardinal, declaring the magnificence of Cardinal College buildings, etc."

43. To Cardinal Wolsey

PRO SP1/50/81–2 September [1528]
LP, IV, 4697; 8 [London or Westminster]

APART FROM the obvious relationship between this letter and others to Wolsey about Cardinal College, the passage relating to Wolsey's foundation at Ipswich helps put in perspective both the Cardinal's hopes and Cromwell's labors for Wolsey. While Oxford was the scene of Wolsey's triumphs on a grand scale, in Ipswich lay interests closer to his heart. He was a native of the town, and its educational problems were matters of his per-

[9] A number of rights of patronage inhered in the chancellorship, especially the gift or right to present to a living or benefice in the church. The fact that presentation to benefices often rested in lay hands was one of the great problems of the period. While Wolsey was a great churchman, the effective disposition of offices of this kind was understood to be a personal and political matter.

[10] It seems likely that the man was a relative of Dr. John Byrton or Burton, who was prior of St. Frideswide's and afterward the abbot of Osney. Osney or Oseney, in Worcestershire, was on very low, island ground, and Dr. Byrton complained often of his poor fate. But we may spare our sorrow; while in Oxford he was the target of frequent complaints pertaining to his highhandedness.

sonal knowledge. St. Mary's College, which he built on the site
of the Priory of St. Peter and St. Paul, an Augustinian house,
was to remedy the defects of that establishment, where there had
been no schoolmaster in 1514 and again in 1526. For the foundation Wolsey not only wrote statutes, he also composed the only
book of his long career, *Rudimenta Grammatices* or *Funda-
mentals of Grammar*, a work in which humanist notions of educational reform had pride of place. The great minister of state
spared himself no pains in supervising the smallest details of
the planning and building of his school, though to Cromwell
fell the actual enforcement of the cardinal's designs. Between 6
March 1527, when the priory surrendered to his agents, until
September of the next year, his men hastened the erection of
the college. While the foundation stone was in place by 15 June
1528, we know that this letter must be of September of that
year when the dedication took place and when, upon Cromwell's
advice, ten shillings were given to the town fathers "to make
merry."

Please it your grace to have in remembrance your finers* of
Durham,[1] whose continuance here is not only to their great
cost and loss of time but also to the great hinderance of your
works there. And also, they be very poor men. Your gracious
pleasure therefore would be known: whether they shall resort
to your presence or how otherwise your grace will that they
should be ordered?

I have according to your most gracious commandment sent
hereenclosed the clear yearly values of all such lands as you
have purchased in the counties of York and Buckingham and
also the clear yearly value of the late monastery of Wallingford.

If it may stand with your pleasure to appoint in whose name
your grace intends to dedicate your college in Ipswich[2] and
by what name the master and fellows shall be called, the license

[1] The meaning of this term is not absolutely clear from the context. A
"finer" may well refer to a collector of revenues arising in Wolsey's
bishopric of Durham—as "one who collects fines." But the most likely
meaning is one who refines or purifies substances, a person or persons
refining metals, for example. In 1528 Wolsey was especially concerned
with the exploitation of minerals in the bishopric as a way of providing
an added income for his bastard son Thomas Winter, who spent rather
lavishly. Exercising his jurisdiction in Durham, Wolsey leased to Winter
all mineral rights (worth about £185 net annually in 1535). But the
lease was partly negated by the fact that Wolsey seems to have collected
and retained most of the income.
[2] St. Mary's College.

of erection, the letters patent, private seals and other things necessary for the same might be put in readiness, so that no time shall be lost.[3] I have caused such bills as have already been signed to pass the privy signet and private seal and shall now put to writing the letters patent for the broad seal, so that after the two months expired your grace may give the lands contained within the same according to your gracious pleasure. It shall be well done that your grace have in remembrance the appropriation of the benefices to your college in Oxford[4] and that an end may be taken with all ordinaries,[5] which I think is not yet done.

I have spoken with Master Babington,[6] now lord of Kylmayne, for the exchange to be made between your college in Oxford

[3] The license of erection was the actual building permit, which seems to have been obtained *after* the building was completed. The references to letters patent, seals of various kinds, and other administrative processes refers to the ordinary practice by which a royal wish was made effective. Bills were requests or petitions to the crown which, if approved, were officially drafted as warrants, to which the seal (signet) in the hands or keeping of the king's secretary was affixed. Before the crown's agents acted in any matter ordered by a signet bill, however, the privy seal was used to issue another warrant, this time directed to the chancery, where the great seal of the kingdom (broad seal) was kept and administered. Thus, before effective action resulted, several layers of what we might call the royal secretariat, or writing departments, acted on a piece of business. By the early Tudor period, both the privy and broad seals reflected centuries of administrative experience and organization, while the signet in the custody of the secretary of the king was still a less formal, less bureaucratized instrument expressing the king's pleasure. Letters patent under the great seal were "open" or patent, because they expressed to every reader the truth of a grantee's claim that he indeed had a right to whatever property, office, or privilege was at stake.

[4] Appropriation was the act of transferring tithes and other endowments intended for the maintenance of a parish incumbent into the hands of a monastery or other corporation, lay or religious. Often appropriation was a step toward the impoverishment of a benefice and consequent irregularities of absenteeism and pluralism, as clergy struggled to meet the rising cost of living.

[5] An ordinary here was a bishop or other ecclesiastical authority who by his own right rather than by special deputation (i.e., the legatine commission of Wolsey) exercised immediate jurisdiction over the clergy of a diocese. The meaning here seems to be that Wolsey had not yet arranged the details of some assertion of authority over clergy normally responsive to the bishop of their diocese.

[6] Sir John Babington, Knight Hospitaler or Knight of Rhodes, was not as far as I can determine "lord of Kylmayne" (see *LP*, IV, p. 3210). He was authorized along with others to exchange Sanford (see note 7 below) with Wolsey, by the grand master of Rhodes, P. de Villers, in a letter dated 2 June 1528 (*LP*, IV, 4322).

and his religion for Sanford.[7] It may therefore please your grace that your pleasure may be known, whether this vacation your council[8] shall further commune with him and other which have authority in that behalf or not, which in mine opinion should be well done and will set your purpose in a great forwardness.

It may also please your grace that these instructions herein enclosed may be sent to Master Holgill,[9] for the ordering of himself in taking possession, livery and seisin[10] at Rudby,[11] which instructions were devised by the judges. And it shall be necessary that he have them with speed. Your gracious pleasure known touching the premises, I shall most humbly devoir* myself according to my duty to accomplish your most gracious commandment, as knows the Holy Trinity, unto whom I shall daily during my life pray for the prosperous conservation of your good grace. Your most humble servant.

Autograph signature; the letter is in a clerk's hand. Addressed: "To my Lord his grace" in Cromwell's hand. Endorsed: On the recto of fol. 81: "1527, from Mr Cromwell touching Rudby."

---

[7] Sanford was a house of Knights Hospitalers at Oxford. The exchange was carried out by 14 July 1530 (*LP*, IV, 6516, no. 15), although first proposed 18 January 1527 (*LP*, IV, 2810).

[8] The council here meant must be Wolsey's personal council and not the royal council. That nobles and great ecclesiastics kept such governing bodies throughout the medieval period is well known. Cromwell was a member of Wolsey's council and addressed as such in 1529 (*LP*, IV, 5492). Since he did not become a royal council member until 1531, there is no ambiguity of fact here.

[9] William Holgill, master of the Savoy, was the head of that Hospitalers' foundation erected by Henry VII and a creditor of Wolsey. He was also a commissioner of the peace in the north and west ridings of Yorkshire.

[10] While possession is the actual holding or occupancy of property, livery and seisin refer to the delivery of property into the corporal possession (seisin) of a person, accompanied by some symbolic act—in the case of a house, by giving the ring latch or key; in the case of land, by delivering a twig, piece of turf, or other object signifying the thing given.

[11] Rudby, a Yorkshire site in the north riding, some three miles west of Stokesley.

44. To Cardinal Wolsey

PRO SP1/57/294–7   18 August [1530]
LP, IV, 6571; 18   London

WE HAVE already noted Wolsey's journey into his diocese. There,
far from court and influence, he urged the cause of his two colleges, which the king had marked for suppression on the ground
that Wolsey's foundations were built through the exercise of that
legatine jurisdiction condemned in the *praemunire* action that
had tumbled the cardinal. Dean Capon of Ipswich had failed
in efforts to convince Henry VIII to spare St. Mary's. Cromwell
and others, at whose sleeves Wolsey now clutched like a beggar,
fared no better with Oxford, since the king had already determined to convert Cardinal College from Wolsey's monument to
his own. But a more interesting element of this letter, at least
for the student of Cromwell's later career, is that which relates
to the flowering of spirituality in Wolsey. While Wolsey had
made his melancholy progress northward, he had stopped at the
charterhouse at Richmond in a house built by Colet, who many
years before had preached to Wolsey about service and humility.
There he met in prayer with meek and lowly Carthusians, men
with hair shirts next to their skin, servants of God in the poorest
and meanest monastic order. The great minister who had intended to reform orders was now given the model whereby he
might reform himself. It is that resolve to which Cromwell
addresses himself, to the world of the spirit far from the vain-
glory of the world. There the cardinal sat "in godly contemplation," as his gentleman-usher Cavendish reports. But not all
courtiers accepted that the proudest prelate who ever drew
breath was converted. The Duke of Norfolk and others met
Cromwell and expressed their hostility and skepticism, to which
he responded by urging upon his master the reality of the virtues
that Wolsey made some show of to the world. But Wolsey could
no more leave off show than could a leopard change its spots.
And so as summer came on, he built new buildings at Southwell and kept great state, despite Cromwell's warnings. Also,
in this letter we hear of Cromwell's new importance, quite apart
from Wolsey's service.

Please it your grace to be advertised that, after the receipt of your letters dated at Southwell[1] on Saint Lawrence day,[2] I perceived how that your grace remained in some displeasure and anxiety of mind, for that I, by my letters, had before certified you of the finding [of] certain offices concerning your bishopric of York. The finding whereof, as I perceive by your letters, you do suppose should be much to your dishonor and detriment. For the which, intent that your grace may put yourself in repose and quietness of mind, I have sent unto you this bearer, who shall at length declare unto you, besides the demonstration of the copies of such offices as be drawn for that purpose, that the finding of the said offices, saving only that in the preamble of the same there is touched the connection of your grace in the *praemunire*,[3] which all the world already knows, shall be for your good, only profit and avail. And yet your pardon and restitution[4] stand in good and perfect effect, so that your grace shall have no need, neither to be in fear of loss of any your spiritual or temporal goods or to be troubled, nor also to be put to any new suit in the obtaining of any other pardon or restitution. And if in case your said pardon and restitution were in any part insufficient, I assure your grace I know that the king's highness would it should be made as good as by any counsel it could be devised. And doubt you not but his highness is your gracious and benign sovereign lord and would in no wise that you should be grieved, molested or troubled. Whereof it may please your grace to quiet yourself and to take the finding of these offices patiently; and upon the return of the same there shall be such orders taken that your grace shall not be interrupted in the receiving of your revenues nor otherwise be molested in any manner [of] case for any new suit.

---

[1] *LP*, IV, 6554, in which Wolsey asked about the well being of his colleges and the inquisition touching his lands in the bishopric of York. Southwell, in Nottinghamshire, is about twelve miles NNE of Nottingham.
[2] 10 August, the Feast of St. Lawrence.
[3] *Praemunire* is the general term for the act of prosecuting in a foreign court suits cognizable in English law, against the intention or subsequent understanding of legislation of 16 R. II. Wolsey was indicted in King's Bench on such a charge on 9 October 1529, essentially because he had procured bulls from Clement VII and used them to usurp English jurisdiction in his legatime court. A good example of the *praemunire* violations alleged against Wolsey is that of an advowson, or presentation of a person to a church living by Wolsey before the owner of the patronage exercised his legal right. Since such presentations were comprehended within the common law of real property, such an exercise of jurisdiction, while technically a violation of acts against premature provision or "prevention," was also against c. 5, 16 R. II.
[4] Wolsey was pardoned by Henry VIII on 12 February 1530.

As touching your colleges, the offices shall be found, howbeit the dean and such other as have sued to the king's highness have had very good answer, whereof I think they have certified your grace or this time.[5] As touching the thousand marks of the revenues of Winchester,[6] I doubt not but it shall be obtained at the audit. And concerning Battersey,[7] it may please your grace that such things as you have sent me the copies of may be sent hither under seal, for they will trust no scrolls, and also, that search may be made for Bishop Booth's[8] will concerning the same. Strangewish[9] continually cries and makes exclamation in the court of you, in so much that the lords of the council have determined to write unto you in that behalf. Would to our Lord your grace were rid of that man! As concerning the prebends of Wetang,[10] doubt you not but in that all thing is and shall be ordered to your good contentation.

Sir, I assure your grace that you be much bound to Our Lord God, that in such wise has suffered you so to behave and order yourself in those parts to attain the good minds and hearts of the people there; the report whereof in the court and elsewhere in these parts is and has been to the acquiring and augmenting the good opinions of many persons towards your grace. Beseeching therefore your grace to continue in the same after such a sort and fashion as you may daily increase not only the favors of the people there but also here and elsewhere, to the pleasure of God and the prince. And notwithstanding, your good, virtuous

[5] William Capon, dean of St. Mary's College, had gone to London in July to engage counsel in behalf of the college and Wolsey's foundation. But the best advice was that any act done on the same authority condemned in the *praemunire* was illegal and so forfeit to the crown, which applied to all the endowment of St. Mary's.

[6] Wolsey was bishop of Winchester from 1528 to 1530, and Cromwell here refers to episcopal revenues promised to Wolsey by Henry VIII as a stipend upon which he could live in exile.

[7] Battersea in Surrey, the site of one of Wolsey's palaces. The business is probably the matter of Wolsey's servant John Oxyherde. Wolsey had granted the use of his house to a son-in-law of Sir Thomas More, who promptly dispossessed Oxyherde, against which action Wolsey protested; see *LP*, IV, 6484.

[8] The reference may be to Lawrence Booth (d. 1480), archbishop of York, who had also possessed the Battersea palace.

[9] Thomas Strangewish or Strangways, a former servant of Wolsey. In 1530 he received £700 from Cromwell in exchange for the wardship of George Bowes (*LP*, IV, 6582 and 6588).

[10] The reference is probably to Agostini Agostini, Wolsey's physician, who had entered the legate's service in 1527 and held the prebend of Wetwang in York Cathedral. Cavendish malignly refers to him as Wolsey's Judas, but the Venetian was Wolsey's faithful agent and friend.

and charitable demeaning and using yourself in those parts is not by your enemies interpreted after the best fashion; yet always follow and proceed you attemperately* in such things as your work and your grace, affections set apart, shall seem to stand best with the pleasure of God and the king. Some there be that do allege [your grace] does keep too great a house and family* and that you are continually building. For the love of God therefore, I eftsoons as I often times have done most heartily beseech your grace to have respect to everything and, considering the time, to restrain yourself for a season from all manner buildings more than mere necessity requires, which I assure your grace shall cease and put silent some persons that much speak of the same. For the geldings which your grace did send me, I most humbly and heartily thank you, beseeching your grace to give further credence to this bearer, who shall declare unto your grace other things not written.

I do reckon your grace right happy that you be now at liberty to serve God and to learn to experience how you shall banish and exile the vain desires of this unstable world, which undoubtedly doth nothing else but allure every person therein and especially such as Our Lord hath most endowed with His gifts to desire the affections of their minds to be satisfied. In studying and seeking whereof, besides the great turmoil and afflictions that men suffer daily, most persons been driven to extreme repentance, and searching for pleasure and felicity find nothing but trouble, sorrow, anxiety and adversity. Wherefore, in mine opinion, your grace being as you are, I suppose you would not be as you were to win a hundred times as much as you were possessed of.

The Bishop of Bayonne[11] is daily looked for, and my lord of Wiltshire[12] is coming home. The saying here is that the Emperor[13] has good obedience of his subjects in all things, saving that they will not dissent from the Lutheran sect. It is also said that the Emperor does make musters for a great army to be prepared against the Turks, to pass into Hungary for the receiving of that region; and that the second son of the Emperor

[11] Jean du Bellay, afterwards bishop of Paris and cardinal. He served Francis I as resident ambassador in England at various times between 1527 and 1533.
[12] Sir Thomas Boleyn, Earl of Wiltshire, lord privy seal and father of Anne Boleyn, who had been in Rome in connection with the Divorce, and who returned to England 30 August 1530.
[13] Charles V.

is departed this present life.[14] The news here is that the Germans will have a general Council[15] for the reformation of many things. The Florentines do still continue and defend* the power of the pope, and it is supposed that they shall vynce* by means that there is a great pestilence fallen amongst them, being in the field of the pope's party.[16] There is also a great scarcity in Italy of all manner of grain, in so much a quarter of wheat is worth generally forty shillings. They look daily for an ambassador from the pope,[17] who at the furthest will be here within thirteen days. The king's highness is this night at Ampthill[18] and there will continue these thirteen days.

It may please your grace to pardon me that I do not repair unto you at this time, for undoubtedly it is not possible, as the bearer shall further declare unto your grace. Our Lord knows my will and mind. And I trust verily that your grace does perfectly think that I would be glad to see you and unfeignedly I would have seen your grace long ere this, if I had not been letted* by important business, whereof I eftsoons* most humbly beseech your grace of pardon. And though I am not with you in person, yet be you assured I am, and during my life shall be, with your grace in heart, spirit, prayer and service, to the uttermost of my poor and simple power; as knows our Lord, whom I most heartily beseech to preserve your grace in long life, good health, with the increase of your heart's desire. At London the eighteenth day of August.

I beseech your grace to dispatch this bearer, whom I might evil have forborn at this time, but only that I perceived by your letters that you much desired to be put in quietation. And besides myself, I could not send any that could certify your

[14] The second son of Charles V, Ferdinand, died in 1529, but the death was made public only after the passage of a year.
[15] This reference is puzzling unless the news of the Council or Diet of Augsburg, which first met 20 June 1530, had not yet reached England. Of course, after Augsburg, there were persistent rumors of a more general council, but the reference seems to be to something specifically German.
[16] Florence surrendered to papal forces 12 August 1530. Cromwell could not know this and thought Florence still besieged. Plague ravaged the besiegers for a short time during the summer of 1530, spreading to Florence itself briefly. Cromwell is supposing that the Florentines will be successful in their defense (vynce) for that reason.
[17] Baron Andrea del Borgo, the new papal nuncio to replace Giovanni Casalis, reached England in mid-September. Clement felt the change necessary in the light of Casalis' weakness concerning the Divorce.
[18] A royal retreat about eight miles south of Bedford.

grace of the effects of such things as you desired to be answered in, but only he. Eftsoons beseeching your grace speedily to send him home, for my business is such that I cannot lack him.

Wriothesley's hand, much corrected by Cromwell; no signature. Addressed: "My lord Cardinal."

45. To Lord Chief Justice Fitz-James[1]

PRO SP1/71/54
LP, V, 1340; 35

24 September [1532]
London

CROMWELL'S BUSY part in royal administration often made him ponder the role of the monasteries in English life. Local gentry exercised great influence over monastic foundation, large and small alike. The matter of being well-friended in the head of a house was of great importance. Economic, social, legal, and educational affairs of the county containing Burton-on-Trent turned, to some degree, on the orderliness with which the abbot conducted the affairs of the community he supervised or, if particular interests took precedence over the general weal of the house, the direction in which patronage was exercised. Much of the business of any monastery was in the hands of laymen by the sixteenth century. In fact, initiative in economic affairs had really passed out of clerical hands before the attacks launched by government in the 1530's. Burton-on-Trent (Staffordshire) was a great house destined to become a college. Struggles over its wealth had engrossed the attention of monks and abbots long before laymen came to exert counterclaims. In the year 1301 the abbot of Burton had been refused rents due him from the prioress of Derby on the grounds that she was a great gentlewoman of Lancashire and Cheshire (she was a Stanley), and that she would not be put upon by any churlish bailiff. We cannot help but notice that the ancient régime in monastic affairs often lacked any hint of concern for the spiritual side of regular life.

---

[1] Sir John Fitz-James, judge and chief justice of King's Bench from 1526 to 1538, was also the nephew of Richard Fitz-James, bishop of London, who had been an active reformer at Oxford prior to his death in 1522. His career led him to a prominent role in the trial of Wolsey and in the actions against More, Fisher, and the Carthusians. He died in 1542, after retiring from the bench in 1538.

My lord, after most hearty commendations, these shall be to advertise your lordship how that I have received your letters[2] and according to the contents of the same moved the king's highness concerning the election of the Abbot of Burton.[3] And like as I wrote to your lordship in my last letters, that you should stay the said election until the king's title might be tried,[4] so his high pleasure is that you shall do, if you see good matter to bear it. Nevertheless, his highness, at the suit of my Lord Lisle,[5] supposing that he and you do both sue for the advancement of one person to be Abbot of Burton foresaid, has, as my lord plainly affirmed to his grace, thereupon directed his gracious letters for that purpose; which, notwithstanding, his high pleasure is if you see cause, that you shall stay the election upon the trial of his title as is aforesaid. And in case your lordship will have that person promoted for whom he has written, his grace is therewith right well contented, so his highness may be remembered somewhat, like as your lordship wrote to me in your last [letters], which he only remits to your wisdom and discretion. For as his highness perfectly trusts that you will substantially look thereunto, who would as feign that you be well neighbored as you would yourself. My lord, this and all other that shall lie in my little power I shall always do as I have promised. And thus most heartily fare you well. At London, the 24th day of September.

Draft; apparently in Wriothesley's hand, corrected by Cromwell. Address and endorsement lacking.

---

[2] On 9 September 1532, Fitz-James wrote to Cromwell of the impending death of the abbot of Burton, complaining that he had been a bad neighbor to the judge. While he knew that the house was not of Henry VIII's foundation, and the founder had given to the community of monks the right of election, he hoped that the king's intercession would help in the election of an abbot more congenial to Fitz-James's interests; *LP*, V, 1304.

[3] Burton-on-Trent was a Benedictine abbey of which William Beyne was head between 1523 and 1532. Whether Burton's new abbot suited Fitz-James is not known.

[4] That is, until we see what happens to any assertion of a royal right in the election.

[5] Arthur Plantagenet, Lord Lisle (1480?–1542), was a bastard son of Edward IV. After early service in Henry VIII's personal bodyguard, Lisle was made deputy of Calais and elevated to the rank of viscount (1533), serving in a kind of political exile against which he complained constantly.

46. To the Abbot of Bury St. Edmunds[1]

PRO SP1/72/60   24 November [1532]
LP, V, 1573; 37   Eltham

BURY ST. EDMUNDS was one of the great Benedictine abbeys of
England, rich in possessions and religious history alike. It had
been the site of pilgrimages for centuries, a place to which
Christians came to see the coals on which St. Lawrence roasted
and the skull of St. Petronilla, far-famed for its healing powers.
It was also a house whose hospitality and possessions were often
exploited by the crown and its servants. It was this fact that
helps to account for another: that when the last abbot surrendered to the royal commissioners, he dealt with men who
were frequently in the past his tenants. This letter is typical of
many in which we can see an abbot exercising patronage in
behalf of some powerful servant of the crown or one of the
local aristocracy or gentry. Much of ordinary monastic revenue
in the years before the Dissolution derived from "spiritual income" in the form of appropriated church tithes, glebe lands,
pensions, and other dues. If the parsonage of Harlowebery illustrates this fact, it also bears witness to the hopes of the abbot
there that a manor let at good terms to Cromwell might bring
a richer return than ever the lands did. The reciprocal system
of favors which tied together religious and lay governors had
more to do with the events disclosed here than we gather from
some historians, who see in every such lease some evidence of
a general impoverishment of the monasteries on the eve of the
Dissolution.

My lord, after my hearty manner I commend me unto you,
advertising you that, for diverse considerations, I am very desirous to have some house in Essex near unto Honysden.[2] And
for as much as your personage of Harlowebery[3] shall shortly be

---

[1] John Melford, *alias* Reeve, was the last abbot of Bury St. Edmunds,
receiving his temporalities 24 April 1514. When Bury was suppressed (in
law it made a voluntary surrender), Reeve was given a pension of five
hundred marks, a sum sufficient to enable him to satisfy his well-developed
tastes for wine and good country gardens.

[2] Honysdon or Honnesdon, Hertfordshire.

[3] Harlowebery or Harlow, Essex, a place about six miles north of Epping.

in your hands and letting, by reason that the lease which Malery and his wife hath is now almost expired,[4] I shall desire and instantly pray you to let your said farm of Harlowebery unto me by lease for term of 40 years, for the same stock rent and farm that has been of all time accustomed, paid and received for the same. In doing whereof, you shall bind me to do you and that monastery such pleasure as may lie in my little power in time to come. And what shall be your toward mind herein I pray you to advertise me in writing by this bearer, my servant. And as for the years that Malery and his wife have yet to come. You shall understand that I have agreed with them for his lease. Thus fare you heartily well. From Eltham[5] the 24th day of November.

Draft in an unknown clerk's hand; without signature or endorsement. Addressed in another hand: "To my lord Abbot of St. Edmunds Bury give this."

47. To the Abbot of Woburn[1]

PRO SP1/77/195   July [1533]
LP, VI, 778; 54

APART FROM any of the particular circumstances of this letter, great interest inheres in it because of the light it throws on the Cistercians (White Monks) and Cromwell's growing power in government. The White Monks in England were governed by the ancient constitutional machinery of their order in the sense that supervision rested with the abbot of Cîteaux. But during the great Schism and afterward, both politics and England's isolation caused the order to grant supervisory powers to a com-

---

[4] Richard Malery, a mercer of London (*LP*, V, 166, no. 54).
[5] Eltham, Kent, a royal palace about two miles south of Woolwich.
[1] Robert Hobbes, abbot of Woburn, a Cistercian foundation in Bedfordshire dependent on Fountains. His house was one in which there was fair observance of the rules of his order. The abbot himself was a man of some learning in theology, with a bent decidedly conservative. He was in fact a critic of the Boleyn marriage, the suppressions of 1536, and Cromwell's encouragement of books he deemed heretical. He was eventually tried for his denial of Henry's supremacy and executed. It is perhaps fair to speculate that his activities against Cranmer's trial of Catherine of Aragon colored Cromwell's view of the incident dealt with in the letter.

mission made up of the heads of the greater Cistercian abbeys
in both north and south England. Throughout the Tudor period,
Fountain Abbey in the north and Stratford and St. Mary's in
the south dominated the commissions. Legally, the abbots were
still bound to attend annual general chapters in France. But in
the circumstances of the early 1530's this seemed strange, a fact
recognized by the general chapter's deputation of the Abbot
of Chalocé to visit and reform the English houses. Henry VIII
would not cooperate, however, and several internal struggles
among abbots raged by 1532. Henry's government reacted by
the creation of a commission exercising royal authority (April
1532), in which the abbots of Fountain and Woburn were joined
by three other heads of houses. Under the commission, the five
abbots were to visit and reform the Cistercian abbeys throughout England. What title to do this inhered in the crown must
remain vague. While the king was declared supreme head in
January 1531 by a church convocation, the parliamentary act
declaring the Supremacy was still two years in the future. But
it may well be that contemporaries understood the concession
of 1531 to imply a right to supervise discipline. More peculiar
than this, peculiar as it is, is the fact that Thomas Cromwell
seems to have taken charge of various Cistercian affairs. His
papers are filled with material relating to the internal squabbles
of the order. Yet he had no ecclesiastical office, nor even a secular one, to justify his meddling in religious matters. He was still
a year away from being secretary of state, and his vice-gerency
in spiritual affairs came only in 1535. What in fact he was is
clear: the chief holder of *political power*. How he exercised
that power in a matter of religious reform and discipline is
clearly shown here.

My lord, after my duty remembered. So it is that I am credibly
informed how that you, bearing inward grudge and displeasure
to my well-beloved friend the Abbot of Vaudy,[2] intend, study,
and go about by such means to depose him from the abbacy
for the promotion thereunto of one of your own monks, being
the cellarar[3] of your house. My lord, I pray you use yourself
unto my said friend as accords to your religion. For I know
certainly that he is a good religious man and that his house,

[2] The last name of the abbot of Vaudy is not given in Dugdale's *Monasti-
con* or Knowles' history of the religious orders. *LP*, V, 1477, states clearly
that he was Henry, abbot of Vaudy; the abbey was located in Lincolnshire and was dependent on Fountains. It was dissolved in 1536.
[3] The cellarar held the monastic office charged with supervising the provisions for table and the storerooms.

which was in great debt at the time of his promotion, is now by his good policy reduced to good and wealthy state and condition, as well in cattle as in corn furnished with other requisites and necessaries. Wherefore my lord, my trust is that you will circumspectly look thereupon, bearing your good and lawful favor unto them, like as good charity requires; and the rather at my desire and request, ascertaining you that I have at this time written my semblable letters in the favor of my said friend unto the Abbot of Fountains,[4] not doubting that he, at my requisition, will lovingly use and entreat my said friend in all his business.

And, whereas you have with your own monks of the said house of Vaudy one Davy Edward, Clerke,[5] which you know well has greatly mis-ordered himself, I trust that you will instruct him so fruitfully that he shall not need to be further reconciled to amend his living; whereby ye shall not do very good and charitable deeds, [as] knows God, who keep you.

Draft; with no signature, but many corrections, all in a clerk's hand. Addressed in another contemporary hand: "A letter for the Abbot of Woburn."

48. To the Abbot of St. Austins[1]

PRO SP1/85/85   25 July [1533]
LP, VII, 1007; 78   London

THE DETAILS of the case presented in this letter are quite obscure. Obviously, Cromwell thinks the monks of St. Austins, Canterbury, or at least their abbot, have been guilty of some underhanded acts. What is specifically of interest is Cromwell's role

4 Robert Thirsk. Fountains was in the western part of Yorkshire. Dissolved in 1539, it figured in Cromwell's correspondence throughout the 1530's. Elton, in his *Star Chamber Stories* (London: Methuen, 1958), pp. 147–73, throws a clear light on Cistercian problems at the time.
5 The reading of the manuscript is difficult at this point. Merriman has "Davys Edward Clerke." But it seems more likely that the best reading is "Dauvy Edward, Clerke," though the person remains beyond identification whatever reading we choose.
1 The abbot of St. Augustine's (Austins) was John Sturrey, alias John Essex, who from 1522 to 1538 headed the Benedictine abbey at Canterbury. He was a scholar of British antiquity and Latin classics. With John

as an arbitrator of grievances between subjects of the king. It
is one we shall see him playing on other occasions. He seems
to have had a desire to keep people from the rigors and delays
of the law, where possible, in the pursuit of equitable settle-
ments. In this he continued a practice of Wolsey and also carried out one of the fervent hopes of the reform-minded humanists of his day. Such men never tired of complaining about the
corruption of justice, and the clergy were frequently as much
their targets as were gentry or allegedly avaricious townsmen.
His position as the king's secretary and the chief lay expert on
monastic life made it nearly inevitable that he would intervene
in such cases. Instances like the one here given were just the sort
of thing that encouraged rampant anticlericalism of the kind that
informs the reports of visitors in the course of the Dissolution,
when complaints of forged wills and violated trusts are not rare.
That it should arise in the Benedictine community of St. Austins
is at first sight a bit of a surprise, since that house had a prior
who was himself a humanist and musician, while the abbot was
a scholar and antiquary quite well thought of in his own time.
Be that as it may, at this time the monks of St. Austins seemed
very amenable to Cromwell's pressure, if we can judge from
other events of 1533. When the Nun of Kent affair threatened
to touch their community, the monks joined Christ Church,
Canterbury, in dissociating themselves from the Observant Friars
of the area. Knowles speaks of the monks as men who abjectly
sought refuge under Cromwell's wings (*The Religious Orders*,
III, 191).

My Lord Abbot I commend me unto you, etc. And whereas
George Goldwin[2] the bringer hereof has been a continual suitor
unto me a great time to have award[3] made between you and
him, I shall heartily desire and pray you upon the sight hereof
to take some reasonable way with him, so that I be no longer
molested by him and his continual suit. And whereas his father

---

Dygon, the prior there and himself a great Renaissance musician, Essex
figures in a vivid sketch written by John Twyne: The abbot, summering
in his manor of Sturrey, in the Stour Valley east of Canterbury, is visited
by the prior and a young lawyer, Henry Wotten, soon to be Cranmer's
dean. They talk about many things, with Twyne reflecting on the sad
fate awaiting the abbot after the Dissolution. But after surrendering his
house to Henry VIII, Essex enjoyed the life of the country gentry at
Sturrey, with a £61 per annum pension from the crown.
[2] It has not been possible to identify Goldwin.
[3] Merriman's reading "A Warde" is incorrect. The reference does not seem
to be to wardship in the feudal sense, but rather to an award touching
the outstanding disputes between Goldwin and Essex.

might have had of your lordship and your predecessor diverse offers, who yet nevertheless always refused them, me thinks your lordship now can no less do than grant him so much as you would have given his father. For he is much charged with the debts of his father, as he affirms, and also with the finding* of his brothers and sisters. Therefore, in mine opinion it shall be well done that you shall take an end with him.[4] You know his father died in prison at your suit. And thus, committing the matter to God and your consciences, I thank you for my hawks and bid you heartily for him.

Draft, much corrected in Cromwell's hand. Endorsed: folio 85, dorse; "minute of a letter."

49. To the Abbots of Fountains[1] and Bylands[2]

PRO SP1/80/97   8 November [1533]
LP, VI, 1408; 59   London

WE LAST saw Cromwell's involvement with the Cistercians in England with regard to an alleged attempt of the Abbot of Woburn to depose the Abbot of Vaudy. On that occasion we noticed the breakdown in the machinery of government which traditionally regulated the order. In the present letter we have another very good case of Cromwell's work with the monastic orders before the hectic period of the Dissolution. Rievaulx was a Cistercian abbey near York which earlier in 1533 had been under the command of one Edward Kirkby. But Kirkby had

[4] In Cromwell's corrected draft a specific composition had been suggested and then struck out. That crossed-out passage reads: "Wherefore my lord, in discharge of your conscience, and at my desire, I pray you to give him a hundred pounds, which you took from his father; and further, to give him some reward. . . ." This is very interesting in the light of a letter from the abbot to Cromwell of 4 August 1533 (*LP*, VI, 937), in which Essex complains that Goldwin continues to ask an unreasonable sum, since the father owed the abbey £100 when he was committed to prison. Yet, he will give him something for Cromwell's sake! The date of this letter is supplied from another crossed-out passage.

[1] Fountains, under Abbot William Thirsk, like Bylands, surrendered to the crown in the suppressions of 1539.

[2] Bylands was under Abbot John Ledes; it was a Yorkshire abbey.

been deposed, chiefly at the instigation of Thomas Manners, the earl of Rutland and heir of the founder of the house, who was certainly justified in his interest in the affairs of the house. Rutland had received appeals from a group of monks who described themselves as "of your honorable lordship's party" at Rievaulx. Cromwell responded by sending Rowland Lee, his friend and Rutland's cousin, to investigate conditions at the abbey. Lee recommended Kirkby's dismissal and, after a formal commission headed by Thomas Legh visited the house, Kirkby was removed. Meanwhile, Legh reported that the order as a whole needed a thorough reform, the more so since the Abbot of Fountains seemed to side with Kirkby in the dispute, which was also true of the majority of the monks. A pretty situation existed, since the new election rested in the hands of the monks themselves, with the permission of the founder. But founder Manners thought Kirkby justly dismissed, while the monks refused to move to a new election, on the grounds that Kirkby had been wronged. Having gone so far into the affairs of the order, Cromwell could not draw back. In the king's name a commission was issued on 13 September 1533, ordering the abbots of Fountains and Bylands to hold an election, with Manners' license. By 16 October the commissioners had not procured any effective action, as we know from Byland's report of that date. It was in that context, then, that Cromwell addressed this letter, which Elton once called "one of his more formidable rockets" (*Star Chamber Stories*, p. 164).

After my full hearty manner I recommend me unto you. And whereas it has pleased the king's highness to direct his most gracious letters unto you now at this present time, for the election of a new Abbot of Rievaulx, wherein his grace has been advertised you have not heretofore endeavored yourself to the accomplishment of the same according to his said letters and commandment, whereof I marvel not a little that you would incur his high displeasure for the non-executing of the same. Therefore, I hereby require you and nevertheless do advise you, in eschewing of further inconveniences and displeasures that may thereby ensue (all affections set apart), you do accomplish the said election according to the tenor and purpose of his most gracious letters directed unto you and to the convent of the same monastery in that behalf.[3] And thereby you shall not only deserve the king's most gracious thanks but also have

[3] On 10 December 1533, Thomas Legh reported to Cromwell that a new abbot was elected and installed at Rievaulx, while the assignment of stipends was in the hands of Rutland (*LP*, VI, 1513).

me to do for you in all your good causes the best I can, as knows Our Lord who keep you. Written at London, the 8th day of November.

Clerk's hand; no signature; no endorsements. Addressed: "To the right honorable in God my Lord Abbot of Fountains and Byland and to either of them."

50. To an Unknown Abbot

PRO SP1/94/222   [1535]
LP, VIII, 1122; 134

As THE summer of 1535 waned, Cromwell's visitors rode over the countryside on a mission that was to end the life of more than 800 religious houses in a scant four years. With them they carried no order to destroy or suppress. Instead, they had parchment bills containing injunctions directed toward the reform of monastic life. These injunctions, like those issued in 1536 and 1538 for the church as a whole, reveal the reform temper of Cromwell as few other documents do. They reminded the communities of religious of the oaths they had sworn touching the Supremacy and Succession and enjoined the abbots and other heads to keep and procure to be kept all statutes pertinent to the changes in polity, especially such as had to do with the bishop of Rome's feigned jurisdiction. These were accompanied by injunctions dealing with the daily life of the monks; in every particular they were traditional and mindful of medieval ecclesiastical legislation. Indeed, they have been seen as conservative echoes of St. Louis and Innocent III (Coulton, *Five Centuries of Religion*, IV, 661). But in some sense they were novel and severe. One article ordered that no monk or brother be allowed to go "forth of the precincts" of the enclosure of the monastery. If the terms monk and brother were strictly understood, an economic and administrative crisis would have ensued, for the house would have been unable to work its glebe lands without dispensations, nor would its head have been able to care for the business of the house as it touched the congregation as a whole. The problems were real rather than theoretical, and Cromwell was at once besieged with requests for clarification and dispensation. He gave both. That fact, so clearly conveyed in this letter, strikes a blow against the cynical assertion that Cromwell made the injunctions draconic as the first step in the campaign to close the monasteries. He specifically argued the point with one of his visitors, Dr. Legh, who wanted the full rigor of the injunction enforced and protested against Cromwell's granting of exceptions. What we see here instead is the realization that a long-needed reform cannot be made to work by excessive zeal, that spiritual rebirth is not the result of rules, no matter how strict. It is remarkable, therefore, that most writers fail to comment on the rest of the injunctions, which are a direct consequence of the New Learning, and which Dom Knowles describes as "Erasmian teaching" (*The Religious Orders*, III, 277).

You shall understand that I have received your letters. And touching that you desire amongst other things licence for your self and certain of your brethren to walk to your manors and other places about your monastery, you shall understand that in consideration of the good and toward mind that I have found in you towards me and my servants diverse ways, I, of the king's highness, have obtained license for yourself that you may resort unto your manors and other convenient walks nigh unto your monastery. So that no common bruit* may be raised thereby, not doubting but you will use yourself so (as for the good will and mind I bear toward you) it may be to the good zeal of religion and as I may thereby receive no disworship thereby. So that always your brethren must needs use and order themselves according to the injunctions in that case given unto them in that behalf.[1]

Draft, much corrected in Cromwell's hand.

[1] The most remarkable sections of these injunctions are not those involving restrictions and reminders of old monastic rules. Among the Erasmian articles mentioned in the headnote are the following: the reading of an hour-long lesson of scripture to the brothers every day, over against the two-centuries-old reading of divinity enjoined by Richard Kidderminster at Winchcombe; a long disquisition on the unprofitableness of ceremonies, offices, rites, and processions; that no one under twenty-four years of age be professed (see editor's Introduction on this point); a command to avoid superstition, especially the exhibiting of relics for money; a reminder that money donated by pilgrims must be distributed to the poor; and so on.

51. To the Prior of Tywardreath[1]

BM Additional Mss. 6416, fo. 31   21 May [1535]
LP, VIII, 743; 103   London

IN THE rural world of sixteenth-century Cornwall, townsmen competed with gentry, several aristocrats, and monks for dominance in their own communities. While some sixteenth-century towns made strides toward self-government, this was not everywhere true; and the Tudors attacked town charters as often as they enlarged them. In a small group of Cornish towns appeals for town rights were not against gentry or aristocrats but against churchmen, against whom Henry Tudor had drawn his sword in the severely anticlerical reforms led by Cromwell. Before 1536 five Cornish boroughs had come under the wing of the church in the shape of religious houses to which had been given franchisal rights in town matters. Bodmin, the largest of the towns of Cornwall, belonged to the priory there. The same was true of Newport, Penryn, St. Germans, and Tywardreath. At Bodmin and Tywardreath there was a good deal of hard feeling between the town and the monastery. And the crown, especially concerned about the loyalty of always difficult people at a time when an invasion in the southwest was feared, tended to side with the burgers for reasons apart from the impending attack on the religious. The challenge given to the priors by the townsmen found a receptive audience in Cromwell, who appointed a commission, strong and wholly secular, to go into these complaints. What was true at Bodmin was true at Fowey, where the leading inhabitants were anxious to jockey the monks out of their dominant position. There, the feeble state of the house and its prior made things easy for Cromwell's friend Thomas Treffry, a son of the most prominent gentry family of the area and a reform-minded member of Parliament who worked closely with the secretary.

Mr. Prior, as unacquainted, I have me commended unto you. And where as it is come unto the king's highness' knowledge

---

[1] Trewardeth or Tywardreath, a Benedictine priority in Cornwall, about three miles from Fowey. The prior there was Thomas Collins, a hard drinker for whom Wolsey had only contempt and against whom dislodgement was attempted on a number of occasions before 1535.

that the town of Fowey[2] is sore decayed and the occasion thereof partly is that in the said town is no order of justice, because the liberties concerning the same granted by the king's highness and his noble progenitors to your predecessors and by them unto the inhabitants of the said town, remain in your hands and keeping, so that between you no manner [of] good order, equity nor justice is exercised and used within the said town. Wherefore, I require you to condescend and agree with the inhabitants of the said town, so that you, having your reasonable approved duties, they may have their liberties, to be used and extended amongst them within the said town, to the increase of good order within the same.

And as ye shall agree therein, to certify me in writing by Mr. Thomas Treffry,[3] bearer hereof. For his highness thinks that the said port of Fowey ought to be his and to be holden of him, so that his grace intends from henceforth to have it as well provided for with good governance and of defense for utter enemies as other his towns and ports within those parts. Whereunto, you, for your parts, before this time had little or no regard, neither to the good order, rule and defense thereof, nor yet to the good rule and governance of yourself, your monastery and religion, as you be bound. Wherefor, his highness thinks that you be very unworthy to have rule of any town that cannot well rule yourselves. And that I may have answer by this bearer what you intend to do, I require you, to the intent I may certify his highness thereof. And thus fare you well. At London, the 21st day of May. Your friend,

Clerk's hand, autograph signature. Addressed: To the Prior of Trewardreth in Cornwall be this given."

---

[2] Fowey, on the English Channel, about three miles from Tywardreath, and perhaps twelve from Tudor Bodmin.

[3] Thomas Treffry of Fowey, often Cromwell's agent in various matters (cf. *LP*, VIII, 50, 149, 676) and the son of William Treffry. The family had grown rich in the last two centuries and built a castle overlooking the town of Fowey, where they still are prominent. Thomas served under Edward and Mary, though he had difficulties after 1554 on account of his known Protestant sympathies.

52. To the Bishop of Lincoln[1]

PRO SP1/101/227   1535-1536[2]
LP, X, 176; 176

THE SUMMER of 1535 was wet with rain and heavy with the sighs
of English monks faced with the visitors sent out by Thomas
Cromwell. Spalding Priory in Lincolnshire was among the monasteries that needed visiting. Though it had been twice sub-
jected to ordinary visitations by the bishops of Lincoln in the
sixteenth century, Spalding was a house with a history of scandal
and incipient disorder. The small community there, ten monks
in all, had suffered the breakdown of the daily routine of hours
(*horarium*); attendance at choir was either scanty or totally
neglected; one of the canons wandered frequently to fish and
hunt, even to spend weeks on end at a brother's house, and
had on four or five occasions offered to fight the prior. On one
pretext or another, or rather on solid grounds, the prior, abbot,
and incontinent canons had been suspended. Strict episcopal injunctions of unusual severity seemed to have had little effect
when, at some time between August 1535 and March 1536 Cromwell's agent visited the house. But the bishop seems to have
resented Cromwell's intrusion on what he took to be his rights
as ordinary nearly as much as the monks had resented the
bishop on earlier occasions. This reply by Cromwell was to be
but the opening round of an escalating war of words, which we
will have occasion to listen to again.

[1] The letter is neither addressed nor endorsed. Since there are no corrections it would appear to be a copy of the original, whether by the sender's
clerk or the recipient's we cannot tell. But that John Longland, bishop of
Lincoln, was the recipient is beyond doubt. He served in that capacity
from 1521 to 1547. He is a man of extraordinary interest among Tudor
bishops, an early friend and patron of Erasmus, a man of sterling personal reputation, learned and able in pastoral care and a brilliant preacher,
a strong advocate of the supremacy, and, withal, a desperate upholder of
high views of the episcopal privilege and an opposer of the 1532 submission of the English clergy. Of more immediate concern to readers of
this letter is the fact that by 1536 he had grown suspicious of further
reform and from that time stood with Gardiner and the conservatives.
[2] The date must fall between 1 August 1535, when the first visitations
began, and early May 1536, when the act dissolving the lesser monasteries
was before Parliament.

My lord in my hearty wise I commend me unto you. And where I visited lately by my deputy[3] the Priority of Spalding[4] and substantially reformed such things as were then to be reformed, as I have to show by the injunctions which were given;[5] for as much as that house pertains to my care and not to yours, being neither founder nor benefactor of the same, as I will show unto you more at large when it shall fortune me next to speak with your lordship,[6] I desire and require the same to suffer and permit the Prior and the convent there to live in quiet and that certain busy fellows of the town of Spalding be not maintained by your lordship against the said Prior because he will not let the farms of his house to the great damage of the same; for denying whereof the said Prior has been put to much trouble and inquietness, as I am credibly informed. In which case I must and will aid and succour the said Prior, as it appertains to mine office and to such trust as the king's grace has put in me concerning the religious persons and other of the clergy of his realm.

Either a copy or a draft: no corrections; no address; no endorsement.

[3] The deputy cannot be identified. The chief visitors were Richard Layton, Thomas Legh, John ap Rice (alias Price), and John Tregonwell. We have detailed itineraries of the visitations made in many shires but no letter describing a visit to Spalding. What is very strange here, however, is that no less an authority than Knowles, *The Religious Orders in England*, III, 286, states that many shires were altogether exempt, among them "Lincolnshire, particularly rich in religious houses. . . ." It may well be that all other Lincolnshire houses went unvisited in 1535–1536, perhaps because Longland had spent three years in visitations of an episcopal character (1525–1531, but especially 1525–1528). This may also help to explain the keen resentment to which Cromwell reacts in this letter.
[4] Spalding Priory, a Benedictine house at Spalding, Lincolnshire.
[5] The injunctions were one of the two sets of documents carried by the visitors of the monasteries, the other being the questions to be administered to the head and inhabitants and upon which the infamous *comperta* rested.
[6] An interesting point! Bishops had sharp limitations imposed upon their visitation rights. Exempt from ordinary visitations were Cluniac, Carthusian, and Cistercian monks, all friars, and Gilbertine and Premonstratensian canons. But Benedictine nuns and monks *were* within his powers before 1534. Cromwell appears to be asserting an authority as vicegerent in much the same way that Wolsey exercised legatine jurisdiction. But Longland had little ground for complaint. He had on occasion asked for help.

53. To Thamworth and Markby, Priests

PRO SP1/102/67   22 February [1536]
LP, X, 334; 138   London

IT HAS not been possible to throw any light on the persons or
the crime mentioned in this letter. And yet the inclusion of it
here seems clearly warranted. Whoever Thamworth and Markby
were, they stood accused of defeating the legitimate interest of
a man who was probably the beneficiary of any valid will in
the case. Priests and monks not infrequently in previous centuries had forged bequests benefiting themselves or, with nobler
motives, their order or house. Complaints of this kind might
easily come to Cromwell's attention for a number of reasons.
As the king's secretary he normally received petitions and requests of many types. As vicegerent for spiritual affairs he
would obviously be concerned in any perversion of a will, since
the witnessing and proving of wills were ecclesiastical functions.
An even more basic reason for his receipt of this complaint may
be the fact that in 1536 he became lord privy seal. The opinion
of Sir Edward Coke was that the lord privy seal was *ex officio*
president of the court of requests, where poor men's causes were
heard and expedited in the interest of equity. But Dr. Elton has
shown that Cromwell did not take an active part in the judicial work of the court, which was in his period simply one
aspect of the king's council. Thus, there was a "determined divorce" between theory and practice in so far as Cromwell's
tenure of the privy seal was concerned. But of the 172 cases
so far attributed to the years 1536–1540, there were two cases
before the court which were in fact dealt with personally by
Cromwell, with the effective disposition of the case being made
by his personal letters. This certainly seems to be the case here,
where the mere sight of Cromwell's letter is to be sufficient
warrant for the priests to come to London to attempt to clear
themselves.

Forasmuch as it is in a complaint afore me that you have
heinously transgressed the law, offended the common wealth
and greatly hindered the complainant, whose name is Richard
Godwyn, by forging of a will, the inanity of which offense so
aggresses the goodness of God and the conscience of all honest

men, that be you sure if you be with this fault lawfully charged you cannot scape unpunished. And, if you be not, then I would your honesty were defended; for this cause I will say that upon the sight of this my letter you hasten hither to London, to make such answer in this cause as truth and honesty bids you. At London, the 22nd day of February. Your friend Thomas Cromwell.

Clerk's hand; but autograph signature clause. Addressed: "To Thamworth and Markeby priests and to either of them. At Boston."[1]

54. To the Prior of St. Faith's[1]

PRO SP1/106/189   23 September [1536]
LP, XI, 484; 163   London

THE ACT of Suppression of 1536 contained a clause reserving to the king freedom to permit any houses he might select to remain in being. Nearly one out of every four houses listed for dissolution was so licensed to continue. The fact of the royal license has been often overlooked by historians, who prefer to see in the survivals some dark plot of Cromwell to enrich himself. Most of the houses that survived did pay for the privilege. But the beneficiary was the king and not his minister. Some heads of religious houses, however, did write to Cromwell, offering inducements to him to place their own communities on the exempt list. It seems clear that many of the houses *had to survive*, since the statute gave to the inhabitants the choice of remaining in their order or seeking a "capacity" or license to live in the uncloistered world. When sufficient numbers requested continuance in their vocation, the government had to house them to avoid the staggering job of coercing all to take capacities. These facts make the present letter of great interest. It would seem clear that, whatever abbots offered, evidence that

[1] The town of Boston in Lincolnshire, one of the great cities of the kingdom, had a number of small parish churches as well as four houses of Augustinian friars. The clergy there were as a whole poverty-stricken, as we know from the reports of Cromwell's visitors. But nothing concrete has been discovered about either of the priests or Richard Godwyn.
[1] John Sarisbury, suffragan bishop of Thetford. St. Faith's was a Benedictine priory in Horsham, Norfolk.

Cromwell was corrupt in his role as reformer of the monasteries must depend on documents showing him actively soliciting rewards in exchange for the continuance of a community. And while many requests were accompanied by gifts, which was the normal practice of the Tudor system of fee and favor, the question of whether the vicar-general "had no scruple in asking for what he wanted" rests on Merriman's printing of two letters of that sort. Dom Knowles (*Religious Orders in England*, III, 337) cites the two letters and Merriman's conclusions about them without noting that the letters are the *only examples* of the alleged common practice. It seems clear, however, that the two letters in question are forgeries!

Right reverend Father in God I recommend me unto you. And the cause of my writing at this time is this. For as much as it pleased the king of his royal power to take reformation of all and singular houses of religion within the diocese of Norwich, like as his great houses done in other places, and for the abuses of religion and excesses of living [some] shall be exposed, of the which your house was billed and named to be one. That notwithstanding, by the labor of your friends made to me;[2] with my diligence your house is taken out of the king's books and without danger and so shall remain til the return of this my chaplain,[3] of whose report hangs your information to the council whom I will that you shall receive as my trusty chaplain. And this pleasure considered, as I have deserved to look to my pains, and to the bearer hereof, as you would have further pleasure stayed of me in like manner for the maintenance of your house, I am the more bolder to write; because it has been sumptuous to me of late, as the bearer hereof can express more plainly to you. Written at London, the 23rd day of September. By me Thomas Cromwell.[4]

Addressed: "To the reverend father in God Prior of Saint Faith's. . . ."

[2] On 18 August 1536, Richard Southwell, one of the general surveyors of the Court of Augmentations, wrote to Cromwell in favor of the Prior of St. Faith's, who being a mere suffragan had neither home nor living, and in behalf of the community there.

[3] Dr. Thomas Legh or Leigh, one of the commissioners for the dissolution in East Anglia.

[4] The signature and the letter above it presents themselves as Cromwell's autograph. They are in an old-fashioned "gothic" hand utterly unlike that of Cromwell or any of the clerks or secretary hands familiar in his household or secretariat. The same hand occurs in the only other letter showing

55. To Edward Gostwick[1]
and Master Stompe[2]

PRO SP1/109/195   26 October [1536]
LP, XI, 875; 166   Windsor

THE ACT of March 1536 which provided for the suppression of the lesser monasteries was accompanied by another, that establishing the Court of Augmentations, the agency charged with conducting the business of the suppression and the administration of former monastic properties. The court was responsible for taking the surrenders, for protecting or realizing the liquid assets of a house, and for administering each estate until it was either farmed or granted away. Cromwell's original intention was to increase the capital of the crown by holding former monastic lands and annexing them to the old crown lands. But emergencies drained away the assets of the crown and led to a situation in which capital was liquidated to meet current costs of government or war in the 1530's and 1540's. Toward the ends originally intended, commissioners scurried about the countryside in 1536, often discovering that the crown's needs had been

---

Cromwell requesting payments for continuance (*LP*, XI, 485). The question of the authenticity of these letters must rest on paleographic considerations, and such tests, when applied, lead to the conclusion that Cromwell did not write these letters nor did anybody normally associated with him. Since they are not copies but the very letters signed and sealed "per me" and delivered, the claim that they are Cromwell autographs is crucial. G. R. Elton, asked whether he had unearthed any forgeries in Cromwell's correspondence, replied, "Have you looked at the one to the prior of St. Faith's and its companion?" or something similar to that. How did these letters come to be among Cromwell's papers confiscated in 1540? Perhaps they were recognized as forgeries—and were sent to him by the prior for his inspection.

[1] John Gostwick, treasurer of first fruits and tenths, was not one of the commissioners for North Wales. The man here addressed is doubtless Edward Gostwick. In the dissolution commissions of 1536, the commissioners were to make inquests, take surrenders, compile inventories, and make audits, as well as to dispatch such religious who asked to remain in the regular religious life and to send to the archbishop of Canterbury such as wished to take capacities as secular priests.

[2] Master Stompe was one of the commissioners in North Wales, specifically in Montgomeryshire.

anticipated by those of the religious managers of monastic lands. A number of heads of communities had already alienated property, in some instances to keep their house afloat and in others for baser motives of personal gain. The fact that so much of the monastic land was already leased or rented formed one of the greatest of the problems facing the new administrators under Cromwell. The policy adopted was tolerant. Existing agreements between monks and tenants were honored, even though in many cases they were by statute voidable. From another point of view, however, the fact that economic initiative had often passed to the local gentry—even extending to purchase, as in the case of Lord Powis—was an element of stability in the vast transfer then brought about.

I commend me heartily unto you. And for as much as the monastery of Stradmarsell in Powis land[3] was bargained and sold unto my Lord Powis[4]—and he in possession thereof before the making of the act[5]—I require you to suffer my said Lord Powis to occupy and enjoy the same accordingly until such time that you shall come hither, that I may more largely declare and show unto you the king's pleasure in that behalf. Having regard that you leave such goods and chatells as belonged to the said monastery with my said Lord or his deputy by bill indented betwixt my Lord or his deputy and you, mentioning only things particularly.[6] And the said Lord Powis shall not only make answer therefore but also for the rents and profits thereof, if the case shall so require. Thus fare you well, from Windsor[7] the 26th day of October. Your loving friend.

P.S. Item. There is offered for the farm of Wymonisold[8] 40 pounds, for the which Thomas Swallow[9] and Adam Gascoyne[10] do sue.

[3] Stradmarsell or Strata Marcella was a Cistercian abbey in Montgomery, within the barony of Powys or Powis, then in the hands of the Grey family.

[4] Lord Powis, Sir Edward Grey. On 19 October 1536 he complained to Cromwell that, although he had bought the house from the abbot and convent there, Strata Marcella was being surveyed for the king's use; *LP*, XI, 795.

[5] 27 Henry VIII, c. 28.

[6] This ambiguous phrase must mean only a general enumeration in lieu of a thorough inventory.

[7] Seventeen miles ENE of Reading, Berkshire.

[8] One mile N of Leicester.

[9] A citizen of Westminster: see *LP*, XI, 202(4).

[10] A groom and messenger of the King's Chamber.

Clerk's hand; autograph signature and postscript.
Addressed: "To my loving friends Master Gostwick and Master
Stompe the King's Commissioners in the North and to either of
them." Endorsed: Received the 20th day of March. My lord
privy seal's letter.

56. To an Unknown Abbot

BM Cotton Mss. Cleopatra Eiv, fo. 86   March [1538]
LP, XIII, i, 573; 249

AFTER THE Dissolution of 1536, and because of the wording of
the statute dissolving the lesser monasteries, the remaining religious in England were hopeful that immediate extinction was
not to be their lot. The old forms of monastic life resumed, and
with it episcopal visitations and injunctions which inform us of
the state of some of the large houses in 1537 and early 1538. But
all was not tranquil. Some of the larger houses had been involved in the Pilgrimage and were suppressed. Despite this, in
the summer of 1537 it seemed true that no general plan to put
down all religious houses was in existence and that perhaps
Cromwell spoke truly in the letter we print here. Indeed, some
smaller houses were being refounded by Henry VIII, at least
until May 1538. If it is difficult to spy out the beginnings of the
new policy of general suppression, it is also true that on 11
November 1537 the wealthy priory of Lewes executed a form
of voluntary surrender to the king, an action quite different from
the involuntary suppression by statute of 1536. Earlier, Furness
in Lancashire had surrendered and others had followed. It was
against that background that Cromwell's commissioners in 1538
began yet another visitation in which they offered a prepared
form of surrender, which was commonly signed without protest.
Reluctant monks and abbots there were, but none of them very
successful, except in the sense that some resisted to the point
of indictment for treason on grounds stemming from accusations spoken against them, often from within their own communities.

After my hearty commendations. Albeit I doubt not but having
long since then received the king's highness' letters[1] wherein

[1] I cannot find any letters answering to this reference in *LP*. Merriman
cites Strype, *Ecclesiastical Memorials;* but I found that reference to support 61 in his collection and not 63.

his majesty signified unto you that, using yourselves like his good and faithful subjects, his grace would not in any wise interrupt you in your state and kind of living. And that his pleasure therefor was, in case any man should declare anything to the contrary, you should cause him to be apprehended and kept in sure custody til further knowledge of his grace's pleasure, you would so firmly report yourselves in the tenor of the said letters as no man's words nor any voluntary surrender made by any governor and company of any religious house since that time shall put you in any doubt or fear of suppression or change of your kind of life and policy. Yet the most excellent wisdom of his majesty, knowing as well that of the one side fear may enter upon a contrary appearance, where the ground and original is not known, as on the other side, that in such cases there come not what some malicious and cankered hearts[2] that upon a voluntary and frank surrender would persuade and blow abroad a general and a violent suppression.[3]

To the intent you should safely adhere to the sentence of the said letters by his highness already addressed unto you and like good subjects ensue* the purport of the same in the apprehension and detention of all such persons as would brute or instill the contrary; whereas certain governors and companies of a few religious houses have lately made free and voluntary surrenders into his grace's hands, his grace's highness has commanded me for your reposes, quietness, and for the causes specified on his grace's behalf, to advertise you that unless there had been overtures made by the said houses that have resigned, his grace would never have retained the same and that his majesty entends not in any wise to trouble you or to devise for the suppression of any religious houses that stands, except they shall either desire of themselves with one whole consent and forsake the same or else misuse themselves contrary to their allegiance. In which case, they shall deserve the loss of much more than their houses and possessions, that is the loss also of their lives. Wherefore, in this you may repose yourselves, giving yourselves to serve God devoutly, to live like true and faithful subjects to his majesty, and to provide honestly for the sustenta-

2 "Cankered hearts" was a stock term in Cromwell's circle, applied against anyone hostile to the régime. See the use of it by Layton, Legh, and St. Clare; *LP*, XIV, ii, 272, 185 and XIII, ii, 887.

3 What motives Cromwell had for so writing must remain conjectural. Clearly, however, the desire to avoid a general panic among the religious may have been mixed with honest doubt about the policy of "surrender" and its extensiveness.

tion of your houses and the relieving of poor people with the hospitality of the same, without consumption and willful waste and spoil of things that has been lately made in many abbeys, as though the governors of them minded only their dissolution.

You may be sure that you shall not be impeached by his majesty, but that his grace will be your shield or defense against all others that would minister unto you any injury or displeasure. And if any man of what degree soever he shall be pronounce anything to the contrary hereof, fail you not either to apprehend him, if you shall be able, or if he be such a personage as you shall not dare meddle with, to write to his majesty's highness their name or names and report that he or they so lewdly behaving themselves may be punished for the same as shall appertain.

Draft in Sadler's hand.

57. To Dr. Thomas Legh[1] and William Cavendish[2]

PRO SP1/138/156–7   6 November [1538]
LP, XIII, ii, 764; 278   London

ON THE surface this letter is one of the many which testify to the orderly routine of the suppression of the larger monasteries, though St. Osyth is not of much interest in that context. Beneath the surface lies much of the troublesome detail of Cromwell's work in that regard. In 1538 Lord Chancellor Audley petitioned Cromwell *to spare* St. John's, Colchester, and convert it to use as a college. This bit of background is vital. For were that not the case, we might well see the lines in which Audley is to be remembered for one monastery and Sir Richard Rich for the

---

[1] Dr. Thomas Legh (d. 1545), employed by Cromwell in various ecclesiastical commissions and in the visitation and suppression of the monasteries. He was a lawyer and master in chancery, best remembered for his aggressive remarks and conduct toward the monks.
[2] Sir William Cavendish (1505?–1557), statesman and administrator, especially prominent in securing the lands of dissolved houses. Of vast experience in revenue matters, he had been treasurer of the king's chamber, the central organ of finance before the Cromwellian reforms.

other as a typical piece of "self-interested misgovernment" by
the king's agent and his friends. Whatever the reasons, the abbey
at Colchester had been slated for suppression soon after Audley's
plea. And we can at least suspect that Cromwell had good reason
to suppress the house and its abbot, Thomas Beche (or Marshall), about whom we have already learned in the context of
treason. Be that as it may, Legh and Cavendish did visit the
house. Suppression, however, did not follow. Cromwell had
gotten information that Beche would not surrender his house
voluntarily. For that or some other reason investigations were
set on foot, leading to the abbot's arrest and confinement in the
Tower by 20 November 1538, two weeks after the commission
to Legh and Cavendish. The charges against him came from
monks of his own house and ranged from plotting with the
rebels of 1536 to treason by words against the king and his
council. Knowles does not doubt the truth of the counts against
Beche, despite the abbot's allegation that his delay was only
to secure a better pension! By 1 December trial and execution
had been made, the victim begging forgiveness of Cromwell and
of Audley, the patron of his house.

After my hearty commendations. These shall be to advertise
you that the king's gracious pleasure is that with convenient
speed you, repairing to the monasteries of St. Osyth[3] and
Colchester,[4] shall for certain reformations and other considerations which his grace intends as well there as in other places
dissolve and take the same to his use. And by your discretions,
considering the age, qualities, conditions and towardness of the
persons there, shall assign unto them their annual pensions,
and all other things do according to his grace's commission to
you in this behalf directed. Not omitting to put my lord chancellor[5] or his deputy in possession of the said monastery and Mr.
Chancellor of the Augmentations[6] or his deputy in the possession
of the other, to our said sovereign lord the king's use accordingly.
Thus fare you heartily well. From London, this sixth of
November, the 30th year of his grace's most noble reign. Your
loving friend.

Clerk's hand.
Address: Obliterated, save for Cavendish's name.

[3] St. Osyth, Essex, abbey of Augustinian canons, suppressed in 1539.
[4] St. John's, Colchester, a Benedictine abbey.
[5] Sir Thomas Audley.
[6] Sir Richard Rich.

58. To Sir Richard Rich[1]

PRO E315/245/31   21 January [1539][2]
LP, XIV, i, 105; not in Merriman[3]   London

ONE OF the most common errors about the fate of former religious in the Reformation is that which holds they were ruth-
lessly evicted from a life they had chosen and turned out into
a hostile and pitiless world. The facts are quite otherwise. Not
only were they given a choice between seeking capacities or
transfer to some undissolved house before 1539; they were also
provided with pensions in many cases, sums which varied with
the status of the particular individuals and which were paid out
of Augmentations. In the matter of getting capacities, one of the
more virulent myths about Cromwell is that he acted not as a
reformer but as an avaricious destroyer intent on profiting from
other people's ruin. This letter shows the process by which
Cromwell gathered the reports of visitors and commissioners and
translated them into government action. And it is especially
worth noting for two reasons: the last sentence of instruction;
and the fact that Merriman overlooked this letter in compiling
the collection in which he printed obvious forgeries.

After my hearty commendations. These be the names of the
abbots, priors and convents which lately surrendered their houses
and monasteries into the king's highness' hands, for whom his
grace's pleasure is you shall make forth sufficient capacities*

---

[1] Sir Richard Rich (1496?–1567), lawyer and administrator; chiefly famous
for his part in the martyrdom of More, he deserves to be remembered for
his work in government as lord chancellor of England and his earlier
work as chancellor of the Court of Augmentations, where his reputation
was that of a man who would take no bribes.
[2] Since Eynsham was suppressed in 1538, this letter must be either of
1539 or 1540. I allow the earlier date on the grounds of Cromwell's
usual celerity in dispatching business.
[3] This is one among a number of authentic Cromwell letters unknown to
Merriman. I have discovered several and so has Dr. G. R. Elton. It is
startling that Merriman did not print this letter, since he surveyed the
volumes (Miscellaneous Books of the Court of Augmentations: E315) in
which it appears. Perhaps he overlooked it because he took it to be a
warrant rather than a letter. While in some cases the diplomatic distinction of letters and warrants is tricky, that can hardly be said in this case.

in due form after the accustomable manner, with dispensations to have one benefice with cure,* and the same to deliver without demanding or taking of any money or fee. Thus fare you well, from London, the 21st day of January.

Names of the canons of Netley[4] Richard Ridge, Abbot; Valentine Brown, Prior; John Keney, Sub-prior; William Walker; William Ball; John Poole; John Lynchpole; James Alborough; William Catesby; John Timmons; John Wheeler; Richard Smythe; Richard Barber; Robert Gooday.

Names of the monks of Eynsham[5] Anthony Dunistone, Abbot; Edmund Ranyford, Prior; Gregory Broadhurst, Sub-prior; Thomas Mill, Chanter and almoner; Thomas Phillips; Thomas Knollys; Robert Ford, Capellarious and Cellararious; John Kocksetter; William Burke; John Hedges.

Names of the friars of the Holy Trinity, Dodington:[6] Henry White, Minister; Richard Uncle.

Clerk's hand; autograph signature.[7]

59. To Stephen Vaughan[1]

BM Cotton Mss. Galba Bx, fos. 338–41   May [1531]
LP, V, 248; 21

IN THE mid-1530's Cromwell revived efforts to secure a reliable and reform-minded translation of the Bible. In the very earliest days of his influence with Henry VIII he had been in contact with the earliest and most formidable translator, William Tyndale, who had already been denounced for Protestant heresies in May 1530. In the spring of 1531 the king considered employing Tyndale's pen, and charged Cromwell with the negotiations. In this cause the latter enlisted the aid of his life-long friend, himself a man of advanced Protestant sympathies, the London merchant and Antwerp factor Stephen Vaughan. Cromwell wrote

---

[4] A Cisterian abbey in Hampshire, famous as a hostel for voyagers making their way to the port at Southampton.
[5] Eynsham, a Benedictine abbey near Oxford.
[6] Dodington, or Donnington, a house of Crutched Friars.
[7] The lists and headings in the original are in Latin.
[1] Stephen Vaughan (d. 1549), diplomatist and merchant and Antwerp agent of Henry VIII, 1530–1546. Often employed in Germany as well, Vaughan held few official appointments, though he was a clerk in chancery.

to tell him to find Tyndale and encourage him to return to England. Vaughan sent a double reply, to the king and Cromwell, reporting Tyndale's views, which were substantially that episcopal persecutions made him fear for his safety. The letter to Cromwell had a confidential postscript revealing that his friend was much impressed by Tyndale and had become ardent in his cause. In March Vaughan wrote again to that effect. In April he reported to the king that he had interviewed Tyndale in Antwerp's suburbs, enclosing a copy of Tyndale's *Answer* to More's confutation of his works. Henry's reading of the work convinced him that Tyndale was an opinionated heretic, and he ordered Cromwell to tell Vaughan to cease efforts in Tyndale's behalf. This letter, with its many corrections due either to Cromwell's perturbation or a change of mind in the king, for it bears a postscript authorizing further discussions, was not the end of the affair. Vaughan had two further interviews with Tyndale in May and June. Tyndale expressed a willingness to return and accept punishment if the king would set forth a bare text of the Bible in English. In November Vaughan again wrote in Tyndale's behalf, but Cromwell would go no further. That ended a stage in Cromwell's development as a reform-minded minister and perhaps did much to convince him that radical Protestant ideas were not the vehicle for reformation in England. Five years later Tyndale was entrapped at Antwerp and surrendered to royal agents to die eventually at the stake.

Stephen Vaughan I commend me unto you and have received your letters[2] dated at Antwerp the 18th day of April with also that part of Tyndale's book[3] enclosed in leather which you with your letters directed to the king's highness. After the receipt whereof, I did repair unto the court and there presented the same unto his royal majesty, who made me answer for that time that his highness at opportune leisure would visit, oversee and read the contents aswell of your letters as also the said book. And at my next repair thither it pleased his highness to call for me, declaring unto me aswell the contents of your letters as also much matter contained in the said book of Tyndale.

And howbeit that I might well perceive that his majesty was right well pleased and right acceptably considered your diligence

[2] *LP*, V, 201.

[3] William Tyndale (d. 1536), translator and polemical writer in a Lutheran tradition. He left England in 1524 to visit Luther. He gained royal favor with his Erastian *Obedience of a Christian Man* (1528), only to lose it with his sharp attack *Practice of Prelates* (1530), in which he denounced the Catholic hierarchy, Wolsey's administration, and the Divorce.

and pains taken in the writing and sending of the said book as also in the persuading and exhorting of Tyndale to repair into this realm, yet his highness nothing liked the said book being filled with seditious slanders, lies and fantastical opinions, showing therein neither learning nor truth. And further communing with his grace, I right well perceive that he thought that you bore much affection towards the said Tyndale, whom in his manners and knowledge in worldly things you undoubtedly in your letters do much allow and commend; whose work bears violent slanders and lies imagined only and feigned to infect the people both to lack grace, virtue, learning, instruction and all other good qualities, nothing else pretending in all his works . . .[4] that you in such wise be envious and lack learning . . . by your letters you praise, set forth and advance him, who else pretends to sow sedition among the people of this realm.

The king's highness therefor has commanded me to advertise you that his pleasure is that you should desert and leave any further to persuade or attempt the said Tyndale to come into this realm, alleging that he, perceiving the malicious, perverse, uncharitable and indurate mind of the said Tyndale, is in manner without hope of reconciliation in him and is very joyous to have his realm destitute of such a person . . . *that should Tyndale return unto the same there to manifest his errors and seditious opinions which (being out of the realm by his most uncharitable, venemous and pestilent books, crafty and false persuasions) he has partly done already,* his highness right prudently considers if he were present by all likelihood he would shortly (which God defend) do as much as in him were to infect and corrupt the whole realm, to the great inquietation and hurt of the commonwealth of the same.

Wherefor Stephen, I heartily pray you in all your doings and proceedings and writings to the king's highness you do instantly, truly and unfeignedly, without dissimulation, show your true learning and obedient subjection, bearing no manner, favor, love or affection to the said Tyndale nor to his works in any manner of ways, but utterly to condemn and abhor the same, assuring you that in so doing you shall not only cause the king's royal majesty, whose goodness is at this time so benignly and graciously minded toward you (*as by your diligence and industry to be used to serve his highness and eschewing and avoiding disfavor and allow the said Tyndale his erroneous works and*

---

[4] The ellipses indicate gaps in the manuscript itself, here and in other places. All italics are found in the manuscript.

opinions), so as to set you forwards as all your lovers and friends shall have great consolation of the same. And by the contrary doing you shall acquire the indignation of God, displeasure of your sovereign lord, and by the same cause your good friends which have been ever glad, prone and ready to bring you towards his gracious favors to lament and sorrow that their suit in that behalf should be frustrated and not to take effect according to their good intent and purpose. Having therefor firm trust that for the love you owe to yourself and your friends you will beware and eschew to enter into any opinions whereby any slander, dishonesty, danger or suspicion might ensue towards you, whereof I promise you I would be as sorry as your natural father.

As touching Frith[5] mentioned in your same letters, the king's highness hearing tell of his towardness in good letters and learning does much lament that he should in such wise as he does set forth, show and apply his learning and doctrine in the semination and sowing such evil seeds of damnable and detestable heresies, maintaining, bolstering and admiring the venemous and pestiferous works, erroneous and seditious opinions, of the said Tyndale and others . . . wherein his highness, like a most virtuous and benign prince and governor, having charge of his people and subjects, and being very sorry to hear tell that any of the same should in such wise run headlong and digress from the laws of almighty God and wholesome doctrine of holy fathers into such damnable heresies and seditious opinions, being ever inclined, willed and greatly desirous to foster and provide for the same, and much desiring the reconciliation of the said Frith; and firmly trusting that he be not so far as yet enrooted in the evil doctrine of the said Tyndale but that, by the grace of God, loving, charitable and friendly exhortations and advertisements of good people he may be called again to the right way, has therefor willed me to write unto you that you therefor, according to his trust and expectation, will with your friendly persuasions, admonitions, wholesome exhortations, counsel and advise the said Frith, if you may conveniently speak with the same to leave off his wilful opinions and like a good Christian to return into his native country, where he shall as-

---

[5] John Frith (1503–1533), translator and Protestant martyr. He was imprisoned for assisting Tyndale in an unauthorized Bible translation. Released in 1528, he began to translate and write himself in a decidedly Protestant way, especially in polemics against More and Fisher about purgatory. In 1532 he was imprisoned and a year later burned for heresy.

suredly find the king's highness most merciful and benignly upon his conversion disposed to accept him to his merciful. . . .

Wherefor aftesones* I exhort you and for the love of God not only utterly to foresake, leave and withdraw your affection from the said Tyndale and all his sect, but also, as much as ye can, politically and charitably to allure the said Frith and all such persons being in those parts which in any way you shall know or suppose to be favorers and assistors to the same from all their erroneous mindings and opinions. In which doing, you shall not only highly merit in almighty God, but also deserve high thanks of the king's royal majesty, who will not forget your devoirs* and labors on that behalf, so that his majesty may evidently perceive that you effectually do intend the same.

And as touching your diligent advertisements unto the king's majesty of the number of ships arrived with corn and grain in those parts, he has commanded me in his behalf to give unto you condign* thanks for the same. And being much desirous to know and attain the truth of that matter, his grace has commanded me to write unto you that by all good dexterity, policy and means you shall endeavor yourself to attain to the knowledge of the masters, servants, owners or others that made sale of the said grain brought thither, to the intent that by examination of some his highness might have better knowledge of the rest, and that you shall with all diligence advertise his highness of their names. And in like wise of such other news concerning the Emperor's affairs, the descending of the Turks into Germany, the preparations against him, the gift of money in the low parts,[6] the agreement between him and the Princes of Germany, as you shall hear by merchants or otherwise, most certainly to ascertain his grace by your letters with as much diligence as you can.

Praying you therefor substantially and circumspectly to endeavor yourself to serve the king's highness herein effectually, so that your towardness, good mind, duty of allegiance and service towards his royal majesty may be apparent and notorious* unto the same, which I doubt not shall be to your singular profit and advancement. . . .

Draft, with many lacunae; breaks off abruptly; clerk's hand, much corrected by T. Cromwell.

[6] The Netherlands.

60. To the English Clergy

PRO SP6/6, No. 4/38–43   August [1536]
LP, XI, 377; 159

DURING MUCH of 1535, Cromwell pursued for the king a series of negotiations with the German princes of the new Schmalkaldic League. They demanded financial backing from England as a condition of adherence; but they also wanted the acceptance of the Augsburg Confession as the basis of a Lutheran reformation in England. This price Henry found too high, and it may be doubted that Cromwell found it any more to his liking. But the situation of 1535–1536 did point up the necessity of deriving conclusions from the royal supremacy in religion. The Ten Articles of Religion submitted to Convocation in 1536 answered the need. Their plan is not our main concern here. Rather it is with the more practical matters of reform to which Cromwell gave attention in his circular letter or injunction to the whole of the English clergy. The business of reform did not after all depend entirely on theology, though specific reforms may well be said to rest on theological notions then being contested between conservatives like Gardiner and reformers of a more advanced disposition, Cranmer and Ridley, for example. In the 1536 injunctions, the first of two sets issued under Cromwell's authority as vicegerent, the emphasis clearly is on educational reform of the sort so central to humanist ideas of general reformation. Certainly the most remarkable implication of the injunctions is the layman's responsibility for the quality of religious life in England through an educational program closely associated with the combating of social and economic disorders, which were considered a threat to common well-being.

In the name of God, Amen. In the year of Our Lord God a thousand five hundred six and thirty, and of the most noble reign of our sovereign Lord Henry the Eighth King of England and of France, Defender of the Faith, Lord of Ireland, and in Earth Supreme Head of the Church of England the twenty-eighth year, and the —— day of August, Thomas Cromwell knight, Lord Cromwell, Keeper of the Privy Seal of our said sovereign Lord the King and vicegerent to the same for and concerning all his jurisdiction ecclesiastical within this realm, visiting by the king's highness supreme authority ecclesiastical the people and clergy of the deanery of N by our trusty Commissary Mr. N. N. Doctor of Law, lawfully constitute and deputed for this part, have to the glory of Almighty God, to the king's highness' honor, the public weale of this realm and increase of virtue in the same, appointed and assigned these injunctions[1] ensuing to be kept and observed of the dean, parsons, vicars, curates and stipendiaries resident or having cure of souls or any other spiritual administration within this deanery under the pains hereafter limited and appointed.

The first is that the dean, parsons, vicars and others having cure of soul anywhere within this deanery shall lawfully keep and observe, and as far as in them may lie, shall cause to be kept and observed of others all and singular laws and statutes of this realm made for the abolishing and extirpation of the Bishop of Rome's pretensed power and jurisdiction within this realm and for the establishing and confirmation of the king's authority and jurisdiction within the same, as of the Supreme Head of the Church of England; and shall declare at the least wise once every quarter of a year in their sermons how the Bishop of Rome's usurped power and jurisdiction having no establishment or ground by the law of God was of most just causes taken away and abolished, and that therefore they owe unto him no manner of obedience or subjection. And that the king's power is within his dominions the highest potentate or power unto God, to whom all men within the same dominion by godly commandment owe most loyalty and obedience, afore and above all other powers and potentates in Earth.

Also, in the same their sermons the parsons, vicars and other curates aforesaid shall diligently admonish the parents, masters and governors of youth being within their cure to teach, or cause to be taught, their children even from their infancy their *pater noster*, the articles of the faith, and the ten commandments in their mother tongue. And the same so taught shall cause the said youth often to repeat and understand. And to the intent this may be the more easily done the said curates shall in their sermons deliberately and plainly recite one clause of the said

---

[1] Injunctions were a familiar device of ecclesiastical reform and were of many kinds. Wolsey gave injunctions as legate; bishops gave injunctions in their capacity as ecclesiastical visitors exercising their "ordinary" jurisdiction. Cromwell had earlier given injunctions to the religious orders, as we have already noted.

pater noster, articles or commandments one day and another day til the whole be taught and learned little by little and shall deliver the same in writing or show where printed books containing the same be to be sold to them that can read and will desire the same. And thereto, that the said parents, masters and governors do bestow their children even from their childhood, either to learning or to some other honest exercise, occupation or husbandry, least at any time afterward they be driven for lack of some mystery* or occupation to live by to fall begging, stealing or some other unthriftyness. Since we may see daily through sloth and idleness diverse valiant men fall, some to begging and some to theft and murder, which after brought to calamity and misery, imputes a great power thereof to their friends and governors, which suffered them to be brought up so idly in their youth. Where, if they had been well educated and brought up in some good literature, occupation or mystery, they should, being rulers of their own family, have profited as well themselves as diverse other persons, to the great commodity and ornament of the commonwealth.

Also, that the said parsons, vicars and other curates shall diligently provide that the sacraments and sacramentals be duly and reverently ministered in their parishes. And if at any time it happen them, either by the cases expressed in the statutes[2] of the realm or of the spiritual license given by the king's majesty to be absent from their benefices, they shall leave their cure not to a rude and unlearned person, but to a good, learned and expert curate, that may teach the rude and unlearned of their cure wholesome doctrine and reduce them to the right way that do err; and always let them see that neither they nor their vicars do seek more their own profit than the profit of the souls that they have under their cure or the glory of God.

And to the intent that learned men may hereafter spring for the execution of the premises,[3] every parson, vicar, clerk or beneficed man within this deanery having yearly to dispend in benefices or other promotions of the Church a hundred pounds shall give competent exhibition[4] to one scholar and for as many hundred pounds more as he may dispend to so many scholars

[2] There were often acts of Parliament designed to reform abuses of absenteeism and pluralism, the most recent being those of the 1529 sessions.
[3] That is, that learned men may be produced in order to carry out the provisions of the injunctions.
[4] That is, that a stipend for the exhibition or maintaining of a scholar be established.

more shall give like exhibition in the universities of Oxford and Cambridge or some grammar school, which, after they have perfected in good learning may be partners of their patrons' cure and charge aswell in preaching as otherwise profit the commonwealth with their counsel and wisdom.

Besides this, to the intent that all superstition and hypocrisy crept into diverse men's hearts may vanish away, they shall not set forth or extoll any images; reliquies or miracles for any superstition or lucre, nor allure the people by any enticements to the pilgrimage of any saint (otherwise than is permitted in the articles lately and condescended upon by the clergy of this realm in convocation),[5] as though it were proper or peculiar to that saint to give this commodity or that, since all goodness, health and grace ought to be both asked and looked for only of God, or of the very author of the same. For without him it cannot be given. But they shall exhort aswell their parishoners as other pilgrims, that they do rather apply themselves to the keeping of God's commandments and fulfilling of his works of charity; and persuade them that it does conduce more toward their soul-health, if they do give that to the poor and needy, that they thought to bestow upon the said images and reliquies.

Also, the said clerks shall in no wise any unlawful time nor for any other cause than their honest necessity haunt or resort to any taverns or alehouses. And after their dinner and supper they shall not give themselves to drinking and riot, sitting all day at tables or cards playing or any other unlawful game, and specially with unhonest or unthrifty persons; but when they have such leisure, they shall read or hear somewhat of Holy Scripture, or shall occupy themself with some other like honest exercise. And let them always do those things which may appertain to good congruence and honesty with profit of the commonwealth, having always in mind how they ought to excel all other in purity of life and should be example to all other to live well and christianly.

To this, because the goods of the Church are called the goods of the poor, and at these days nothing is less seen than the poor to be sustained with the same, we will that all parsons

---

[5] Convocation was the legislative assembly of the church in the English provinces of Canterbury and York. One of the consequences of the royal supremacy was that when Convocation opened in 1536 a layman, Sir William Petre, proctor for the vicegerent Thomas Cromwell, took a place above the bishops and archbishops in their own assembly. The Ten Articles were enacted on 11 July 1536.

and vicars and other beneficed men and pensioners within this deanery not being resident upon their benefices, which may dispend yearly twenty pounds or above, either within this deanery or otherwise, do distribute hereafter yearly amongst their poor parishoners or other inhabitants there, in the presence of the churchwardens or some other honest men of the parish, the fortieth part of the fruit and revenues of their said benefices, least they be not unworthily noted of ingratitude which, reserving so many parts to themselves, cannot vouchsafe to impart the fortieth portion thereof amongst the poor people of that parish that is so fruitful and profitable unto them. Also, that all parsons, vicars and clerks having Churches, chapels or mansions within this deanery shall bestow yearly hereafter upon the same mansions or chancels of their churches, being in decay, the fifth part of that their benefices, til they be fully repaired, and the same so repaired shall always keep and maintain in good state.

Item. Whereas certain articles were lately devised and put forth by the king's authority and condescended upon by the prelates and clergy of this realm in convocation, whereof part are necessary to be holden and believed for our salvation, and the other part do concern and touch certain laudable ceremonies, rites and usages of the Church meet and convenient to be kept and used for a decent and a politic order in the same;[6] the said dean, parsons, vicars and other curates shall so open and declare the said articles unto them that be under their cure that they may plainly know and discern which of the said articles be necessary for their salvation and which of the same do but concern the decent and politic order of the said Church; and the first diligently to plant and inculcate into the minds of their parishoners and to show the other to be laudable and expedient and not to be condemned, albeit that no man may reckon himself to be saved by the observing of them. Moreover, that

---

[6] The character of the articles of religion of 1536 was truly adiaphorist, or based on the distinction between things necessary and things indifferent to salvation. Auricular confession and penance are maintained, along with prayers for the dead; but no doctrine of purgatory is given. On justification Melanchthon is cited, but sinners are said to attain justification by contrition and faith joined with charity. The articles are similarly ambiguous with regard to the sacraments; three only are mentioned (baptism, penance, and the eucharist) and defined in an orthodox way. But the validity of the four "lost" sacraments accepted by Catholics is not denied. This ambiguity was both politically and diplomatically wise; it also conformed to an emphasis on a middle way that corresponded to a humanist wish to avoid too strict doctrinal formulations, since such were considered a general cause of disaffection in the life of the church.

they shall declare unto all such as be under their cure the articles likewise devised, put forth and authorized of late for and concerning the abrogation of certain superstitious holidays, according to the effect and purpose of the same articles and persuade their parishoners to keep and observe the same inviolately, as things wholesomely provided, decreed and established by common consent and public authority, for the weale, commodity and profit of all this realm.

All which and singular injunctions we will shall be inviolately observed of the said dean, parsons, vicars, curates, stipendiaries and other clerks and beneficed men, under the pain of suspension and sequestration of the fruits of their benefices, until they have done their duties according to these Injunctions.

Copy; few corrections. Addressed: "Injunctions for the clergy published by the Lord Cromwell Vicegerent to the King, etc., A. 28 H. 8." Endorsed: "To Mr. Wriothesley. Injunctions for the Clergy."

61. To Doctor William Sandwich[1]

PRO SP1/123/174   July [1537][2]
LP, XII, ii, 412; 197

CROMWELL VIGOROUSLY exercised the patronage inherent in his vicar's power over the Church of England. One of the most important instruments of communicating the motives of government to influential segments of the population was the pulpit in the yard of St. Paul's, Paul's Cross as it was commonly known. Whatever had been the state of preaching in England before the Reformation, from the year 1533 government programs received their best explanations Sunday by Sunday at Paul's Cross, beginning with the campaign in behalf of the Act of Appeals in 1533. The control of that pulpit by Cromwell may in fact be viewed as a sign of his power and continued good standing

[1] William Sandwich, warden of Canterbury College, for whose career there is no account whatsoever; see *LP*, XII, i, 437.
[2] The date of the letter as 1537 can be calculated from the perpetual calendar given in C. R. Cheyney, *Handbook of Dates for Students of English History* (London: Royal Historical Society, 1955), pp. 104–5, table eleven, which gives 19 August 1537 as the twelfth Sunday after Trinity Sunday.

with the king. It is also of interest that he chose a man especially versed in holy letters in naming Sandwich. Perhaps the
most famous preachers at St. Paul's Cross were Colet and Latimer in the sixteenth century and John Donne in the early seventeenth.

In my right hearty manner I commend me unto you. And
whereas for the honest report of your learning in holy letters
and incorrupt judgement in the same I have appointed you
amongst others to occupy the room of a preacher one day at
Paul's Cross, these be as well to signify unto you that the said
day so limited for you is the twelfth Sunday after Trinity, being
the nineteenth day of August; as also to require you that you
fail not to be there at the same day, preparing in the mean
time with such good sincereness truly to open the world of God
at the said day, as I may thereby take occasion to think the
report made of you to be true. Whereby you shall not only do
a right good deed, but also minister unto me a thankful pleasure
which I shall not fail to requite as occasion may there unto serve.
And thus fare you well. Your friend.

Clerk's hand; autograph signature. Addressed: "To my loving
friend Doctor Sandwich of Canterbury College in Oxford."
Endorsed: "Mr. Cromwell commanding him to preach at Paul's
Cross."

62. To Roland Lee [1]

PRO SP1/131/126–7   April [1538]
LP, XIII, i, 765; 256

ALMOST IMMEDIATELY after Cromwell gained a hold on power in
Henry VIII's council in 1533, he turned his attention to the
problems of Wales. Indeed, in April 1533 he already intended

[1] Roland Lee (d. 1543), ordained priest in 1512 after a Cambridge education. He followed a legal career and was patronized liberally by Wolsey
before becoming a royal chaplain and master in chancery. From 1534
until his death in 1543, he doubled as president of the Council in the
marches of Wales and bishop of Coventry and Lichfield. His name is
still a term of disdain in Wales, where his effective suppression of march
disorders was his preoccupation from 1534 to 1540.

a council of the marches, as we know from his published memorandums. And in 1534 he appointed the most famous of all march administrators, Roland Lee, to the presidency of the Council of the Marches, only a short time after nominating him to the king for the bishopric of Coventry and Lichfield. After legal training, Lee had entered Wolsey's service where he befriended Gardiner and Cromwell, acting with them in the suppression of religious houses between 1525 and 1528. His friendship with Cromwell was an extraordinarily close one, extending to a common loyalty to Wolsey and the guardianship of Cromwell's son Gregory. A man of great courage, physical vigor, loyalty to the dynasty, he had aristocratic connections with the Manners family and early enthusiasms for humanistic learning and reform. He was a member of Doctors' Commons and an enthusiastic supporter of the Reformation of the 1530's. The most salient feature of his career until 1540 was that he always made sure of Cromwell's attitude about matters within his jurisdiction, civil or ecclesiastical. A steady stream of letters from Lee to Cromwell requests the secretary's advice, opinion, and support. He was always Cromwell's agent, never the independent proconsul. This seems to have been Cromwell's purpose in 1534, for the episcopal appointment provided the funds to support the large entourage of the president of the Council, and it also ensured that all march affairs and those of the diocese of Coventry and Lichfield would be immediately subject to Cromwell's authority in a personal sense. Thus the patronage problem reflected in this letter serves to remind us of something Cromwell's friends knew well when one of them wrote about Lee's promotion to the bishopric: "I shall reckon you bishop there yourself" (*LP*, VIII, 839).

After my right hearty commendations unto your lordship. Forasmuch as my nephew Richard[2] is much desirous to have the disposition and assignment of a prebend* in your Church of Lichfield[3] to prefer a right honest man and a special friend[4] of his thereunto, and for the accomplishment thereof has sent unto you an advowson* all ready written to have a presentation and title of preferment of one of the three named in the said

[2] Richard Williams, alias Cromwell, who took the name of his uncle and served him in household and administrative roles. He was an accomplished soldier and courtier and a favorite of the king even after the execution of his namesake. Oliver Cromwell was his great-grandson.
[3] Lichfield, Staffordshire, 17 miles SE of the county town.
[4] Merriman notes the friend as Simon Jakes, abbot of Killingworth. There is no record of a monastery by that name. The reference must be to Kenilworth Abbey, a house of Augustinian canons in Warwickshire.

vowson, which first shall chance to become vacant there; these shall be to desire and most heartily pray your lordship to tender my said nephew's suit and to send unto him by this bearer the said advowson signed and sealed as well under your seal and the chapter seal of the said church accordingly. Where in your so doing you shall administer unto me such thankful pleasure as I shall not fail to have the same in remembrance when occasion shall occur. Further desiring your lordship to advertise me by your letters of your good conformity herein. Thus most heartily fare your lordship.

Draft, corrected by Cromwell. Endorsed: "The abbot of Kenilworth."

63. To the Bishop of Salisbury[1]

BM Cotton Mss. Cleopatra Eiv, fos. 81–5   March [1538]
LP, XIII, i, 572; 248

CROMWELL'S ACTIVITIES as a patron of reform had brought him into close relationship with both Hugh Faringdon (alias Cook), the remarkable abbot of Reading mentioned in this letter, and with Nicholas Shaxton, his nominee for the bishopric of Salisbury in the year 1535. The latter became one of the stalwarts of reform, often in close association with Cranmer, and always in friendship with the lord privy seal. It was not strange, therefore, to see the reforming bishop in league with Cranmer and Latimer in early 1538 in efforts to enforce royal proclamations commanding the justices of the peace to see that the clergy preached the word of God truly and sincerely. When the Bible in English was ordered set up in every parish, Shaxton ordered his clergy to read a chapter a day and to learn by heart a chapter a fortnight; and he urged every parish to buy an English text from parish funds. His zeal for reform may be said to match that of Cromwell, which we may infer from the fact that he and Latimer were the only bishops to resign in 1539 in protest against the Six Articles. These facts must make more important the letter given here, in which we see Shaxton and Cromwell near the end of a long and deeply argued dispute triggered by

[1] Nicholas Shaxton (1485–1556), favored Henry VIII's views on the Divorce and was promoted at Cromwell's urging in 1535 to the bishopric of Salisbury.

the rather conservative preaching of a monk of Reading, against whom Shaxton made complaints and in whose behalf Cromwell seems to have intervened in defiance of Shaxton's hurt protests about usurpations of episcopal jurisdiction. There is perhaps no finer Cromwellian text for the reader weighing for himself the relevance of the legend of the evil careerist against the picture presented in this Introduction. One still questioning Cromwell's ultimate sincerity, his zeal to edify and create, as Professor Dickens wrote, must look long at this emotional and heartfelt letter of the vicar general, with its prayer and its explicit sense of vocation, and ask why these things meant for a friend's correction should be hypocritical?

My lord, after hearty commendations. I cannot but both much marvel that you, whom I have taken to be my truest friend, should judge me, as I may perceive by your letters[2] you do, and also be glad, that you so frankly utter your stomach to me. I would thank you for your plain writing and monitions, saving that you seem fuller of suspicions than it becomes, as I think, a prelate of your sort to be, and, to say that makes me more sorry, much worse persuaded of me than I thought any of your learning and judgment could have been.

I took a matter out of your hands into mine, if upon consideration mine ofice bid me to do so.[3] What cause have you to complain? If I had done this either upon affection, or intending prejudice dire to your estimation, you might have expostulated with me. And yet, if you then had done it, after a juster sort, I should both sooner have amended that I did amiss and also have had better cause to judge your writings to me of a friendly heart towards me. If you be offended with my sharp letters, how can your letters' words, I had almost given this another name, delight me? I required you to use no extremity in your office; *durus est sic sermo;*[4] you toss it and when you have done, you begin again, even as though all being said, all were still behind. If you have used no extremity, I am, I assure you, as

---

[2] On 21 March, Shaxton wrote to Cromwell that somebody misinformed the minister about his reasons for inhibiting the reader at Reading. He accuses the reader of heresy and states that the preferment is not his concern, but only that heretics be displaced. (*LP*, XIII, i, 571; see also, XIII, i, 147 and 264.)

[3] Cromwell's vicegerency in spiritual matters.

[4] This is a hard sentence! Cromwell refers here to his requiring Shaxton to use no extremity in his office and Shaxton's fierce reaction to that letter in *LP*, XIII, i, 571.

glad of it as I ought to be. And though you do not, yet upon a complaint mine office bids me to succour him that says he is overmatched and is compelled to sustain wrongs.[5] I was thus informed and by persons to whom I gave much credit than I intend to do hereafter, if they have abused me, as you would make me believe they have. They thus complaining, could I do any less than grant unto them such remedy as the king's highness and his laws give indifferently to all his subjects? Might I not also somewhat gather that you proceded the sorer against the Reader, Roger London,[6] when I had seen how much you desired the preferment of your servant to that room?[7]

My lord, you had showed yourself of much more patience, I would not say of much more prudence, if you had contented yourself with their lawful appeal and my lawful injunctions, and rather have sought fully to instruct me in the matter, than thus to desire to conquer me; by shrewd words to vanquish me, by sharp threats of scripture, which, as I know to be true, so I trust to God, as great a clerk as you be, you allege them out of their place. It becomes me not, whether yet I am wont, to vaunt myself of well doing. I know who works all that is wrought by me and who, as he is the whole doer, I intend not to offer him this wrong: he to labor and I to take the thanks. Yet, as I do not cease to give thanks that it has pleased his goodness to use me as an instrument and to work somewhat by me, so, I trust, I am as ready to serve him in my calling, to my little power, as you a priest to write worse of me than you ought to think. My prayer is that God give me no longer life than I shall be glad to use mine office in edifications and not in destructions, as you bear me in hand I do. God, you say, will judge such using of authority, meaning flatly that I do abuse such power as has pleased God and the king's highness to set me in. God, I say, will judge, such judges as you, and charity also such thoughts as you misuse.

You do not so well as I would you should do, if you think of me as your letters make me think you do. The crime that you charge me withal is greater than I may or ought to bear,

---

[5] Either Roger London or the abbot of Reading, Hugh Faringdon. For the fate of the Reading community, see Knowles, *The Religious Orders in England,* III, 378f.

[6] Roger London, reader at the Benedictine abbey at Reading, Berkshire.

[7] On 12 February 1538 Salisbury thanked Cromwell for letters written to Faringdon on the behalf of his (Shaxton's) servant; *LP,* XIII, i, 264.

untruer I trust than they that would feign shall be able to prove. It is a strange thing you say, that I would neither write nor send you word by mouth what you should do with the popish monks of Abingdon,[8] and that the Abbot of Reading[9] could get straight away my letters to inhibit your just doings. I wiss* that was not my mind, when I wrote. I did not intend to let your just doings, but rather to require you to do justly. Neither I was swift in granting my letters to him; albeit I am much readier to help him that complains of wrong than priest to further on that desire punishments of a person whom I am not sure has offended. I made you no answer: a strange thing, I wiss, my Lord. I thought you had better known my businesses than for such a matter to esteem me not your friend. You might have better judged that I was too much cumbered with other affairs, that those who sued for the abbot could better spy their time than you could. Some men will rather think you utter displeasure conceived before than that you have any urgent occasion here to misjudge my mind towards you. As concerning your matter, you must use your privileges as things lent unto you, so long as you shall occupy them well, that is according to the mind and pleasure of them that gave you them.[10]

I took neither the monks cause nor any other in my hands to be a bearer of any such whom their upright dealing is not able to bear. No. You know I think that I love such readers of scripture as well as you do. Would God men of your sort were as diligent to see that in all their dioceses good were made as I am glad to remove the evil, when I know them. If you had taken then even half the pain to send up such things against him as you now send, neither you should have had cause, no, nor occasion, thus rashly to determine of my good or evil will toward you, nor I have been encumbered with this answer.

My lord, I pray you which I am, your friend, take me to be so. For if I were not, or if I knew any cause why I ought not, as I would not be afraid to show you, so you should well perceive that my displeasure should last no longer than there were

---

[8] Abingdon, a Benedictine abbey in Berkshire. Shaxton wrote Cromwell on 14 February 1538 asking for instructions concerning a papist monk of that house too ill to travel to London for interrogation; *LP*, XIII, i, 275.
[9] Hugh Faringdon or Cook, a remarkable abbot and the last at Reading, executed in 1539 for treason related to his resistance to the surrender of his house, but earlier a supporter of many humanist enterprises of reform.
[10] Cromwell here states facts and also perhaps threatens.

cause. I pass over your *nemo l—itur nisi a seipso*[11] I pray with
you this first part: our Lord have pity upon me. The other part
is not in my prayers, that God should turn my heart. For he is
my judge: I may err in my doings for want of knowledge, [but]
I willingly bear no misdoers. I willingly hurt none whom honesty
and the king's laws do not refuse. Undo not yourself. I intend
nothing less than to work you any displeasure. If hitherto I
have showed you any pleasure, I am glad of it. I showed it to
your qualities and not to you. If they tarry with you, my good
will cannot depart from you, except your prayer be heard; that is
my heart be turned. I assure you I am right glad you are in the
place you are in and will do what shall lie in me to aid you in
your office, to maintain your reputation, to give you credit
amongst your flock and elsewhere, as long as I shall see you
desireful to do your duty according to your calling. I will not
become your good lord, as your desire is; I am and have been
your friend and take you to be mine. Caste out vain suspicion.
Let rash judgment rule men of lesser wits and discretion. Will-
fulness becomes all men better than a bishop, which should
always search in to lack gladly our own will. Because you may
not have your own will herein *deus pauperem facit et ditat,* with
dominus dedit et dominus abstulit:[12] to what purpose? *Sit nomen
domini benedictur*[13] can never lack his place; it comes always
in season, or else, as great a divine as you are, I would say it
were not even the best place here, except you had meant better
you had lost all than any part of your will. I pray you, teach
patience better in your deeds, or else speak as little of it as
you can.

My lord, you might have guilted another in my place that
would have used less patience with you, finding so little in you.
But I can take your writings and this heave of your stomach
even as well as I can. I must beware of flatterers. As for the
Abbot of Reading and his monks, if I find them as you say
they are, I will order them as I think good. You shall do well
to do your duty; if you so do, you shall have no cause to mistrust my friendship. If you do not, I must tell it you, and it
somewhat after the plainest sort. To take a controversey out
of your hands into mine I do but my office. You meddle further

[11] *Nemo leditur nisi a se ipso!* No one is harmed except he harm himself.
The text is at this point actually too blemished to read. But Shaxton-
Cromwell, BM Cotton Mss. Cleopatra Eiv, fos. 79–80, supplies Shaxton's
words, which Cromwell quotes.
[12] God makes the pauper and enriches him! The Lord gives and takes away.
[13] Blessed is the name of the Lord!

than your office will bear you, thus roughly to handle me for using of mine. If you do no more, I let pass all that is past and offer you such kindness as you shall lawfully desire at my hands. Thus fare you well.

Draft in Richard Moryson's hand; corrected by T. Cromwell.

64. To an Unknown Bishop

BM Cotton Mss. Cleopatra Eiv, fos. 9–10   [June 1538]
LP, XIII, i, 1304; 266

CROMWELL'S EXPECTATION that a Bible would be available in English in the autumn of 1538 was upset by events in Paris at the Sorbonne, where the French printing of Grafton's "Great Bible" was seized and not released for a very long time, with the consequence that it was not before April 1539 that that book appeared for sale in London. But the general expectation of a Bible in English was welcome to reformers, and Latimer had anticipated its availability when in late 1537 he ordered each clerk in his diocese to obtain by Christmas a Bible (New Testament only) in Latin and English, and to read a chapter daily. It was that expectation to which the royal proclamation of early 1538 also referred and to which Shaxton looked in the orders he made within his diocese. And it was to that proclamation and the printing projects sponsored by himself that Cromwell looked in the spring of 1538, when he issued a circular letter to all or some of the bishops. That letter was meant to bring pressure to bear in behalf of reform. Hearing that the king's ordinances are sometimes not observed closely, he commands the bishops to open the English Bible in their own houses and to otherwise provide and exhort to the reading of scripture. We know from later evidence that the degree of compliance with Cromwell's letter and the later injunctions in which the subject of the Bible figured largely was not constant. In Lincoln diocese, for example, by autumn 1539 many parishes had no Bibles as yet, either because there were no copies or because of slackness and apathy among some clergy and some parish vestrymen, to whom the expense was appointed.

After my right hearty commendations. Whereas the king's highness, minding to set forth the glory of God and the truth of his Word, has as well in his own person and by other his ministers travailed to bring the same plainly and sincerely to the knowledge of his subjects; and for that purpose not only in the late visitation exercised by authority of his majesty but also at other times and other ways has ordained many godly ordinances and injunctions and given also sundry straight commandments, as well to you as to all other persons ecclesiastical of all sorts and degrees within this his realm; for as much as it is come to his grace's knowledge that his said ordinances, commandments and injunctions have been very remissly hitherto observed, kept and obeyed within your diocese, and his highness' people there for want of the sincere and true teaching of the Word of God suffered to live and dwell continually in their old ignorance and blindness, his grace's pleasure and express commandment is that you, having a more vigilant eye and better respect to his highness' said commandments and ordinances, cause the same and every of them to be duly published and observed. Forseeing as well in your own person and by your archdeacons, chancellors, officials, deans rural and other ministers that all curates and other persons ecclesiastical as after these many callings over shall be found negligent, remiss or stubborn in the fulfillment of them or any of them, receive for the transgression in that behalf such punishment as in the said ordinances is contained and more, as to your discretions shall be seen mete and convenient. And further, his grace's pleasure and high commandment is that you with no less circumspection and diligence cause the *Bible* in English to be laid forth openly in your own houses[1] and that the same be in like manner openly laid forth in every parish church, at the charge and costs of the parsons and vicars; that every man having free access to it, by reading of the same may both be the more apt to understand the declaration of it at the preacher's mouth, and also the more able to teach and instruct his wife, children and family at home; commanding nevertheless all curates and other preachers within that your diocese that they at all times, and specially now at the beginning, exhort and require the people to use and read the *Bible* so left amongst them according to the tenor of my instructions, which you shall receive herein enclosed,[2] to be sent to every curate

---

[1] Since the address is lost, this clause is vital for the inference that this may be a draft form of a circular letter.

[2] These instructions cannot be the injunctions of 1538, as those were not issued until September. See Dickens, *The English Reformation*, pp. 131–4.

within a certain day by you to be appointed, within the which the *Bible* in English be as is aforesaid laid forth in every church.

Draft, William Petre's hand; corrected by T. Cromwell.

65. To the Clergy of England

PRO SP6/3/No. 1   5 September [1538]
LP, XIII, ii, 281; 273

THE OFFICIAL formularies of the faith of the new church in England began with the Ten Articles of 1536 and Cromwell's injunctions of that year. These were followed by the Bishop's Book in 1537, the result of a commission of ecclesiastics, the king, and Cranmer debating together the necessary truths of religion. In the summer of 1538 that book was given unofficial approval, and the new injunctions were shortly thereafter put forward. These may be said to mark the high-water level of humanist influence on English Reformation thought, since in the following year the conservative Six Articles clearly retreated from the principles that had dominated from 1536 to 1539. While the Ten Articles had exhibited the basically Erasmian distinction of things necessary and things indifferent to salvation, they were an ambiguous and mild amalgam of tradition and innovation. But in Cromwell's two sets of injunctions we have a very direct statement of humanist criticism and goals. Those of 1538 may in fact be said to embody most of the major tenets of the humanistic religious ideal of the *philosophia christi*, from the vernacular Bible through the reformation of the preaching clergy and popular instruction in the essential truths of the religion. The emphasis on family instruction, the reduction of holidays and ceremonies, the critique of pilgrimages and other observations together constitute a program expounded by Erasmus and other critics of a humanist bent, without labels as deceptively simple as Catholic and Protestant. And through it all shines the insistence on the availability of scripture. Cromwell's role in the Reformation was symbolically as well as directly expressed in the Bible of the "largest volume," for the famous engraving on the title page, possibly Holbein's art, showed Cranmer distributing the book to the clergy and Cromwell to the laity under the supreme government of the king. It was a pictorial statement of official reform.

Exhibit quinto die mensis Septembris Anno domini 1538.

In the name of God Amen. By the authority and commission of the most excellent Prince Henry, by the grace of God king of England and France, defensor of the Faith, Lord of Ireland and in earth supreme head under Christ of the Church of England, I Thomas Lord Cromwell, lord privy seal, vice-gerent to the king's said highness for all his jurisdiction ecclesiastical within his realm, do for the enforcement of the true honor of almighty God, increase of virtue and discharge of the king's majesty give and exhibit unto you ———— these injunctions following, to be kept, observed and fulfilled upon the pains hereafter declared.

First, that you shall truly observe and keep all and singular the king's highness' injunctions given unto you heretofore in my name by his grace's authority, not only upon the pains herein expressed, but also in your default now after this second monition continued upon further punishment to be straightly extended towards you by the king's highness arbitrement or his vice-gerent aforesaid.

Item. That you shall provide on this side [of] the feast of All Saints[1] next coming one book of the whole bible of the largest volume in English[2] and the same set up in some convenient place within the said Church that you have cure of, whereas your parishioners may most commodiously resort to the same and read it. The charges of which book shall be ratably* born between you the person and the parishioners aforesaid, that is to say the one half by you and the other half by them.

Item. That you shall discourage no man privily or apertly from the reading or hearing of the said bible, but shall expressly provoke, steer and exhort to every person to read the

---

[1] The first of November.

[2] Cromwell was working feverishly to secure a Bible that would answer the demand made in the injunctions. He had collaborated with Miles Coverdale in establishing a publishing venture based in Paris and supervised by Richard Grafton and Edward Whitechurch. But that plan was displaced by Francis I's yielding to the Sorbonne authorities and seizing the book before it could be assembled and exported. The Paris Bible and the substitute upon which Richard Taverner was then hard at work figure prominently in an episode of diplomacy in which Cromwell may well have bargained jurisdiction in the Rochepot Affair (see letter 41) for the release of his precious Paris Bible. Mr. Abe Hoffman of my doctoral seminar recently studied the evidence linking the Bible and the case of Rochepot, the constable of France's own brother, and convincingly concluded that Cromwell's interest in the Rochepot affair was not one of personal enrichment, a charge against which he had to defend himself in 1540, but rather one of reform.

same as that which is the very lively word of God that every Christian person is bound to embrace, believe and follow, if they look to be saved; admonishing them nevertheless to avoid all contentions and altercation therein, but to use an honest sobriety in the inquisition of the true sense of the same and to reserve the explication of obscure places to men of higher judgement in scripture.

Item. That you shall every Sunday and holiday through the year openly and plainly recite to your parishioners twice or thrice together or oftener, if need require, one particle or sentence of the *pater noster* or creed in English, to the intent they may learn the same by heart; and so from day to day to give them one like lesson or sentence of the same, till they have learned the whole *pater noster* and creed in English by rote. And as they be taught every sentence by rote, you shall expound and declare the understanding of the same unto them, exhorting all parents and householders to teach their children and servants the same, as they are bound in conscience to do. And that done, you shall declare unto them the ten commandments, one-by-one, every Sunday and holiday, till they be likewise perfect in the same.

Item. That you shall in confessions every Lent examine every person that comes to confession unto you, whether they can recite the articles of our faith and the *pater noster* in English and hear them say the same particularly; wherein, if they be not perfect, you shall declare to the same that every Christian person ought to know the same before they should receive the blessed sacrament of the altar, and monish* them to learn the same more perfectly by the next year following or else, like as they ought not to presume to come to God's board without perfect knowledge of the same. And if they do, it is to the great peril of their souls. So you shall declare unto them that you look for other injunctions from the king's highness, by that time to stay and repel all such from God's board as shall be found ignorant in the premisses whereof you do thus admonish them; to the intent they should both eschew the peril of their souls and also the worldly rebuke that they might incur hereafter by the same.

Item. That you shall make or cause to be made in the said Church and every other cure you have one sermon every quarter of a year at the least, wherein you shall purely and sincerely declare the very Gospel of Christ and in the same exhort your hearers to the works of charity, mercy and faith specially pre-

scribed and commanded in scripture and not to repose their
trust or affiance in any other works devised by mens' phantasies
besides scripture; as in wandering to pilgrimages, offering of
money, candles or tapers to images or relics or kissing or licking
the same, saying over a number of beads not understood or
minded, or in any other such like superstition; for the doing
whereof you not only have no promise of reward in scripture,
but contrarywise, great threats and maledictions of God, as
things tending to idolatry and superstition, which of all other
offenses God almighty doth most detest and abhor for that the
same diminished most his honor and glory.

Item. That such images as you know in any of your cures to
be so abused with pilgrimages or offerings of anything in aid
thereunto, you shall for avoiding of that most detestable offence
of idolatry forthwith take down and deley* and shall suffer
from henceforth no candles, taper or images of wax to be set
afore any images or picture, but only the light that commonly
goes across the Church by the rood loft,* the light afore the
sacrament of the altar and the light about the sepulchre, which
for the adjourning of the Church and divine service you shall
suffer to remain still; admonishing your parishioners that images
serve for no other purpose but as to be books of unlearned men
that can [read or do] no letters; whereby they might be otherwise admonished of the lives and conversation of them that the
said images do represent, which images, if they abuse for any
other intent than for such remembrances, they commit idolatry
in the same, to the great danger of their souls. And, therefore,
the king's highness, greatly tendering the weale of his subjects'
souls, has in part already and more will hereafter travail for
the abolishing of such images as might be occasion of so grave
an offence to God and so great danger to the souls of his loving
subjects.

Item. That in all such benefices or cures as you have whereupon you be not yourself resident, you shall appoint such curates
in your stead as both can by their ability and will also promptly
execute these injunctions and do their duty otherwise that you
are bound to do in every behalf accordingly and may profit their
cure no less with good examples of living than with declarations
of the word of God; or else, their lack and defaults shall be
imputed unto you, who shall straightly answer for the same if
they do otherwise.

Item. That you shall admit no man to preach within any of
your benefices or cures but such as shall appear unto you to be

sufficiently licensed by the king's highness or his grace's authority by the archbishop of Canterbury or the bishop of this diocese; and such as shall be so licensed, you shall gladly receive to declare the word of God, without any resistance or contradiction.

Item. If you have heretofore declared anything to your parishioners to the extolling or setting forth of any pilgrimages, relics or images or any such superstition, you shall now openly afore the same recant and reprove the same, showing them (as the truth is) that you did the same upon no ground of scripture but as one being led and seduced by a common error and abuse crept into the Church through the sufferance and avarice of such as felt profit by the same.

Item. If you do or shall know any man within your parish or elsewhere that is a letter* 'of the word of God to be read in English or sincerely preached or of the execution of these injunctions or a servitor of the Bishop of Rome's pretensed power, now by the laws of this realm justly rejected and extirped, you shall detect and present the same to the king's highness or his honorable council or to his vice-gerent aforesaid, or to the justice of the peace next adjoining.

Item. That you and every parson, vicar or curate within this diocese shall for every church keep one book of register wherein you shall write the day and year of every wedding, christening and burial made within your parish for your time and so every man succeeding you likewise, and shall there insert every person's name that shall be wedded, christened or buried. And for the safe keeping of the same book the parish shall be bounded to provide of their common charge one sure coffer, with two locks and keys, whereof the one to remain with you and the other with the said wardens, wherein the said book shall be laid up. Which book you shall every Sunday take forth and in the presence of the said wardens or one of them write and record in the same all the weddings, christenings and buryings made the whole week before; and that done, to lay up the said book in the said coffer, as before. And for every time that the same shall be omitted, the party that shall be in the fault thereof shall. forfeit to the said church 3s. 4d., to be employed on the reparation of the same church.

Item. That you shall one evening every quarter of a year read these and the other former injunctions given unto you by authority of the king's highness openly and deliberately before all your parishioners, to the intent that both you by the same may be the better admonished of your duty and your said parishioners the more incited to deserve the same for their part.

All which and singular injunctions I minister unto you and your successors by the king's highness' authority to me committed in this part, which I charge and command you by the same authority to observe and keep upon pain of deprivation, sequestration of your fruits or such other coersion as to the king's highness or his vice-gerent for the time being shall be seen convenient.

Wriothesley's hand; autograph signature, with few corrections. Endorsed: "Injunctions devised by the Lord Cromwell vice-gerent to the King for all his jurisdiction ecclesiastical."

66. To Sir Thomas Wyatt

BM Harleian Mss. 282, fos. 217–8   28 November 1538
LP, XIII, ii, 924; 281   London

In July of 1538 Francis I and Charles V had met at Aigues-mortes, the ancient port of departure for Crusaders, apparently in fulfillment of the obligations of the Holy League—from which England had been excluded. Paul III was also present. But, as the summer wore on, it appeared that another Crusade, this one against the Turk on the Thames, might be intended. Reports began to come in of papal agents negotiating with the Geraldine Earl of Desmond in Ireland. Also, informers in the west of England were uncovering what looked like an alarming conspiracy in which the White Rose of York, represented by the Pole family, in alliance with the Courtenay Marquis of Exeter, had linked its future with that of Rome in England. At the same time severe internal disturbances were occasioned by the campaign started by Cromwell against the shrines and pilgrimage stations of England and its dominions. By December the so-called Exeter conspiracy was over and the leading plotters executed. But on 28 November that pass had not been reached. And above all, there was the increasingly vexing question of what to do with truly radical religious ideas, especially those that touched the sacrament of the altar, a problem we have seen developing at Calais and now in the center of the kingdom of England itself. Cromwell's description of the king playing his quasi-sacerdotal role throws light on the king, certainly; but it throws even more light on the degree to which king and minister alike distrusted radical reform in doctrine as distinct from practice. When writing of these things to his close associate, Cromwell had no need to dissemble, for Wyatt was a friend of reform perhaps more to the left than was Cromwell. The minister clearly thought the ambassador would be in agreement with him in detesting sacramentarians. Other matters intrude in a busy letter, and there is the charming touch in which we see Cromwell gently acknowledging that he supports the debts of friends perhaps too willingly. Diplomacy, reform, treason, and *res privata* mixed in him so easily; that is both his enduring importance and his greatness.

Mr. Wyatt, after my hearty commendations. I have received by this bearer, Nicholas[1] the courrier, your letters[2] directed to the king's highness, signed by you and my friend Hoby,[3] and also another letter in cipher, the which have been both delivered unto his majesty, like as by the answer his grace sends unto you you may amply know. Doubtless I think no need to require you to use your accustomed dexterity in setting forth the same after your best sort and to utter every point thereof in such terms, order and place as upon the disposition, inclination, answers, occurences and circumstances there you shall by your discretion know most convenient to bring his majesty's purposes to pass and to the conclusion his highness most desires. I assure you your diligence and dexterity to be used therein shall be much commended and praised, if as my hope is, the things by your good setting forth may take effect; nevertheless, the same to be thankfully taken, however the matters shall succeed.[4] For it is well known you want no good heart and alacrity, and that his majesty considers well and continues your gracious and benign lord. For my part, you may be certain that I bear unto you no less good will and sincere affection than I was wont. The effect has been and shall be my witness thereof.

Concerning the two hundred pounds which you lent to Sir Francis Brian:[5] whosoever owes them, I have disbursed them

---

[1] Nicholas de Pelle or Pelley, a courier.

[2] *LP*, XIII, ii, 786, Wyatt to Cromwell, 9 November 1538, concerning the Infant of Portugal as a partner for Mary.

[3] Sir Philip Hoby (1505–1558), diplomatist, accompanied Wyatt on his embassy; later ambassador to Charles V and also Francis I.

[4] The prospective betrothal of Mary and the Infant.

[5] The king's friend, Anne Boleyn's cousin, ambassador to Clement VII, and a great courtier-poet.

and paid to Mr. Bonvixi.[6] Other men make in manner of their debts mine own. For very oft where they have borrowed I am feigned to pay. You have to mine opinion by way of Flanders been advertised how the lord Marquis of Exeter[7] and the Lord Montague,[8] with a sort of their adherents, of many of late and no estimation, have greatly been commanded to the Tower, to prison there, for sundry great crimes of lèse majesté traiterously imagined and uttered as far as they durst, against the king's royal person, his issue, his council and the whole realm, so that it abhors any man to hear of it. And the same their offenses be not known by light suspicions, but by certain proofs and confessions. I doubt not but when their conspirations shall be disclosed and their ingratitude towards the king, their sovereign lord, to whom they [ought] to give most humble thanks for all that they had and for that state they were in, all honest hearts shall have abomination at their miserable wretchedness and traiterous malice.

Other occurences of importance we have none here. The king's majesty, my lord prince's grace, my ladies his daughters and the rest of the council be all merry and in good prosperity.

The 14th day of this present, the king's majesty for the reverence of the holy sacrament of the altar, did sit openly in his hall and there presided at the disputation, process and judgment of a miserable heretic sacramentary, who was burnt the 20th of the same month.[9] It was a wonder to see how princely, with how

---

[6] Antonio Bonvisi (d. 1558), a merchant of Italian descent, although probably born in London. He dealt in wool, jewels, and luxury goods; he was also banker to Henry VIII. He was among Cromwell's close friends.

[7] Henry Courtenay (1496?–1538), marquis of Exeter and earl of Devonshire. He was a grandson of Edward IV and thus had a close claim to the throne. His involvement with the Pole group gave Henry the legal reason to cut off yet another stem of the White Rose.

[8] Sir Henry Pole, Lord Montague (1492?–1538). He was very much against the Dissolution and the abrogation of the pope's power in England, but he remained loyal to the king until the confession of his brother, Sir Geoffrey, involved him in the Exeter conspiracy, for which he was executed.

[9] John Lambert's trial well illustrates the difficulties of Cromwell and his supporters. A fellow of Queen's College, Cambridge, Lambert was converted to Protestantism by Thomas Bilney. At Antwerp he was associated with Frith and Tyndale, where he was entrapped and, on More's insistence, sent back to England. After house imprisonment in Warham's house at Otford, he was released at the archbishop's death, when he went to London and kept a school there. In 1536 Norfolk attacked him for heretical views about the saints. Cranmer, Latimer, and Shaxton were named by Cromwell to hear the charges, and the case was composed by

excellent gravity and inestimable majesty his highness exercised there the very office of a supreme head of his Church of England, how benignly his grace assayed to convert the miserable man, how strong and manifest reasons his highness alleged against him. I wished the princes and potentates of Christendom to have a mete place for them to have seen it. Undoubtedly they should have much marvelled at his majesty's most high wisdom and judgment and reputed him none otherwise after the same than in manner the mirror and light of all other kings and princes in Christendom. The same was openly done with great solemnity, whereby I doubt not but some of your friends that have good leisure shall by their letters advertise you of the whole discourse thereof.

So without further recit* (save to indicate unto you) that forasmuch as it is by sundry complaints showed unto the king's majesty that his grace's subjects, John Toles, Richard Fermour and other their consorts, merchants of London,[10] and besides them sundry of his grace's subjects both of this realm and other dominions, be protracted there without any expedition of sundry processes and suits they have, touching many depredations and robberies by the Emperor's subjects committed against them; as it is like they have had recourse some of them unto you, you shall at your opportune occasion after dispatch of his grace's affairs take your time to solicit the Emperor to ordain that they may have brief justice and reason by his judges manifested unto them there and that they may be no longer tracted* and delayed in their suits, to the utter undoing of one of them. The king's highness has granted unto them a letter to the said Emperor of the same tenor, requiring him to cause justice to be ministered, with declarations that his majesty has appointed you to solicit their expedition. You shall do well and charitably to help them of your intercession, both to the Emperor and to his privy council, to obtain short judgment and final end in their matters.

---

them to allow him to maintain that prayers to the saints, while not necessary, were not sinful. This Lambert refused to do. He was then kept in prison by Audley for a while. But after so much luck and protection from Cromwell's allies in reform, in 1538, while again at liberty, Lambert foolishly wrote some very dangerous opinions on the eucharist, which were turned over to Robert Barnes, a member of the commission to extirpate Anabaptist errors. Henry debated with Lambert, dressed in white, as if to symbolize "an awful purity." Cranmer tried to reason gently with Lambert; but the king was relentless, and finally Cromwell had to read out the sentence of death.

[10] I cannot further identify these merchants.

Also to desire you that you shall call upon the Emperor to send
instructions full and ample into Flanders for expedition of the
matters, and that the king's highness' ambassador shall not remain there without business, but everyone provide to the expedition of their affairs. Not failing after your accustomed fashion to
use diligence in giving advertisements of all the answer you
shall have, their occurrences, and other things whereof you may
attain any familiarity, being of any importance. I commit you
to our Blessed Lord's custody and keeping, who preserve you;
from London, this 28th day of November, 1538. Your assured
loving friend.

P.S. At the time of the condemnation of the sacramentary, the
king's highness caused some proclamations to be made, the
copy whereof in private you shall receive herein.[11]

Clerk's hand; Cromwell's signature. Addressed: "To my very loving friend Sir Thomas Wyatt Knight, the king's ambassador with
the Emperor." Endorsed: "From my Lord Privy Seal, the 28th
of November, letter by Nicholas the Courrier."

[11] The proclamation meant is doubtless the one prohibiting unlicensed
printing of scripture, exiling Anabaptists, depriving married clergy of their
benefices, and removing St. Thomas à Becket from the calendar of saints'
days; 16 November 1538, the draft of which survives in BM Cleopatra
Eiv, fo. 431. For the best printed version, see Hughes and Larkin, *Tudor
Royal Proclamations*, I, pp. 270–6.

67. To Bishop Robert Holgate[1]

BM Cotton Mss. Cleopatra Eiv, fo. 8   7 January [1539][2]
LP, XIII, i, 40; 236   The Rolls

THE CONTEXT of this letter from Cromwell to his staunch ally and dependent is easily established. In 1538 the new injunctions and the setting up of the Bible in English had been ordered. But this had an effect ·sometimes the reverse of that intended and, instead of providing a basis for new harmony, often set men contending about the new guides to devotion and their interpretation. The problems were of a serious enough nature to warrant the issuance of a circular letter from the crown to the bishops and curates, and also to prompt proclamations prohibiting the unlicensed printing of scripture and the excessive exposition and reading of holy letters. Holgate was not one of the bishops with whom we would expect Cromwell to have trouble, since the former head of the Gilbertine house at Sempringham was favorable to reform. This letter must perhaps be read in the context of a circular letter of general address to the bishops as a body of men responsible for the enforcement of the king's letters and proclamations rather than as a complaint addressed to the president of the Council of the North only.[3]

---

[1] Robert Holgate (1481–1555), bishop of Llandaff, later president of the Council of the North and archbishop of York. He was nominated to the prior's post at Sempringham with Cromwell's help and advanced by him to the very vital post of president, though he was a relatively obscure divine and administrator. Holgate's loyalty to reform and his great accomplishments in the North again are testimony to Cromwell's shrewd reading of men of affairs of the skill of Roland Lee and Holgate.

[2] The date given by Merriman and *LP* is 1538, which seems unlikely to me. The sense of the letter and the reference to the king's charge to the clergy indicate a date after the events referred to in the headnote, and are supported by a reading of Strype, *Ecclesiastical Memorials*, I, 302–4, as well as of the proclamation of 16 November 1538: Hughes and Larkin, *Tudor Royal Proclamations*, I, 270–6.

[3] This letter Merriman attributes to Cromwell and claims it was sent to Llandaff. That Cromwell made corrections in it in his own hand is evident. But the authority for attaching it to Holgate is a note in Robert Cotton's hand at fo. 8, verso, as the flyleaf containing the contemporary address and endorsements is lost. Moreover, Cleopatra Ev, fo. 302 is erroneously described by Merriman as a "copy" of the present document. Cleopatra Ev, fo. 302 is rather another letter *also signed by Cromwell*, a letter show-

After my right hearty commendations to your lordship. You shall herewith receive the king's highness' letters addressed unto you, to put you in remembrance of his highness' travails and your duty touching order to be taken for preaching, to the intent the people may be taught the truth and yet not charged at the beginning with over many novelties, the publication whereof, unless the same be tempered and qualified with much wisdom, do rather breed contention, division and contrariety in opinion in the unlearned multitude, than either edification or remove from them and out of their hearts such abuses as by the corrupt and unsavory teaching of the Bishop of Rome and his disciples have crept in the same. The effect of which letters, albeit I doubt not but aswell for the honesty of the matter as for your own discharge, you will so consider and put in execution as shall be to his grace's satisfaction in that behalf. Yet for as much as it has pleased his majesty to appoint and constitute me in the room and place of his supreme and principal minister in all matters that may touch anything his clergy or their doings, I thought it also my part, for the exoneration of my duty towards his highness, and the rather to answer to his grace's expectation, opinion and trust conceived in me, and in that among other committed to my fidelity; to pray and desire you in such circumstantial sort and manner to travail in the execution of the contents of his grace's said letters, namely for avoiding of contrariety in preaching and of the pronunciation of novelties without wise and discreet qualification and the repression of the temerity of those that either privily or apertly, directly or indirectly, would advance the pretended authority of the Bishop of Rome.

As I be not for my discharge both enforced to complain further and to declare what I have now written unto you for that purpose, and for to charge you with your own fault and to devise such remedy for the same as shall appertain, desiring your lordship to accept my meaning herein, tendering only to an honest, friendly and christian reformation for avoiding of further inconvenience and to think none unkindness; though in this matter wherein it is almost more than time to speak, I write frankly, compelled and enforced thereunto both in respect of my private duty and otherwise for my discharge, for as much as it pleases his majesty to use me in the lieu of a councillor,

---

ing only minor variants from this one, and those in phrasing only. This is indicative of the fact that Cromwell may well have sent a letter of this sort to all, or a number of, bishops in order to reinforce the king's will.

whose office is as an eye to the Prince, to forsee and in time to provide remedy for such abuses, enormities and inconveniences as might else with a little sufferance engender more evil in his public weale, than could be after redubbed with much labor, study, diligence and travail. And thus most heartily fare you well, from the Rolls, the 7th of January. Your lordship's friend.

Clerk's hand; autograph signature.

68. To the Bishop of Salisbury [1]

PRO SP1/160/113–4   31 May [1540]
LP, XV, 717; 346   London

THIS LETTER to John Capon, with whom Cromwell had been for years associated in Wolsey's service, reminds us that a good number of the bishops alive in 1540 were nominated to their sees by Cromwell. Along with Capon, we find Holgate and Lee at the top level of reform-minded administrators. Cranmer, Latimer, Aldridge of Carlisle, Bird of Bangor, Bonner, Edward Fox, Goodrich of Ely, John Hilsey, and Shaxton also secured appointments during Cromwell's ministry and in the aura of his patronage. Such facts help us to account for the obvious ease with which Cromwell exploited patronage in church matters, quite apart from any less friendly assertion of his power in mid-Tudor politics.

   After my right hearty commendations unto your good lordship. These be for as much as my friend John Walgrave Esquier,[2] patron of the parsonage of Hilperton[3] in the county of Wiltshire and in your diocese, has presented unto you a sufficient clerk to be parson there upon the death of the late incumbent;[4] to

[1] John Capon (alias Salcot; d. 1557), a Benedictine monk and lawyer in Wolsey's service. Like so many of the cardinal's men, he turns up in Cromwell's affinity after 1532.
[2] John Walgrave or Waldegrave, perhaps a relative of Edward Waldegrave, a receiver in Augmentations and relative of Cromwell's agent Thomas Wriothesley.
[3] Hilperton, Wiltshire, two miles NE of Trowbridge.
[4] I have been unable to identify any incumbent deceased in 1540. The meaning may well be that the patronage is an expectancy or reversion.

require you to admit the said clerk without any delay, as to your office does appertain. Whereby besides that you shall do therein that right and reason require you shall administer unto me right thankful pleasure, which I shall be glad in semblable wise to requite. Thus heartily fare you well. At my house in London the last day of May. Your lordship's assured.

Wriothesley's hand; autograph signature (Thomas Essex).[5] Addressed: "To my very good lord the Bishop of Salisbury." Endorsed: "My LPS to the Bishop of Salisbury ultimo Maii."

69. To Lord Lisle

PRO SP3/2/118   3 March [1536]
LP, X, 405; 140   London

CONCERNING LORD LISLE (ARTHUR PLANTAGENET)

THE EIGHT letters from Thomas Cromwell to Sir Arthur Plantagenet, Lord Lisle, presented here were written between early 1536 and the summer of 1539. Because they all deal with one of the most difficult problems faced by the Tudor monarchy, that of adequately supervising the last of England's possessions on the Continent, it will be convenient to give some connected account of the matters pertaining to Calais by way of introduction to the entire group of the Cromwell-Lisle letters.

Calais and the "Pale," or surrounding lands, were in essence an English march lordship adjacent to France and the Low Countries. The territory or dominion, as it was often called in the sixteenth century, was conquered for England by Edward III in 1347. The legal basis for England's hold over it came about in 1360, in the Treaty of Brétigny, which ended one of the many successive phases of the Hundred Years' War between England and France. From that time until the Reformation, Calais and its environs were intended to serve as a naval base to guard the Straits of Dover, as a military enclave to secure English conquests in France, and also as a colony of merchants, the great government monopoly over the export of wool called the Calais Staple.

[5] From the signature "Thomas Essex" we may conclude that this letter is of 1540, since Cromwell's elevation to the Essex earldom came in April of that year.

From the late fourteenth through the second half of the fifteenth century, Calais served the intended purposes. The Staple merchants exported almost all the English wools and skins through the port of Calais. In exchange for certain privileges they gave to the kings of England a sum of money in excess of £10,000 a year, out of which the costs of various aspects of civil and military government were met. But with the end of the Hundred Years' War and the arrest of English ambitions on the mainland of Europe, that process of redirecting policy began which was to make the island empire of the future. The decline of the Staple set in also as new patterns of commerce appeared, in which the English exported cloth more often than wool and favored merchant adventurers and oceanic ventures over the primary products of the Staple. By the early Tudor period, therefore, Calais served increasingly as an outpost of England against any French threats across the Channel and as a staging ground for any English military adventures in Europe. The growth of French power after 1450 witnessed the beginning of a process of territorial unification which was to continue for several hundred years and which always looked to English eyes to be directed at Calais.

Calais was from the first difficult to manage. It attracted foreigners in large numbers, especially merchants and victualers anxious to deal in English wool or to make a profit out of the fact that a large English military garrison and civilian establishment was separated from the homeland by water. Military and civilian affairs were, as we have noted, managed by the Staple and also by a number of royal officials, the foremost of whom came to be called the king's lieutenant, or deputy of Calais. On the ecclesiastical side, Calais had parishes subject to the discipline of the bishop of Thérouanne, an anomaly somewhat resolved by an agreement in 1379 whereby jurisdiction was transferred to Canterbury.

Many problems of government in the Pale were often short-lived, but there were certain features of a constant nature. The port and surrounding land were difficult to supply from England, even more difficult to defend, hard to govern efficiently through officers sent out from England, and extremely difficult to integrate into any consistent pattern of administration by virtue of the fact that the population of Calais was by no means English. This last was a catalyst which kept the brew of supply, defense, and administration at a boil. And when the era of religious revolution arose, public uniformity in matters of religious reform was to prove impossible to attain. In the late fifteenth and early sixteenth centuries, royal control in Calais steadily increased, while at the same time the port's commercial prosperity was eclipsed. Beneath the surface of integration there were unre-

solved tensions with regard to the people and government there.
In the 1530's, as we know from a recent thorough study of
Calais in the early Tudor period (P. T. J. Morgan, "The Government of Calais: 1485–1558" [Oxford, D. Phil. unpublished,
1966]), the most serious efforts at reform were made through
government subsidies as the Staple payment lagged and by acts
of Parliament designed to achieve some final integration of Calais
into the English monarchy.

The minister chiefly responsible for the enormous increase in
activity concerning Calais was Thomas Cromwell. His correspondence shows a vital concern for government reform at every
level and for social and religious reform as well. Since Lord
Lisle was the king's deputy at Calais from 1533 to 1540, at
which time he was involved in an alleged plot of treason, most
of the letters from London to Calais are now to be found either
in the state papers of Henry VIII, which are for the 1530's
chiefly papers confiscated from Cromwell after his own fall in
1540, or in the Lisle papers, also confiscated by the council's
agents in 1540 upon the deputy's arrest. Routine and even trivial
matters of administration may be followed in the two collections
of letters. Often the entire course of a particular request for patronage can be followed. Not always, but frequently, we can
see the difficulties of administration at a distance in an age of
backward communication and transportation facilities. It is seldom that we cannot read there the increasing anxiety of Henry
VIII's great minister about how secure Calais was.

This anxiety arose out of the feeling that the largely foreign
population was untrustworthy, especially the Flemish and
French. It also stemmed from the recognition that efforts to
anglicize the people were hopeless. Again, the officials there
formed a uniquely independent social and political force, of
which Tudor sovereigns were made painfully aware when forces
hostile to Henry VII and Queen Mary tried to use Calais as the
base for military actions against the crown.

But none of these fears or weaknesses caused the English as
much trouble as did the political problems raised by religious
divisions. The garrison at Calais was infected with extremes of
Protestantism. A good part of the town and the Pale seemed
much taken by "sacramentaries," or heretics who doubted the
doctrine and practice of the eucharist or Lord's Supper. In the
heightened religious fervor of partisans, faction found its natural
breeding place, and London watched anxiously every sign of
disharmony.

Well might she do so. Worship and politics were twin aspects
of the single problem of uniformity. While the government might
imagine that religious uniformity could be commanded as a simple matter, this was the case even less in the Pale, so remote

from the immediate power of the crown, than it was in England itself. Before the Reformation no special religious qualities seemed in evidence in the Pale. Charities and parishes mixed with regular religious houses of monks and nuns in abundance. There were some twenty parishes in the territory under English rule and a Carmelite friars' house and two nunneries. There was also a Hospitalers' hospice and a number of chantries, all nominally under Canterbury's supervision, but in fact dependent upon Cranmer's representative or commissary there. Many of the clergy were foreigners, being "provided" to their livings under patronage agreements with the Roman curia and French court. Few of the priests were English before the Reformation, a fact of the greatest importance to Cromwell, who saw the necessity of converting the entire Pale to the religion of England, if that threatened outpost was not to be worse than an Achilles' heel to England.

The problems of uniformity were enormous. In the eastern parts of the Pale, Flemish was the language spoken. In the western areas it was French that people used in daily life. Thus, even if there had been enough resident English priests, it was hardly likely that any large-scale uniformity could be obtained. Moreover, the Pale was by its very geography doomed to nonconformity of one sort or another. Not only was it adjacent to territories of the French Catholics; it also touched Spanish territory. Reformed doctrines from Germany could enter freely from the sea. As early as 1525–1526 religious disagreements appeared. The radical Protestant, William Roy, dedicated a Lutheran treatise to his native townsfolk of Calais. The parson of the Staplers, one Philip Smith, was charged in 1528 with keeping some two dozen heretical books, among them works of Melanchthon, Luther, and Erasmus. He corresponded with reformers in Paris, only to be seized by one John Butler, Wolsey's agent. But Smith, after being examined by the cardinal and Campeggio, was released. That is not to say that all of the danger stemmed from Germany. There is even a report that Sir Thomas More sent a necromancer to Calais in 1533, whether to conjure against the king we do not know.

Be that as it may, there was no large-scale disaffection before 1536. In 1536 Cromwell had secured an act of Parliament and subsequent injunctions for Calais commanding every person to speak English, to have an English name, to be provided with an English priest, and to have preaching and catechism in English. In 1534 isolated cases of serious heresy and faction were reported, with Lord Lisle and his wife, Honor Grenville, revealing that the new deputy's influence in religion would be conservative. They were old-fashioned Catholics at heart. And though they were not powerful in Tudor court circles or politics, they did have connections among powerful men of a conservative disposition: the Duke of Norfolk and Sir Anthony Browne, to name two of Cromwell's most effective opponents in religious matters.

By 1535 Cromwell and Crammer began to suspect the Lisles. Cranmer protested to Cromwell that preachers he had sent out to carry the gospel to Calais were being influenced by the Lisles against the intention of the laudable acts of Parliament. John Butler was appointed commissary in that year especially to enforce the acts of the Reformation Parliament. Beyond the Lisles, Cranmer and Cromwell were convinced that a number of their friends exercised a perverse influence. Moves and countermoves were made, with the vicegerent in ecclesiastical matters and the archbishop infiltrating their own reform-minded men into Calais in order to counteract the influence of the Lisles' chaplain, Gregory Botolph. The Carmelite abbey at Sandingfield was put in the hands of Sir Thomas Palmer who was certainly a client of Cromwell. In 1536 Cranmer and Cromwell used their patronage to send two preachers (Dr. Hoore and Dr. Champion) for the express purpose of converting the Pale, under the aegis of the king's privy council.

The council was vitally interested in the sources of trouble at Calais. Popish priests were carefully reported upon. Thomas Wakefield, a friend of Cromwell, was given a benefice there. Men sent out from England on military purposes were questioned about religious unrest, often through the commissary John Butler. Lisle, in defense, complained regularly about men like Butler, especially when the archbishop's friend began to destroy the idols of the Pale, an episode which for the first time showed evidence of a widespread, popular Protestantism and a reform-minded element anxious to serve the ends Cromwell had made his policy. In the struggles over images two defrocked friars were licensed to preach in French against images! Despite simple successes, most of the Calais inhabitants were very upset early in 1538 when Butler pulled down the shrine of Our Lady at the Wall. The council and Cromwell received complaints against Lisle's obstructions, while the deputy, for his part, wrote his objections through various agents, especially the member of Parliament chosen by the council for Calais, Thomas Boyce.

The relative uproar of the controversy about idols and images was nothing compared to the fury of the faction fighting that came to the Pale in 1538, about Easter, in the person of Adam Damplyp, a former chaplain to Bishop Fisher. Damplyp charmed the Lisles, who offered him the Friary (the chapter house of the White Friars) as a place to preach. The prior, John Dove, complained bitterly to Cranmer, alleging that Damplyp was a dangerous heretic. But Dove seemed also to resent the favor shown

Damplyp as much as his doctrine. By June 1538 the council at
Calais took notice of the preacher's heresies, a little annoyed by
the fact that he found their morals wanting. They complained
to the London authorities, who responded by asking Dove to
present the Lisle side of the matter. Cranmer heard Dove, but
ended by supporting Damplyp and urging the prior to ask the
preacher's forgiveness. At Whitsuntide, the king apparently sided
with Cranmer and Cromwell by ordering the destruction of the
shrine of the Resurrection. Damplyp preached vigorously against
the pretended relics of the shrine and did so with such vigor
that he was asked to defend himself before the privy council.
He was accused of sacramentariañ views. His response was a
brisk defense in writing and a precipitate retreat into hiding in
the west of England.

Amid moves and stratagems, the conflict over doctrine was
slowly taking on the aspect of a contest for power, with Lisle
anxious to convince the king that he was in control of the
situation. He was fretful and resentful over Cromwell's interference in the administration of Calais on many counts, but on
none more than in the affairs of religion. While outwardly con-
forming to the spirit of reform, for example by placing English
Bibles in parish churches in accord with the 1538 injunctions,
Lisle secretly plotted against Butler, Wakefield, and others
among the Cromwellians at Calais, and against the king's minister himself. This movement on Lisle's part coincided with the
first wave of what we might call the reaction in England.
Throughout 1538 and 1539 Lisle kept up the pressure of his
correspondence, accusing Cromwell and "protestantism" of mis-
governing the Pale.

Hordes of people were staying away from religious services
in one of the first manifestations of voluntary separatism. Lisle
accused half the garrison of being treasonable heretics. Cromwell responded by begging Lisle to arrest a mere half-dozen,
in what was to be the opening salvo in the dispute between
the two about the building of peace and harmony at Calais.
Lisle kept back some evidence, as he had done in hearing the
Damplyp case, to spring it on Cromwell after the minister had
declared himself. With the success of the Damplyp case behind
him, Lisle felt the tide to be in his favor. He told Cranmer not
to interfere in the Pale. The government was so annoyed and
worried that informers were invited to London to give more
evidence about the condition of Calais. A commission of inquiry
sat and after gathering much evidence punished Butler and
another Cromwellian. The Duke of Norfolk complained that the
garrison of Calais was "Lollard," a suitable anachronism for
that reactionary politician! By the end of 1539, most of the
Calais reformers connected with Cromwell were in exile, in

hiding, or in prison. Lisle and his allies were preparing evidence
agitating against Cromwell himself. And in that frantic atmosphere Cromwell discovered that Lisle's chaplain had made a
secret trip to Ghent to talk with Cardinal Pole. That was close
to treason in 1539–1540, and it was enough to bring Lisle down.
But not before the letters printed here were exchanged; and
not before Cromwell's position as a reformer had been revealed
in a way filled with danger for both Cromwell and reform.

In the last of the eight letters composing this group, Cromwell has skirted the issue of Lisle's efforts to lead him into
maintaining Damplyp's cause only to be trapped by the further
show of evidence about Damplyp's views. Instead of taking up
that matter at any length, Cromwell uses the constant complaint of Lisle as a device inviting a lecture on what I have in
the Introduction called "civic" philosophy. Here the unfanatical
Cromwell can be seen at his best, setting forth the governing
conditions of the Reformation: the effort not to cut windows into
men's souls, there to see their secret thoughts, but the effort at
a Christian conspiracy driven by charity. It was his reiteration
of something he had written to the council at Calais as early
as 1532: "You shall nourish and bring a very union and concord
between all them there and conduce them to such a knot as
there shall be perfect union amongst them, without strife, which
one of the strongest fortresses that can be in any such town
of war, as the same is. . . ." (PRO SP1/152/209–10.)

After my right hearty commendations unto your good lordship. These be to desire you to send unto me a bill signed with
your hand for a protection[1] for a poor merchant stranger, according as I have caused it to be written and sent unto your lordship here enclosed. The which I pray you to write and send
again under your sign and seal in your accustomed manner.
Whereby, I assure you, you shall do a meritorious and very
good deed, as God know, who preserve your lordship. At my
house in London, the third day of March. Your lordship's assured.

Clerk's hand; autograph signature. Addressed: "To my very good
Lord the Viscount Lisle the King's Deputy in Calais."

---

[1] A written permission granting immunity from arrest or lawsuit to one
going abroad with the king's permission.

70. To Lord Lisle

PRO SP3/2/122
LP, XI, 55; 155

10 July [1536]
London

After my right hearty commendations unto your good lordship. These shall be to advertise the same that I have received your letters and perceive as well by the same as by other report that you should take unkindly my letters lately sent unto you, taking thereby occasion to judge me to be displeased with you. I assure your lordship howsoever wrote I meant no ill. But, forasmuch as your former letters and mine were so written that neither of us understood the same well, as your lordship's loving friend, I wrote the more plainly for the time to give you occasion to set forward that weighty business as the necessity thereof did then require, meaning nothing else touching any displeasure than your very perfect friend might do. I have been once in hand with the king's highness to obtain licence that your lordship might come over to meet with his said highness at Dover, when he should come thither. But as yet I have no determinate answer therein. But when I shall receive the same I shall more largely advertise your lordship thereof, by Husey[1] your servant who attended here (as he says) for that purpose. Thus the Blessed Trinity preserve your good lordship. At the Rolls, the 10th of July. Your lordship's assured.

Clerk's hand; autograph signature. Addressed: "To my very good Lord the Viscount Lisle lord Deputy of the Town of Calais and the Marches of the same." Endorsed: "My lord privy seal."

---

[1] This reference is to John Husee or Husey, industrious and talkative London factor, or agent, of Lisle, especially busy about the court and with Cromwell, Wriothesley, and Sadler in suits of Lisle's touching lands contested between the deputy and Sir Edward Seymour in 1536.

71. To Lord Lisle

BM Cotton Mss. Cleopatra Eiv, fo. 55   17 July [1537]
LP, XII, ii, 267; 194   Sutton

After my right hearty commendations. The king's highness
being informed that there be two priests in that town, the one
called Sir William Minstarlew,[1] which is now in ward,* the
other called Sir William Richardson,[2] otherwise Good Sir William, has commanded me to signify unto you that, like as his
pleasure is that upon receipt hereof, you should send both the
said priests as prisoners in assured custody. So his grace cannot
a little marvel to hear of the papistical faction that is maintained
in that town, and by you chiefly that be of his grace's council.[3]
Surely his majesty thinks that you have little respect either to
him, to his laws or to the good order of that town, which so
little regard him in a matter of great weight; which also his
majesty has so much to heart and willed me plainly to intimate
to you, all and every of you, that in case he shall perceive from

[1] Sir William Minstarlew or Minsterley, author of a book setting out an
exaggerated doctrine of the powers of priests. He was punished by the
council for popery.
[2] William Richardson was apprehended for popery at the same time as
Minsterley. His specific offense was maintaining the feast day of St. Thomas
à Becket contrary to royal order. But Lady Lisle eventually secured Richardson's release. It was at this time that Cromwell secured the nomination
of his friend Wakefield.
[3] The council at Calais was the chief body through which the crown
attempted to subordinate Calais to the English government at home.
Through it and its secretary passed all of the important administrative
and judicial work of the Pale. Royal commissions worked through it and
its chief members, all of whom below the deputy were of real standing
locally, and a few of whom had strong peerage and gentry connections in
the southeastern counties of England. Some kind of council had existed
at Calais since the English conquest. Clerks of the council are in evidence
by 1450. But it was only with the decline of the Staple and its control
over government that the council at Calais became a true reflection of
conciliar government of the same type that flourished in the marches of
Wales and along the northern borderlands of England. After 1522, the
council consisted of the deputy, the commander of Guisnes, the high
marshal, high porter, controller, under-marshal, mayor of the town and
lieutenant of the Staple.

henceforth any such abuses suffered or winked at, as have been hitherto in manner in contempt of his most royal estate maintained, his highness will put others in the best of your rooms* that shall so offend him, by whom he will be better served.

It is thought against all reason that the prayers of women and their fond flickerings should move any of you to do that thing that should in any wise displease your Prince and sovereign lord or offend his just laws. And if you should think any extremity in this writing, you must thank yourselves that have so procured it. For neither of yourselves have you regarded these matters nor answered to many my letters written for like purposes and upon like occasions. Wherein, though I have not made any accusation, yet being in the place for those things that I am, I have thought you did me therein too much injury and such as I am assured, his highness, knowing it, would not have taken in good part. But this matter needs no aggravation nor have I done anything in it more than has been by his majesty thought mete, percase not so much.[4] And thus fare you heartily well, from Sutton, the 17th day of July. Your lordships assured.

Clerk's hand; autograph signature.

72. To Lord Lisle

PRO SP3/2/121   14 May [1538]
LP, XIII, i, 996; 263

After my right hearty commendations to your lordship. By your letters of the 7th of this month which I have received with the other writings sent with the same, I do perceive both the ruin of certain parts of that town meet to be repaired and the dissention amongst you upon certain hard words and the pulling

---

[4] The specific offenses against the king's laws can only be guessed at. But there were some cases involving palavering ladies of Calais. One Mrs. Talbotte, apparently a Protestant, went about maintaining she was as good as the Virgin Mary. The "flickerings" are doubtless those of Lady Lisle herself, for Thomas Palmer, Cromwell's friend, reported through Sir Richard Lee (military engineer) of Lady Lisle's being gone over to things "a little papist." In early 1537 she apparently opposed the campaign against statues and images.

down of the images of Our Lady in the wall.[1] Touching the reparations, I shall move the king's majesty therein and obtain, I trust, such order for the same as shall be convenient for his honor and the surety of his town.

Touching the words pretended to be spoken in contempt of the sacrament.[2] If your lordship, joining with some others of the council with you, will take pain to examine the very truth of them upon your advertisement such direction shall be taken for the reformation of such as shall be found offenders therein as shall be consonant to justice. And, as concerning the pulling down of the image, though it be thought that many abuses and fond superstitions were maintained by the same, yet, if it were taken down after any such sort as implied a contempt of royal authority or might have made any tumult in the people, upon your signification thereof such like order shall be taken therein as shall be thought most expedient. Thus fare you heartily well. From St. James, the 13th day of May.

Post Scriptum: I thank you very heartily for your letters and advertisements. And whereas you write unto me that there is plenty of wine and one tun* of French wine of the best and send it unto me by the next [ship], signifying the price thereof, and you shall have the money repayed with condign* and right hearty thanks. And the same pleasure to be requited and remembered accordingly. And thus fare you right heartily well. Your lordship's assured.

Clerk's hand; autograph signature. Addressed: "To my very good lord the Viscount Lisle Deputy of the Town of Calais and the Marches of the Same." Endorsed: "My lord privy seal."

[1] John Butler, Cranmer's commissary at Calais, began to pull down idols in 1537. In the early spring of 1538 he destroyed the shrine of Our Lady at the Wall. Some resentment manifested itself, and Butler countered by allowing the defrocked French friars to preach against images. Aliens had been prohibited from preaching by the Calais Act of 1536, but Butler trusted that Cranmer could dispense from the act. It was Butler's feeling that reform was held back by the fact that few of the Calais clergy were evangelical in orientation.

[2] The reference must be to Adam Damplyp or Damplip, who is the chief figure in the storm over sacramentarian doctrines at Calais. But the events or words here meant cannot be Damplyp's vigorous attack on the contents of the shrine of the Resurrection, which took place only after Whitsunday (9 June 1538). Damplyp appeared in Calais between Easter Sunday (21 April 1538) and Whitsunday and immediately attracted notice for his sermons on the sacrament of the altar. For additional material on Damplyp see the notes to the following letters.

73. To Lord Lisle

PRO SP1/134/174–5   16 July [1538]
LP, XIII, i, 1386; 268   Chelsea

After my right hearty commendations to your lordship. I have received sundry your letters[1] and right well perused and noted the contents thereof, whereby I perceive that in the same the king's town of Calais there is some infection of certain persons denying the holy sacrament of Christ's blessed body and blood, of such opinions as commonly they call sacramentaries.* For remedy whereof, the king's gracious pleasure is that you shall cause the said persons suspected to be thoroughly, groundly and substantially examined, aswell upon the formal and material points thereof and well weighing their sayings. In case it shall appear unto you that they well maintain any errors against the true doctrine, you shall not only cause them to be punished, to the example of all others; but also provide that no such error pernicious be spread abroad there but utterly suppressed, banished and extincted as it appertains.

I perceive also of the variances between the Friar[2] and a preacher there.[3] I require you likewise to cause them to be well

[1] By June 1538 the Council of Calais had begun to take note of Damplyp's alleged heresies and reported on them to London; see *LP,* XIII, i, 1219 (June 1538).

[2] The "Friar" is the Carmelite prior, John Dove, to whose own pulpit Damplyp was licensed by Lord Lisle. Dove and Damplyp engaged in a series of debates which apparently became the occasion of public disorder. Cranmer eventually called Dove to England, where the Carmelite was informed that Damplyp taught the truth, even if it appeared sacramentarian, and that he was to make an apology to his new preacher. Foxe, *Acts and Monuments,* V, 501, states clearly that Cranmer connived in Damplyp's favor.

[3] Adam Damplyp was a Lancashire man whose real name was George Bowker and who had served Bishop Fisher as chaplain. After the execution of Fisher, English Catholics sent Damplyp to Rome, where Reginald Pole befriended him. But Damplyp voiced criticisms of the Roman Curia and shortly afterward turned to Protestant ideas, wandering and teaching in Italy and Germany. By 1538 he planned to return to England on the assumption that the régime there would prove amicable. At Calais, Damplyp was delayed by a series of storms, meanwhile growing friendly with one William Stevyns, who persuaded Lisle and others to allow

and formally examined and their allegations heard on both parts;
and thereupon [su]che inquisition . . . examination, search and
trial as shall be ex[pedient] . . . in all your proceed[ings]
therein to advertise me with convenient diligence, to the intent
I may signify the same to the king's majesty and thereupon
know his further pleasure for a direction to be taken in the
same.[4]

As for your desires and suits, I trust to send you shortly comfortable word of his majesty's determinate pleasure, such as I
hope shall be to the satisfaction both of you and of my Lady,
to whom I pray you to have me heartily commended. Thus
fare you right heartily well, from Chelsey, this 16th of July.
Your lordship's assured.

Wriothesley's hand; autograph signature. Addressed: "To my
very good Lord the Viscount Lisle, lord Deputy of the King's
Toun of Calais and the Marches."

74. To Lord Lisle

PRO SP1/151/241–3   27 May [1539]
LP, XIV, i, 1029; 312   St. James's Palace

After my right hearty commendations. These shall be to signify unto you that I have received your letters of the 18th of
this present with a book of such depositions as you have taken
upon my advertisement made unto you the 6th of the same, by

Damplyp to read the Bible to the people. Lord and Lady Lisle entertained Damplyp and were much taken with him, offering him the chapter
house of the White Friars as a pulpit. His oratory attracted praise from
the people and the enmity of Dove and the councilors there. Damplyp
attacked official immorality as well as various superstitions. He ridiculed
relics and shrines in general, and in particular the supposed miraculous
holy wafers of the Resurrection shrine. It was the outspoken attack on
the sacrament that caused Damplyp to be summoned to London, whence
he fled, leaving only a Latin *apologia*. Dove returned from his own hearings a chastened man, burdened with the task of surrendering his house
in October 1538. Of Damplyp we have little information after 1538. But
at least one source reports him in the entourage of the Bishop of Salisbury.
Foxe tells of him keeping a good school in the remote west of England.
[4] The few sentences transcribed here are in part conjectural; the manuscript is badly torn at this point.

the king's majesty's commandment.[1] And having thoroughly perused both your common letters[2] with the private letters of you
my lord deputy and my lord chamberlain[3] and also the said
depositions; forasmuch as the king's majesty, travailing most
catholically, christianly and charitably to set a general quiet and
unity in all those matters, has not hitherto had time to read or
hear your collections, which, as it appears you have with much
travail gathered; and that I think it nevertheless to be most
necessary that such slanders might be appeased as give courage
to his grace's enemies to note more division amongst us, which
may embolden them to advance evil practices against his majesty and enfeeble men's spirits that be of true faith and meaning
toward God and his highness; I have thought convenient not
only to give you mine advice for the ordering and quieting of
things till in those matters you shall know further of his majesty's
pleasure, but also to declare some part of mine opinion touching
the effects of the said depositions and concerning the quieting
of the bruits* and rumors which have risen and be spread abroad
by your advertisements and earnest proceedings in these matters
and examinations.

I think that like as the king's majesty cannot better or more
highly advance the honor of God nor more prudently provide
for his own surety and the tranquility of the realm, dominions
and subjects than in the discrete and charitable punishment of
such as do by any means labor and purpose to sow sedition,
division and contention in opinion among his people contrary
to the truth of God's word and his grace's most christian ordinances; so, I think again on the other side that he or they,
whatsoever they be that would without great and substantial
grounds be authors or setters forth of any such rumor, may ap-

[1] While Damplyp and Dove went before the council in England, Commissary Butler and others pushed iconoclastic and seemingly heretical views
at Calais. Throughout the winter of 1538 and early 1539 Lisle and others
at Calais looked in dismay at what seemed the encouragement of dangerous ideas. With Lisle stood John Wallop, the ambassador to France, and
Lord William Sandys, the captain at Guisnes. A number of letters are in
LP, while Foxe also gives some very detailed information about the drawing of factional lines. Lisle and the council collected information or depositions, apparently at Cromwell's request. But this is only to be understood
in the light of the Lisle-Cromwell exchanges, in which it is clear that
Cromwell was actually protecting the Calais Protestants and trying to blunt
the thrust of all efforts to make them the cause of unrest in the Pale.
[2] The common letters are those of the council of Calais.
[3] William Sandys, captain of Guisnes (d. 1540), was also lord chamberlain of Calais.

pear rather desirous of sedition than of quiet and unity, and may therein show themselves rather devisers how to put men in trouble and despair that be peaceable, quiet and faithful, than how to reform what is amiss and with consideration of the matter, the time and other circumstances meet to be pondered, to preserve the number in that courage towards truth to God and their Prince that their bounden duties at all times do require. And therefore, mine opinion is that you shall by all means divise how with charity and mild handling of things to quench this slanderous bent as much as you may, ever exhorting men discreetly and without rigor or extreme dealing to know and serve God truly and their Prince and sovereign lord with all humility and obediance.

As touching the substance of the depositions. It is sore to note any man for a sacramentary, unless he that shall be the author of the infamy know well what a sacramentary is. And yet it is more sore to note a commune* officer, put in place to advise and reform others, of so heinous a crime, except it might be duly and evidently proved against him. I mean this by the Commissary,[4] the depositions against whom be not most weighty and substantial. Against the other few accused of the same crime, the accusations seem to weigh somewhat deeper. And yet the final number that be accused of that offence might have been punished without an infamy to the whole town. And as for the rest of the depositions that be made specially touching the preacher,[5] though per case he and others might in their proceedings have done more circumspectly in some things, yet they seem to help little to fortify that there should be such a general division among you.

[4] The substance of the depositions against the commissary was contained in charges that he destroyed images and attacked the sacrament of the altar by stating that brandy sold by any grocer would do a man as much good as the sacrament. Butler informed Cranmer that there were three great papists at Calais, but not a sacramentary (*LP*, XIII, i. 813 and 934). Butler's alleged offenses were also grounded in a Calais council judgment that whoever gave Damplyp license to preach was a supporter of his heresies, for which see *LP*, XIII, i, 1219. Cromwell is at his best in his protest that the council at Calais is stirring the waters of sedition in their too active inquisition into the secret hearts of men. Lisle and Calais officials with him had apparently been so zealous in their complaints as to allow Cromwell to accuse them of drawing a blanket indictment against the men of the Pale as a whole.

[5] Adam Damplyp. Even in his case, Cromwell did not seem to feel that the facts warranted the stir Lisle was making. It is a thinly veiled threat to Lisle and his supporters that Cromwell makes in the last paragraph by raising the question, Who are the real enemies?

Finally, I shall advise you to use things with charity and with such wisdom to suppress as much as in you in this general slander that there may be a towardness of a quiet amongst you, which the king's majesty will shortly I doubt not make perfect, to the comfort of all that be well disposed and the punishment of all such as at present appear or shall upon just and indifferent examination be found hereafter to maintain evil and corrupt opinions or to be inclined to sedition. And thus most heartily fare you well, from St. James, the 27th day of May. Your lordships assured

Clerk's hand, autograph signature. Address: "To my very good lords and friends and other the king's highness' council at Calais."

75. To Lord Lisle

PRO SP3/2/124   1 June [1539]
LP, XIV, i, 1060; 313   St. James's Palace

After my right hearty commendations to your lordship. With your letters of the 29th of the last month addressed unto me upon the arrival there of my servant Thomas Palmer,[1] I have received the two prisoners Rafe Hare[2] and the barber of Mark,[3] who shall be duly here examined upon such points as be de-

---

[1] The Palmers were prominent in Calais government. Henry Palmer was bailiff of Guisnes. There were apparently two Thomas Palmers there, both of them in Cromwell's circle of friends and supporters. One was Henry Palmer's brother, Sir Thomas, who, as we have already noted, held the abbey of Sandingfield *in commendam* from 1535. The other seems to have been a messenger and perhaps a soldier of the garrison, but definitely not the knight porter of Calais mentioned above.

[2] Ralph Hare was a soldier of the garrison at Calais. He and others, among them Henry Tourney, were strong supporters of reform and in regular contact with Cromwell. Lisle had gotten rid of Tourney in 1535. William Stevyns was another of the lord privy seal's friends there, who often complained about the popish priest William Blagges, the vicar of Hervelingham. But Hare was the most intriguing. He was arrested in the circumstances alluded to here. His crime seems to have been the keeping of an unlicensed school and congregation! This is a quite remarkable and early instance of that voluntary separatism Patrick Collinson has noted as a salient characteristic of Elizabethan popular Protestantism and Puritanism. See *LP*, XIV, i, 1319.

[3] I am not able to identify the "barber of Mark."

posed against them; and remitted thither if they shall be found
culpable, to be punished according to the qualities of their
offenses.

And where as your lordship writes that you be no man
malicious, nor have for malice theretofore written anything but
such as has been brought unto you and proved by honest persons; my lord, I assure you that I never took you to be a man
of such sort, but have ever thought you to be a good and gentle
natural disposition. Marry,* when I have perceived anything
in you that I supposed could not fend* in fine* to your commodity I have sometime friendly written to you my mind as to
him whose continued prosperity I have more desired than I
shall need now to recount and express. And as for other men's
advertisements, which as it appears you conject should be made
against you and your doings, so you write that if you can find
no remedy for the same at my hand rather than you would be
used as you have been in times past you would choose to lie
in perpetual prison during life, adding that you will so write in
that case to the king's majesty; I shall advise your lordship to
suspect no man further than need [be] which should trouble
yourself and breed some inconvenience amongst you.

And as concerning redress of anything that does or should
molest and inquiet you, surely, my lord, as I know not wherein
I have hitherto failed you or been remiss in any your pursuits,
causes and requests reasonable; so, if it shall like you plainly
and specially to write unto me your griefs, I shall myself declare the same to the king's majesty and join with you for the
healing of them as the case will permit and require. Wherein,
if you do mistrust me, you may without offense to me seek
such other remedies as your lordship shall think most convenient
and propicious for your purpose.[4] And thus most heartily fare
you well. From St. James, the 1st of June. Your assured friend.

Post Scriptum. I thank your lordship for your gentle present
of the porpoise. Your men be committed to the gatehouse til
they be examined.

Clerk's hand; autograph signature. Addressed: "To my very good
lord the Viscount Lisle deputy of the king's Town and Marches
of Calais."

---

[4] For the many suits and problems Lisle encountered therein, as well as
for Cromwell's just claim that he had done all that was possible in maintaining them, see Michael Bush, "Protector Somerset," (Ph.D. dissertation,
Cambridge, 1966), and his essay on the Lisle-Seymour disputes in *Historical
Journal* (1966).

76. To Lord Lisle

PRO SP1/152/55–6   8 June [1539]
LP, XIV, i, 1086; 314   St. James's Palace

After my right hearty commendations. These shall be to advertise the same that I have received your letters dated in this month with a schedule of certain articles preached by one Adam Damplip, as it is alleged, by the permission of the Commissary, which Damplip you judge to have been the author of the erroneous opinions which have lately appeared in Calais and those parts. Which articles I have perused and find them very pestilent, much marvelling that the same were not presented heretofore against him, when he was accused of the matter of transubstantiation. But if it be true that he taught them, then taught he most detestable and cankered heresy. And if the Commissary consented to that doctrine, I must needs think him unmete for such an office and judge him also worthy great punishment. And for his examination therein and in the other matters laid to his charge by the deposition which you sent lately unto me, the king's majesty's pleasure is that you shall deliver both the said Commissary and parish priest[1] that hath been the preacher unto this bearer, who has charge to see them surely and yet honestly conveyed hither.

Now, to answer to the points of your said letters. As I wrote before that I thought it necessary that such slanders chancing to rise amongst you, the same should be rather discreetly and charitably appeased, and the offenders quietly punished, than so handled as should give courage to the king's majesty's enemies to note much division amongst us and percase cause them the rather to advance sundry evil practises. Even so must I advise you again, being the same counsel that I would in like case follow myself, not seeing but offenders may aswell be punished

---

[1] We have already had more than one occasion to note the displeasure of Lisle at John Butler's conduct as Cranmer's commissary in Calais. But he was in 1539 clearly a pawn in the attacks of Lisle and his supporters in Calais and England upon the reformers at Calais and Cromwell. The parish priest sent up with Butler was William Smith, who seems to have been related to another Smith, the Staple chaplain arrested as early as 1528 for the possession of heretical books.

without too great a tumult, as if the faults of a few in respect
of the multitude there were bruited through an whole world.
And this gives no judgement against the truth of your advertisements, but shows a mean how, if they be good and just, by
honest circumstance you may make them yet better.

And as to the second point of your letters, touching the occasioners of the bruits which have been spread of these matters.
I meant none other than to ascribe the same chiefly to those
which were the first setters forth of any erroneous opinions. And
yet to be plain with you as with my friends, many times many
diseases that be of their own nature disposed to very evil effects,
if it chance them to be espied by a good physician, his learning,
wisdom, knowledge and good disposition may in such wise provide remedy, as the patient shall with little pain attain perfect
health. Whereas, if the physician should, upon respect wink*
til the infection were more deeply settled, percase all his cunning
to be practiced upon the sick man should not be able to help
him, though he should daily rack him with his medicines. And
surely we be no less but more in fault which labor not to avoid
evil from our neighbors where we see the same imminent, then
if we should be ourselves the very authors and workers of the
same evil towards them.[2]

I have informed the king's majesty of all your letters and of

---

[2] The context is vital. Cromwell and Cranmer were alarmed by the split
in the Calais community. Cromwell was all too keenly aware of the permanent problems besetting Calais to be indifferent to serious disharmony of
a religious sort, whatever his own views might be. The Lisles were informing on officers of Protestant opinions—that Sir Robert Wingfield ate
meat at times of fast, for example. William Smith had discovered that
Lord Lisle disobeyed a royal order for the destruction of the shrine of St.
Thomas à Becket. Smith preached publicly that the deputy had merely
painted out St. Thomas' name and put another in its place. In such
circumstances Cromwell could not let it appear that reform and misgovernment went together at Calais. So it was indeed on his own order as
vicegerent that Butler and Smith were called before the privy council in
June 1539, under the escort of John Barthelot (*LP*, XIV, i, 1042). In
May the Six Articles had been introduced by Norfolk. And at Calais the
reform supporters were not able to outface the Lisle-led conservatives. It
was in this circumstance that Lisle complained that half the garrison were
heretics and Cromwell challenged him to arrest half of them, if that were
true. The government was deeply disturbed, and pressure for a commission
of inquiry, which Cromwell resisted, finally proved too strong. As a result,
Butler was punished. Smith, ordered to recant, attacked Lisle and his
judges, deeming them maintainers of the "mere bran" of ceremonies and
the "Iscariots of Calais." But ultimately Lisle and the Earl of Sussex
surprised the king by how few indictments their committee could make.

your book of depositions, whose highness has already taken
order for the examination of all those matters, the resolution
whereof shall be signified unto you. The evil (as you write
therein truly) will labor to pervert the good. And even so, those
that be well disposed will both lament the folly of the evil and
do what they can to make them better. He that either fears not
God nor esteems the king's majesty's injunctions, precepts, ordinances and commandments, is no meet herb to grow in his
majesty's most catholic and virtuous garden. If you know, therefore, any more of that sort to be opened than you have already
revealed by such examinations as you lately sent unto me, I
doubt not but without respect you will give the king's majesty
advertisement of them. And where I wrote the matter deposed
against the Commissary not to be most heinous, now you answer
that he is the maintainer and very supporter of all this evil,
bringing in the foresaid matter of Damplip for a justification
thereof. Surely, if he shall be found as great an offender as the
articles note and as you report him to be, I will not only help
to have him from thence avoided, but also do for his further
punishment that shall appertain.

As touching the vintners* and constables* which have been
noted of the saddest sort of men of that town and almost in
greatest trust under you of the council; if they have offended,
it shall be better that you show to the king's majesty secretly
your old ordinance for their punishment than thus to put all
men generally and openly in fear of the loss of their livings. It
might turn to a matter of great importance, and the consequent
such as I will not nor can alone define. And to conclude: doubt
you not but the wisdom of the king's majesty, seeing the experience of many inconveniences, will very shortly so play a part of
a most noble king and arbiter amongst us, as all parties shall
be brought to a godly order, with relief of the honest and the
punishment of the malefactor accordingly. Thus fare you most
heartily well. Your lordship's assured.

Clerk's hand; autograph signature. Addressed: "To my very good
lord and loving friend the Viscount Lisle, Lord Deputy of the
King's Town and Marches of Calais and to the rest of his grace's
council there."

GLOSSARY

Advowson The patronage of an ecclesiastical office or religious house; the right of presentation to such an office or benefice.

Allect To allure or entice.

Anempst With respect to, concerning, on even ground, level with.

Apairment To impair or harm.

Assign To sign (very obscure and archaic).

Attemperaunce Temperance

Bedesman A man offering prayers for another, with an implied reference to the beads of the rosary.

Bruit Rumor or report.

Bruyllie *The Oxford English Dictionary,* vol. I, gives only this letter of Cromwell's as a source and considers his use to be an error, perhaps for "cruyltie." But the manuscript is clear. In northern dialects *brulliement* is a broil, riot, or tumult; in some cases *broylery* appears in the same sense. Halliwell's *Dictionary of Archaic and Provincial Words* gives *brulyie, brulzie,* and *brully* as rare synonyms, with obvious relations to the Italian *broglio* and French *brouille,* a confused disturbance, from the Old French *bruller* and *builler,* to burn or broil.

Burgess A member of the lower house of Parliament.

Cankered Consumed or totally infected in a malignant way; also, envious, spiteful, and ill-tempered.

Capacities Licenses given to regular clergy, granting to them the right to hold benefices of the kind held by parish clergy. These were offered to monks and friars after the Dissolution.

Cauteles Crafty devices; tricks or deceptive practices.

Choler Temperament ascribed to the superfluity of one of the four humors, bile; hence, heat, anger, irascibility, or a person with such qualities.

Commissary A bishop's administrative agent in a part of his diocese.

COMMISSION Usually letters patent from the king, granting certain rights or power to the person addressed.

COMMUNE A municipal corporation; a man with communal powers is thus a commune officer.

COMPROMIT To bind mutually; to settle by arbitration.

CONDIGN Wholly worthy; merited; adequate.

CONSTABLE The chief officer of a court or household; the conservators of the peace in subdivisions of the shire were so named.

COUNTERFEYED To put on with an intent to deceive; used here in a rare variant of the more common "counterfeight."

COVIN A private agreement between two or more people tending to the hurt of another.

CURE The office or function of a curate; the spiritual care of parishioners. Clergy from the houses dissolved in 1536 and 1539 were licensed to hold benefices *cum cura,* with the cure of souls.

DEFEND To fight against; to ward off attacks.

DELEY A variant of delay; to defer or postpone.

DEMORE A form of demur; a delay, hesitation, or state of irresolution.

DETAINDOR The condition of being forcibly restrained in one's movements.

DEVOIR One's duty; a thing or service owed to another.

EFTSOONS Again; afterwards; or soon afterwards (archaic).

ENGRIEVE To cause grief to another.

ENSEARCHING To seek; inquire; make search after (archaic).

ENSUE To follow; conform to; to imitate.

ENSUMMONING Convoking; calling together (archaic).

EVIDENCES Information given in a legal investigation to establish points of fact; hence, answers to questions about monastic property.

FAMILY The entire body of servants of a house; a household or all persons living in it.

FEES Estates, or heritable lands, held on condition of homage and service to a special lord or superior; a fief or feudal benefice.

FEND Defend; ward off; argue against; keep off.

FINDING The act or instance of declaring the result of an inquiry in judicial form; the result of such process; also, the support given to another person, as in the "finding" of an orphan by a legal guardian.

FINE Used in the idiom "fend in fine"; to redound to one's credit; to argue favorably for a person.

INDAINED Appointed; ordered; or ordained (obscure and rare).

LET Used in a sense opposite to the modern one of allowing or permitting; hence, to hinder; or, used as a noun, one form of obstacle or another; a LETTER is thus one who prevents another from doing something or hinders any action. Also, to be "letted" is to be obstructed in the performance of any task.

LETTERS PATENT Letters of instruction or information of a public character, open to all, and given under the Great Seal of England or another royal seal and signifying entitlement, the enjoyment of privilege, office, or reward, or the right to exercise authority inherent in the crown and its servants.

MARRY From the oath invoking the Virgin Mary; hence, an oath or exclamation, usually of surprise, indignation, or affirmation (archaic and dialectical).

MELANCHOLILY In a melancholy manner.

MONISH To admonish (rare).

MYSTERY Service, occupation, or office; ministry, craft, or art used by a guild master.

NOISOME Harmful; injurious; noxious and disagreeable.

NOTORIOUS Well known, but without the modern overtone of noted for some bad quality or practice.

OFFICES Inquests concerning the king's possession of or rights to land or chattels.

PERPEND To weigh mentally, to ponder or consider (archaic).

PERVICACIE From the Latin *per* plus *vincere,* to conquer heroically or completely; hence headstrong, willful, obstinate, or one having those qualities (very rare and archaic).

PLEDGES Hostages or persons held as security for the good behavior of others; in this case Pilgrims of 1536 put on their own allegiance.

PRATY The quality of arguing excessively about trifles or in a childish way.

PREBEND The tenure of a portion of land or revenue held by a canon or chapter member in a collegiate church or cathedral as his stipend; also applied to the benefice or office held.

PROPENCE Variant of propense; having an inclination or bias toward; disposed to; ready, willing, or partial toward.

PROPONE To propose a matter for decision (rare).

QUICKENED To excite, in the sense of to irritate; this is a very strained usage, derived from the Middle English "quicken," which ordinarily means to make more lively.

RATABLY In just proportion; divided justly, as with taxes.

RECIT A variant of recite; to relate or rehearse.

REDOUB To repair or restore; to correct or to amend, put right, or remedy a defect.

REMOTION The act of taking away or removing something.

ROOD LOFT The loft adorned with a crucifix (rood); this gallery separated the nave from the choir of the church, or, more exactly, the rood screen separated the two parts and was topped by the rood loft.

ROOMS Offices; situations; finite functions.

SACRAMENTARY Name given to a heretic maintaining that Christ was present merely symbolically in the eucharistic sacrifice.

STEAD The place, room, or "lieu" of another; a function, person, or thing held by a substitute; hence, to stand in "stead."

SUPREMITY A variant of supremacy.

TOTE Total amount; sum of anything.

TRACT Drawing out; prolonging; or delaying.

TROW To trust; have confidence in (archaic).

TUN A large wine vessel or cask; also, a measure of capacity with regard to wine.

UTTERED To put goods forth on the market; to vend or sell.

VINTNER One who deals in wine; also, technically, the term applied to the twenty officers of middle rank in the English garrison at Calais.

VYNCE The warlike defeat of another party or person; to conquer (from Latin *vincere*).

WADE To enter or walk through a medium impeding motion.

WARD A room or division of a prison; applied to the person held in custody and to the state of being held in custody.

WINK To close one's eyes innocently; but also to ignore improper actions of which one is well aware.

WISS A variant of the participle of *wit, wot, wist*, from the Latin *video, videre, visus*, "I see, to see, seen;" hence, having personal knowledge of or being aware of; to know how to do something.

BIBLIOGRAPHY

The items in this bibliography are divided under a number of headings to allow easy reference to different aspects of reform and the Cromwellian ministry.

COMPLAINT AND REFORM BEFORE THE DIVORCE

ASTON, MARGARET. "Lollardy and Reformation: Survival or Revival," *History*, XLIX (1964), 149–70.

BEAN, J. W. "Plague, Population and Economic Decline in England in the Later Middle Ages," *Economic History Review*, XV (1963), 423–37.

BOWKER, MARGARET. "Non-residence in the Lincoln Diocese in the Early Sixteenth Century," *Journal of Ecclesiastical History*, XV (1964), 1–22.

DAHMUS, J. H. "John Wyclif and English Government," *Speculum*, XXXV (1960), 51–68.

DUNHAM, WILLIAM H., JR. "Wolsey's Rule of the King's Whole Council," *American Historical Review*, XLIX (1944), 644–62.

FINES, J. "The Post Mortem Condemnation of Richard Hunne," *English Historical Review*, LXXVIII (1963), 528–31.

FOXE, JOHN. *Acts and Monuments*. Edited by S. R. CATTLEY and GEORGE TOWNSHEND, 8 vols., London, 1837–1841. (Popularly known as *The Book of Martyrs*.)

POLLARD, A. F. *Wolsey*. London, 1929.

SCARISBRICK, J. J. "Clerical Taxation in England, 1485–1547," *Journal of Ecclesiastical History*, XI (1960), 41–54.

THOMPSON, J. A. F. *The Later Lollards*. Oxford, 1966.

DIVORCE, SCHISM, AND SUPREMACY

COOPER, J. P. "The Supplication Against the Ordinaries Reconsidered," *English Historical Review*, LXXII (1957), 616–41.

DUNHAM, WILLIAM H., JR. "Regal Power and the Rule of Law: A Tudor Paradox," *Journal of British Studies*, III (1964), 24–56.

ELTON. G. R. "The Evolution of a Reformation Statute," *English Historical Review*, LXIV (1949), 174–97.

———. "The Commons' Supplication Against the Ordinaries," *ibid.*, LXVI (1951), 507–34.

———. "King or Minister," *History*, XXXIX (1954), 216–32.

———. *The Tudor Constitution: Documents and Commentary.* London, 1960.

GAIRDNER, J. A. "The Fall of Cardinal Wolsey," *Transactions of Royal Historical Society*, New Series, XIII (1899), 75–102.

JANELLE, PIERRE. *Obedience in Church and State: The Works of Stephen Gardiner.* Cambridge, England, 1930.

POLLARD, A. F. *Henry VIII.* London, 1902.

———. "The Reformation Parliament as a Matrimonial Agent," *History*, XXI (1936), 219–29.

ROSKELL, J. S. "Perspectives in Parliamentary History," *Bulletin of the John Rylands Library*, XLVI (1964), 448–75.

SCARISBRICK, J. J. "The Pardon of the Clergy," *Cambridge Historical Journal*, XII (1958), 22–40.

SMITH, PRESERVED. "German Opinion of the Divorce of Henry VIII," *English Historical Review*, XXVII (1912), 671–81.

SPEEL, C. J. "Theological Concepts of the Magistracy," *Church History*, XXXII (1963), 130–49.

ULLMANN, WALTER. "The Development of the Medieval Idea of Sovereignty," *English Historical Review*, LXIV (1949), 1–33.

RESISTANCE TO REFORMATION AND THE FALL OF THE MONASTERIES

BATESON, MARY. "Archbishop Warham's Visitations of Monasteries," *English Historical Review*, VI (1891), 18–35.

———. "The Pilgrimage of Grace and Aske's Examination," *ibid.*, V (1890), 330–45 and 550–73.

CHEYNEY, A. D. "The Holy Maid of Kent," *Transactions of Royal Historical Society*, New Series, XVIII, (1904), 107–29.

COULTON, G. G. *Five Centuries of Religion*, 4 vols. Cambridge, 1923–50.

DAVIS, E. J. "The Beginning of the Dissolution: Christ Church, Aldgate," *Transactions of Royal Historical Society*, 4th Series, VIII (1925), 127–50.

DICKENS, A. G. "The Yorkshire Submissions to Henry VIII," *English Historical Review*, LIII (1938), 267–75.

————. *The English Reformation*. London, 1964.

DIETZ, F. C. *English Public Finance, 1485–1558* (2nd ed.). New York, 1963.

DODD, MARY AND RUTH. *The Pilgrimage of Grace and the Exeter Conspiracy*, 2 vols. Cambridge, England, 1925.

HABAKKUK, H. J. "The Market for Monastic Property," *Economic History Review*, 2nd Series, X (1958), 362–80.

JAMES, M. E. *Change and Continuity in the Tudor North*. London, 1964.

KNOWLES, DAVID. *The Religious Orders in England*, vol. III. Cambridge, England, 1959.

LAPSLEY, G. T. "The Problem of the North," *American Historical Review*, V (1900), 440–66.

PRESCOTT, H. M. F. *Man on a Donkey*. London, 1952.

REID, RACHAEL. *The King's Council in the North*. London, 1921.

RICHARDSON, WALTER. *A History of the Court of Augmentations*. Baton Rouge, La., 1961.

SAVINE, A. *The English Monasteries on the Eve of the Dissolution*. Oxford, 1909.

SIMON, JOAN. "The Reformation and English Education," *Past and Present*, XI (1957), 47–65.

SMITH, L. B. "English Treason Trials and Confessions in the Sixteenth Century," *Journal of the History of Ideas*, XV, (1954), 471–98.

STRYPE, JOHN. *Ecclesiastical Memorials, Relating Chiefly to Religion, and the Reformation of It, and the Emergencies of the Church of England Under King Henry VIII, King Edward VI, and Queen Mary I*, 3 vols. In *Works*, Oxford, 1820–1840.

THORNLEY, ISABEL D. "The Treason Legislation of Henry VIII," *Transactions of Royal Historical Society*, 3rd Series, XI (1917), 87–124.

————. "Treason by Words in the Fifteenth Century," *English Historical Review*, XXXII (1917), 555–61.

VAN DYKE, PAUL. "The Mission of Cardinal Pole to Enforce the Bull of Deposition," *English Historical Review*, XXXVII (1922), 422–3.

WOODWARD, G. W. O. "The Exemption from Suppression of Certain Yorkshire Priories," *English Historical Review*, LXXVI (1961), 385–401.

WRIGHT, THOMAS. *Three Chapters of Letters Relating to the Suppression of the Monasteries.* London, 1843.

HUMANISM, FACTIONS, AND DOCTRINE

BASKERVILLE, C. R. "Richard Morison as the Author of Two Anonymous Tracts on Sedition," *Library,* 4th Series, XVII (1936), 83–7.

BINDOFF, S. T. "Clement Armstrong and His Treatise of the Commonweal," *Economic History Review,* XIV (1944), 64–73.

BOONE, H. "L'Infructeuse ambassade du Cardinal Pole," in *Mémoire de la societé d'émulation de Cambrai,* LXXXV (1937), 213–49.

BRIGHTMAN, F. E. "The Litany and Henry VIII," *English Historical Review,* XXIV (1909), 101–4.

CASPARI, FRITZ. *Humanism and the Social Order in Tudor England.* Chicago, 1954.

CHESTER, A. G. "Hugh Latimer at Cambridge," *Crozier Quarterly,* XXVIII (1953), 306–18.

———. *Hugh Latimer: Apostle to the English.* Philadelphia, 1954.

CLEBSCH, W. A. "John Colet and the English Reformation," *Anglican Theological Review,* XXXVII (1955), 167–77.

———. *England's Earliest Protestants.* New Haven, Conn., 1965.

CONSTANT, G. "Formularies of Faith During the Reign of Henry VIII," *Downside Review,* LIV (1936), 155–64.

DICKENS, A. G. "Aspects of Intellectual Transition Among Some Parish Clergy," *Archiv für Reformationsegeschichte,* XLIII (1952), 51–69.

———. "Heresy and the Origins of the English Reformation," in *Britain and the Netherlands,* vol. II, 47–66. Edited by J. S. BROMLEY and E. H. KOSSMANN. London, 1964.

———. *Lollards and Protestants in the Diocese of York.* Oxford, 1959.

DOERNBERG, ERWIN. *Luther and Henry VIII.* London, 1961.

DUHAMEL, P. A. "The Oxford Lectures of John Colet," *Journal of the History of Ideas,* XIV (1953), 493–510.

EMMISON, F. G. *Tudor Secretary: Sir William Peter at Home and Court.* Cambridge, Mass., 1961.

FERGUSON, ARTHUR. "Renaissance Realism in the Commonwealth Literature of Early Tudor England," *Journal of the History of Ideas,* XVI (1955), 287–305.

————. "The Tudor Commonweal and the Sense of Change," *Journal of British Studies*, III (1963), 11–35.

————. *The Articulate Citizen and the English Renaissance.* Durham, N. C. 1965.

GRAY, C. M. *Hugh Latimer and the Sixteenth Century.* Cambridge, Mass., 1950.

GUPPY, HENRY. "The Royal Injunctions of 1538 and the Great Bible, 1539–1541," *Bulletin of the John Rylands Library*, XXII, 31–71 (1938).

————. "William Tindale and the Earlier Translators of the Bible," *Bulletin of the John Rylands Library*, IX (1925), 542–84.

HEXTER, J. H. "Thomas More: On the Margins of Modernity," *Journal of British Studies*, I (1961), 20–37.

HUTCHINSON, F. E. *Thomas Cranmer and the English Reformation.* London, 1951.

LACEY, T. A. *The King's Book.* London, 1932.

LEHMBERG, S. E. *Sir Thomas Elyot.* Austin, Texas, 1960.

MC CONICA, J. K. *English Humanists and Reformation Politics.* Oxford, 1965.

PINEAS, RAINER. "John Bale's Non-Dramatic Works of Religious Controversy," *Studies in the Renaissance*, IX (1962), 218–33.

————. "William Tyndale, Controversialist," *Studies in Philology*, LX (1963), 117–32.

PRUSSER, F. *England und die Schmalkalner* (Leipzig, 1929).

RICE, E. F. "John Colet and the Annihilation of the Natural," *Harvard Theological Review*, XLV (1952), 141–63.

RIDLEY, JASPER. *Thomas Cranmer.* Oxford, 1962.

ROWSE, A. L. "Sir Thomas Wriothesley," *Huntington Library Quarterly*, XXVIII (1965), 105–30.

RUPP, E. G. *Studies in the Making of the English Protestant Tradition.* London, 1947.

SCHENK, WILHELM. "The Student Days of Cardinal Pole," *History* XXXIII (1948), 211–25.

SLAVIN, A. J. "Sir Ralph Sadler and Master John Hales at the Hanaper: A Sixteenth-Century Struggle for Property and Profit," *Bulletin of the Institute of Historical Research*, XXXVIII (1965), 31–47.

————. *Politics and Profit.* Cambridge, England, 1966.

SMITH, L. B. *Tudor Prelates and Politics.* Princeton, N. J., 1953.

STURGE, CHARLES. *Cuthbert Tunstal.* London, 1938.

SURTZ, E. "John Fisher and the Scholastics," *Studies in Philology,* LV (1958), 136–53.

————. "Richard Pace's Sketch of Thomas More," *Journal of English and Germanic Philology,* LVII (1958), 36–50.

————. "Thomas More and Communism," *Publications of the Modern Language Association,* LXIV (1959), 549–64.

THOMPSON, P. "Sir Thomas Wyatt," *Huntington Library Quarterly,* XXV (1962), 79–96.

WHALE, J. S. *The Protestant Tradition.* Cambridge, England, 1959.

WILLOUGHBY, HAROLD. *The First Authorized English Bible.* Chicago, 1942.

ZEEVELD, W. G. *Foundations of Tudor Policy.* Cambridge, Mass., 1948.

THOMAS CROMWELL AND HIS PLACE IN ENGLISH HISTORY

BARNES, T. G. "Star Chamber Mythologies," *American Journal of Legal History,* V (1961), 1–11.

DICKENS, A. G. *Thomas Cromwell and the English Reformation.* London, 1959.

ELTON, G. R. "Parliamentary Drafts, 1529–1540," *Bulletin of the Institute of Historical Research,* XXV (1952), 117–32.

————. *The Tudor Revolution in Government.* Cambridge, England, 1953.

————. "The Political Creed of Thomas Cromwell," *Transactions of Royal Historical Society,* 5th Series, VI (1956), 69–92.

————. "A Further Note on Parliamentary Drafts in Henry VIII's Reign," *Bulletin of the Institute of Historical Research,* XXVII (1954), 198–200.

————, "Henry VIII's Act of Proclamations," *English Historical Review,* LXXV (1960), 208–22.

————. "State-Planning in Early Tudor England," *Economic History Review,* 2nd Series, XIII (1961), 433–9.

————. "The Tudor Revolution: A Reply," *Past and Present,* XXIX (1964), 26–49.

HARRISS, G. L. "Medieval Government and Statecraft," *Past and Present,* XXV (1963), 8–38.

MOSSE, G. L. "Change and Continuity in the Tudor Constitution," *Speculum,* XXII (1947), 18–28.

NEWTON, A. P. "The King's Chamber Under the Early Tudors," *English Historical Review,* XXXII (1917), 348–60.

PARKER, T. M. "Was Thomas Cromwell a Machiavellian?" *Journal of Ecclesiastical History,* I (1950), 61–75.

POWICKE, SIR F. M. *The Reformation in England.* London, 1958.

RICHARDSON, WALTER. *Tudor Chamber Administration.* Baton Rouge, La., 1952.

SCARISBRICK, J. J. *Henry VIII.* London, 1968.

STONE, LAWRENCE. "The Political Program of Thomas Cromwell," *Bulletin of the Institute of Historical Research,* XXIV (1951), 1–18.

WILLIAMS, PENRY. "A Revolution in Tudor History?" *Past and Present,* XXV (1963), 3–8.

——. "The Tudor State," *Ibid.,* 39–58.

ADDITIONAL NOTE ON BIBLIOGRAPHY

The student will find that many new books and articles in Tudor history are listed in the major journals, especially *American Historical Review, English Historical Review, Speculum,* and *Economic History Review.* There are also important review articles from time to time in *Journal of British Studies, Studies in the Renaissance,* and *Church History.* Also, the Conference on British Studies in conjunction with Cambridge University Press has now issued the first volume of their important bibliographic series devoted to English history. In that series Mortimer Levine's volume on the early Tudors now supplements and adds detail to Conyers Read's *Bibliography of British History: Tudor Period, 1485–1603,* 2nd ed. (Oxford, 1959).

INDEX